Europe in the Global Age

Other Books by Anthony Giddens

Capitalism and Modern Social Theory, 1971
Politics and Sociology in the Thought of Max Weber, 1972
The Class Structure of the Advanced Societies, 1973
New Rules of Sociological Method, 1976
Studies in Social and Political Theory, 1977
Emile Durkheim, 1978
Central Problems in Social Theory, 1979
A Contemporary Critique of Historical Materialism, 1981
Sociology: A Brief but Critical Introduction, 1982
Profiles and Critiques in Social Theory, 1983
The Constitution of Society, 1984
The Nation-State and Violence, 1985
Social Theory and Modern Sociology, 1987
Sociology, 1988
The Consequences of Modernity, 1990
Modernity and Self-Identity, 1991
The Transformation of Intimacy, 1992
Beyond Left and Right, 1994
Reflexive Modernisation (with Ulrich Beck and Scott Lash), 1994
Politics, Sociology and Social Theory, 1995
In Defence of Sociology, 1996
Making Sense of Modernity (with Christopher Pierson), 1998
The Third Way: The Renewal of Social Democracy, 1998
Runaway World, 1999
The Third Way and its Critics, 2000
Where Now for New Labour?, 2002

Europe in the Global Age

ANTHONY GIDDENS

polity

Copyright © Anthony Giddens 2007

The right of Anthony Giddens to be identified as Author of this Work has been asserted in accordance with the UK Copyright, Designs and Patents Act 1988.

First published in 2007 by Polity Press
Reprinted in 2007 (twice)

Polity Press
65 Bridge Street
Cambridge CB2 1UR, UK

Polity Press
350 Main Street
Malden, MA 02148, USA

ISBN 978-07456-4011-2
ISBN 978-07456-4012-9 (pb)

A catalogue record for this book is available from the British Library.

Typeset in 11 on 13 pt Sabon
by Servis Filmsetting Ltd, Manchester
Printed and bound in the United States by Odyssey Press Inc.,
Gonic, New Hampshire

The publisher has used its best endeavours to ensure that the URLs for external websites referred to in this book are correct and active at the time of going to press. However, the publisher has no responsibility for the websites and can make no guarantee that a site will remain live or that the content is or will remain appropriate.

Every effort has been made to trace all copyright holders, but if any have been inadvertently overlooked the publishers will be pleased to include any necessary credits in any subsequent reprint or edition.

For further information on Polity, visit our website: www.polity.co.uk

Contents

Preface		*vii*
Glossary of Terms		*xi*
1	The Social Model	1
2	Change and Innovation in Europe	30
3	Social Justice and Social Divisions	59
4	From Negative to Positive Welfare	96
5	Lifestyle Change	135
6	At the Level of the EU	164
7	Eight Theses on the Future of Europe	199
Appendix: Open Letter on the Future of Europe		*231*
Index		*235*

To Alena

Preface

This book was prompted by some comments made by the British Prime Minister, Tony Blair, in a speech to the European Parliament in June 2005. In that speech, he stressed his commitment to the European project and to the European 'social model'. But what kind of social model is it, he asked rhetorically, that leaves almost 20 million people in the EU unemployed? Europe's welfare systems stand in need of radical reform.

The speech, which made a great impression around Europe, was given just before the beginning of the British Presidency of the European Union, which lasted from 1 July to 31 December 2005. Working in loose connection with that Presidency, a group was set up to analyse the state of health of the social model and suggest reforms that might be made. The point was not in any sense to propose an 'Anglo-Saxon' approach, but to look in a neutral way at the issues. Some twenty individuals from a range of European countries were involved in the project, all of whom contributed papers. Seminars organized by the think-tank Policy Network were held in many countries across Europe, involving political leaders and academics.

Two significant publications have come so far from this endeavour. One is a work edited by myself, Patrick Diamond and Roger Liddle, called *Global Europe, Social Europe* (Polity, 2006); the other is *The Hampton Court Agenda: A Social Model for Europe* (Policy Network, 2006). My opening chapter in this book overlaps heavily with chapter 1 in *Global Europe, Social Europe*, which was written first.

This study has been strongly influenced by the many discussions with colleagues in which I took part. I have drawn extensively upon their contributions in what follows, although this book represents a personal statement, not a collective one.

While my discussion concentrates upon Europe, I believe its implications stretch much more widely. All the developed countries face a range of similar problems, bound up with global social and economic changes and with major transformations in work, family and everyday life. I hope therefore that what I have to say will have some interest to those from elsewhere. I would include also the less developed nations. Countries that do not have effective welfare systems – including the rising world powers China and India – will have to build them if they want to create integrated and inclusive societies. In so doing, they can learn from both the achievements and the mistakes of the more advanced states.

The aims of the book are several-fold. They are first of all to identify cutting-edge economic and social policy in Europe and to draw lessons from it. In looking at this issue, I do not confine myself to the European Union alone, but draw also upon evidence from other parts of the world. A continuing, and sharply drawn, debate is going on about whether the European social model confers competitive advantages or whether, on the contrary, it is an economic handicap. There are in fact many European social models, and some fare far better than others. The evidence shows that countries that have been able to reform have done well in the global marketplace and have sustained high levels of social justice. Far from the one standing in the way of the other, they are mutually supportive. The future of Europe – and perhaps even the continuing existence of the European Union as a major force – depends upon these reforms being generalized.

Vital though they might be, such reforms are still not enough. We have to think more adventurously. The intensive discussion of the emergence of the knowledge-based economy that has gone on in Europe has not been matched by equivalent analysis of social changes. Without such an analysis, we cannot hope to have effective programmes of social justice and social welfare.

Some of the challenges to which Europe has to respond apply to all developed societies. Others are more specific to the European context – especially the demise of Soviet-style society in Eastern Europe. One should stop pretending that the European Union post-1989 is simply an enlarged version of what existed before. The identity of the EU simply cannot be the same as it was when there is an open border to the East – and increasingly to the south too.

The European social model was defined in large part through a contrast with the Soviet Union and Eastern Europe on the one hand and American free-market liberalism on the other. That self-definition does not pertain today. In considering reforms and changes, we have to react not only to 1989, but also to the forces and influences that brought it about, which were connected above all with intensifying globalization. That is why, following Martin Albrow, I have chosen to give this book the title *Europe in the Global Age*.[1] The global age is a state of affairs, a set of social conditions signalling many changes in our lives. Globalization, by contrast, is a process, or complex set of processes, referring to the forces and influences responsible for those changes.

There is today a 'struggle for Europe'. The phrase has more than one meaning. There is a struggle for Europe in the sense of a clash between differing versions of what the Union represents, and what form it should assume in the future. But there is also a struggle that Europe has to engage in to assert itself in a world of far-reaching transformation. I am a pro-European and I want the Union to flourish, which I believe it can. But it will not be easy and is in no sense guaranteed. If this book makes even a modest contribution to the current debates about where the Union should go from here, I shall be satisfied.

I would like to thank whole-heartedly all of those who participated in the seminars and discussions. Special thanks are due to Anne de Sayrah, who has played a key role throughout. I owe just as great a debt to Jean-François Drolet for his excellent and dedicated work. Many people made comments on earlier versions of the manuscript, including Neil Kinnock, Shirley Williams, David Held, Roger Liddle, Patrick Diamond, Matt Browne and François Lafond. François played the key role in organizing the Policy

[1] See Martin Albrow, *The Global Age*. Cambridge: Polity, 1996.

Network seminars, ably assisted by Johanna Juselius. I would like to thank all their co-workers at Policy Network too. Victor Phillip Dahdaleh not only funded all our meetings, but actively took part in many of them. Sarah Dancy did an excellent job of copy-editing the manuscript. Thanks are also due to all at Policy Network. As always, Emma Hutchinson and her colleagues at Polity Press did a marvellous production job.

Glossary of Terms Introduced in the Book

Activating labour market policy Policy concerned with helping people successfully master transitions across the life-course

Active trust Trust based on monitoring the integrity of the other in an open and continuous way

Assertive multilateralism Multilateralism deploying various forms of power, and backed up by the potential use of force

Blocked societies Societies in which vested interests, or structural conservatism, or both, inhibit needed changes

Citizen-consumers Citizens have choice within non-market spheres, such as in health care or education, but the quality and efficiency of service have to be guaranteed by public mechanisms

Consumer-citizens Choice in market contexts is the mechanism that drives quality control, by forcing manufacturers to compete on quality and price

Ensuring state The state seeks to empower citizens, but also provides a framework of guarantees, such as a minimum wage

Euro-hypocrisy The propagation of 'European values' without due regard to Europe's chequered past and current policies inconsistent with those values

Glossary of Terms

Eurorealism Taking a sober but ambitious view of the EU's socio-geopolitical capabilities (I do not mean realism in the more technical sense it has in international relations)

Everyday democratization The advance of substantive freedoms in everyday life

Globalization Increasing interdependence between individuals, nations and regions. Does *not* just mean economic interdependence. Involves accelerated and universal communication, and concerns also political and cultural dimensions

Knowledge/service economy An economy in which only a small minority works in manufacture and agriculture; most are in knowledge-based and service occupations

Lifestyle change Positive welfare expressed in terms of changes in harmful everyday habits

New egalitarianism Policies that seek where possible to combine the furtherance of equality with increasing economic dynamism

Passive trust Trust based upon accepted symbols of authority, established by habit or tradition

Politics of second chances Policies providing resources for people to 'start again' in various areas of life

Positive welfare Welfare oriented to positive life-goals rather than only the minimizing of risk

Post-industrial society A society marked by everyday democratization, individualism and cultural diversity; and where knowledge or service occupations dominate

Preventative welfare Welfare policies that seek to intervene at source, rather than only coming into play after things go wrong

Social investment state State-provided or regulated investments in human or social capital

Transitional labour markets Labour markets considered from the perspective of transitions across the life-span

'Youthing' society A society where the life-habits of older people merge with those of younger generations

1

The Social Model

Europe's welfare system is often regarded as the jewel in the crown – perhaps the main feature that gives the European societies their special quality. In May 2003 two of Europe's most distinguished intellectuals, Jürgen Habermas and Jacques Derrida, wrote a public letter about the future of European identity in the wake of the Iraq war. The welfare state's 'guarantees of social security' and 'Europeans' trust in the civilizing power of the state' brooked large.[1] Most other observers sympathetic to the European Union project would agree. The European social model (ESM) is, or has become, a fundamental part of what Europe stands for.

Cue in 'ESM' in Google and 55,800,000 items come up! Such a profusion perhaps reflects the fact that the ESM, like so much else about the EU, is essentially a contested notion. In spite of the fact that it is so central, the idea is somewhat elusive when we try to pin it down. The ESM, it has been said, is not solely European, not wholly social and not a model.[2] If it means having effective welfare institutions, and limiting inequality, then other countries are just as advanced as states in Europe. For instance, Australia and Canada surpass Portugal and Greece, not to mention most of the new states in the enlarged EU25. The ESM is not purely social, since however it is defined, it depends fundamentally upon economic prosperity

[1] Jürgen Habermas and Jacques Derrida, 'February 15, or, what binds Europeans together', in Daniel Levy et al. (eds.), *Old Europe, New Europe, Core Europe*. London: Verso, 2005.
[2] Anna Diamantopoulou, 'The European social model – myth or reality?', Speech at Labour Party Conference, Bournemouth, 29 September 2003.

and redistribution. It is not a single model, since there are big divergences between European countries in terms of their welfare systems.

There are many different definitions of the ESM around, although they all home in on the welfare state. Daniel Vaughan-Whitehead, for example, lists no fewer than fifteen components of the ESM.[3] We should probably conclude that the ESM is not a unitary concept, but a mixture of values, accomplishments and aspirations, varying in form and degree of realization among European states. My version of it would be:

- a developed and interventionist state, funded by relatively high levels of taxation;
- a robust welfare system, which provides effective social protection, to some considerable degree for all citizens, but especially for those most in need;
- the limitation, or containment, of economic and other forms of inequality.

A key role in sustaining these institutions is played by the 'social partners', the unions and other agencies promoting workers' rights. Each trait has to go along with expanding overall economic prosperity and (ideally) full employment.

Underlying the ESM is a general set of values: sharing both risk and opportunity widely across society, cultivating social solidarity or cohesion, protecting the most vulnerable members of society through active social intervention, encouraging consultation rather than confrontation in industry, and providing a rich framework of social and economic citizenship rights for the population as a whole.

Stresses and Strains

It is agreed by more or less everyone, supporters and opponents alike, that the ESM is currently under great strain, or even failing.

---

[3] Daniel Vaughan-Whitehead, *EU Enlargement versus Social Europe?* London: Elgar, 2003.

The welfare state is embattled. It no longer offers the stability and security it seemed to do thirty or so years ago. We should begin, however, by putting this situation into context. Some speak of the 1960s and 1970s as the 'golden age' of the welfare state, when there was good economic growth, low unemployment, social protection for all – and when citizens were able to feel much more secure than today. From this perspective, the ESM has been 'attacked' by external forces, particularly those associated with globalization, and progressively weakened or partly dismantled.

The reality is more complex. For member states such as Spain, Portugal, Greece and most later entrants to the European Union, there was no golden age at all, since welfare provisions were weak and inadequate. Even in those nations with advanced welfare systems, everything was far from golden in the golden age. That era was dominated by mass production and bureaucratic hierarchies, where management styles were often autocratic and many workers were in assembly-line jobs. Few women were able to have working careers; only a small proportion of young people entered further or higher education; the range of health services offered was far below that available now; older people were put out to pasture by a rigid retirement age. In line with the bureaucratic ethos of the time, the state generally treated its clients as passive subjects rather than as active citizens. Some of the changes in welfare systems over the past thirty years have been aimed at correcting these deficiencies and hence have been both progressive and necessary.

The world, of course, has shifted massively since the 'golden age'. The ESM, and the EU itself, were in some large part products of a bipolar world – a recurrent theme of this book. The fall of the Berlin Wall – Europe's 11:9, as Thomas Friedman calls it[4] – more or less completely changed the nature of the EU, giving rise to identity problems that still remain unresolved – and indeed were reflected in the refusal of the proposed EU constitution by the people of France and the Netherlands.

The demise of Keynesianism in the West and the collapse of Soviet Communism were brought about by much the same

---

[4] Thomas Friedman, *The World is Flat: A Brief History of the Twenty-First Century.* New York: Allen Lane, 2005.

trends – accelerating globalization, the rise of a worldwide information order, the shrinking of manufacture (and its transfer to less developed countries), coupled to the rise of new forms of individualism and consumer power. These are not changes that came and went; their impact continues to grow apace.

Two decades ago the countries in the developing world produced 10 per cent of the world's manufactured goods. That proportion has risen to 25 per cent and, if present trends are maintained, will reach 50 per cent by 2020. China has recently overtaken Japan to become the second largest economy in the world as measured in terms of purchasing power. In less than five years it is likely to surpass Japan's economy in terms of market exchange values as well.[5] In 1980, the countries that now comprise EU25 produced 26 per cent of world manufacturing output. By 2003 that proportion had become reduced to 22 per cent and is likely to be no more than 17 per cent by 2015.

The larger companies no longer source their goods and services nationally, but worldwide, intensifying both trade and local specialization. In 2003–4 world trade grew twice as quickly as global output. Transnational trade in services is advancing rapidly, with India in the lead. India's service exports in real money terms grew from a value of $5 billion in 1990 to $40 billion in 2004.

Competition from the developing economies is no longer concentrated only in low-cost goods. China and India have made large-scale investments in technology, especially information and communications technology (ICT), and are each producing four million graduates a year. No one knows how far the outsourcing of services will go, given the fact that it is driven partly by developments in computer technology and by the widening of access to such technology. However, the complexity of the services that can be outsourced is rising rapidly. Financial, legal, high-tech, journalistic and medical services are among those most likely to be directly affected. I shall discuss those issues in more detail in chapter 2.

The social model depends upon overall economic prosperity, to which ideally it should contribute. The EU's economic performance over the past twenty years or so, however, has given rise to

[5] Gordon Brown, *Global Europe*. London: Treasury, 2005, p. 4.

recurrent anxiety. The EU has fallen behind the US according to the standard measures of economic success. (Western) Europe was once in the vanguard of social and economic change; today, the EU risks getting left behind by history. The progress that has been made with consolidating the Single Market, and the introduction of the euro, have not created an economic regeneration.

We know from survey results that the issues which preoccupied voters in the referendums in France and the Netherlands were not in fact primarily constitutional. In France, 75 per cent of those who voted in the referendum and, extraordinarily, fully 66 per cent of 'no' voters, still believed a constitution for Europe was necessary. The position in the Netherlands was more complex, since some 'no' voters were worried about smaller countries becoming too dominated by larger ones. But in both nations, social and economic concerns were of prime importance – mainly worries about jobs and about the adequacy of welfare. Changes happening in the EU, especially to do with its expansion, were seen as likely to make an already difficult situation worse.

A few commentators tend to underplay the economic difficulties faced by Europe, especially when the EU is compared with the United States.[6] Europeans, they say, have made a lifestyle choice. They have traded in a certain level of possible growth for more leisure than is enjoyed by most Americans. Nevertheless, productivity in some EU countries rivals that of the US. Precisely because of Europe's stronger welfare systems, there are fewer working poor in the EU states than in the US.

But these ideas are not convincing, as others have demonstrated.[7] Average growth in the EU15 has declined in relative terms year on year since the 1980s. GDP per head has not got beyond 70 per cent of the US level over that period. Not only has the US had higher growth, it has also had greater macroeconomic stability over that time. About a third of the difference in per capita GDP with the US derives from lower average productivity of labour, a third from shorter working hours and the remaining third from a

---

[6] See, for example, Jeremy Rifkin, *The European Dream*. Cambridge: Polity, 2004.
[7] See especially André Sapir et al., *An Agenda for a Growing Europe: Report of the High-Level Study Group*. Brussels: European Commission, July 2003.

lower employment rate. None of these comes purely from choice, and all affect the viability of the ESM. Unemployment is far higher in the EU than in America. There are 93 million economically inactive people below the age of 60, a much higher rate than in the US.

Very many in Europe, including many young people – and over 60s – want to work but can't. This comment also applies to immigrants. The US has done a better job of integrating immigrants into its labour market than have the EU countries. The jobless rate of non-nationals in the EU15 in 2002 was more than twice the rate for nationals. In the US the two rates are almost the same. The incorporation of ten new member states has brought with it a series of issues that are very remote from a 'preference for leisure'. It has increased the EU population by 20 per cent, but GDP by only 5 per cent. Problems of inequality and cohesion have increased, both across the EU as a whole and within the member states.

Globalization

These are all challenges to which Europe can and must react. They have some major implications for the social model. However, in looking at strains affecting welfare systems, it is a mistake to focus on globalization alone. Some of the core problems faced by Europe's welfare states come from endogenous structural change. These changes are directly connected with globalization (since almost all changes are) but are not wholly driven by it. This point is an important one to register, as some commentators invoke the spectre of globalization to explain away home-grown problems and delay reform.

The changing age profile of Europe is a case in point. In the EU today there are some 70 million people aged 60 and over, making up 20 per cent of the population. Over 30 per cent are aged 50 or more. One factor producing the ageing population is that, on average, people are living longer than in the past. A prime additional reason, however, is the low birth rate. This fact is easily understood if we compare the EU with the US. Following its most recent expansion, the EU has a population of 455 million, compared to 295 million in the US. Yet if current trends were maintained, by mid-century the two populations will be virtually the same.[8] In America, birth rates are at replacement level. In the EU25, by contrast, they average 1.5 per 1,000 women, and in some countries the rate is as low as 1.2. If nothing changes in Italy, for example, the numbers of those of working age (19–65) will decrease by 20 per cent by 2035.

The steep decline in the number of those working in manufacture in the EU countries has been influenced by the transfer of industry to the developing world, and thus by economic globalization. But the main reason is not this. It is the impact of technological change, which in many industries has either reduced the need for human labour power or has simply rendered more traditional production processes obsolete. For instance, car manufacture has been almost wholly automated; the coal industry in most countries has shrunk, largely because of a widespread transfer to natural gas. Of course, it is again the interaction between 'inside' and 'outside' influences that is important. Technological change has accelerated because of growing intensity of competition.

One further example: patterns of poverty and social exclusion, although certainly affected by globalization, are influenced by endogenous changes too, including, in particular, transformations in the structure of the family. In most EU countries, rates of divorce are higher, and rates of marriage lower, than they were in the past. Families are more mobile, and may lack the extended kin relations that were once a source of social support. There is also the rise of the 'non-conventional family' – women having children on their own, same-sex partners living together, and so forth. These trends are complex and often difficult to interpret, but they have strongly influenced the nature of poverty and other forms of deprivation. Women and children make up a high percentage of the 'new poor' in most EU countries.

What globalization is has to be properly understood. Globalization is often seen solely as an economic phenomenon, even by some of the most sophisticated commentators on the subject. Martin Wolf, for example, defines it as 'the integration of economic

---

[8] *The Economist*, 30 September 2004.

activities, across borders, through markets'.[9] The definition is not so much incorrect as too partial. Globalization is so obviously not only economic that it is hard to see how anyone could seriously think otherwise.

Consider, for example, the role of communications media. The world has become interconnected electronically in ways that no one could have even anticipated several decades ago. I would in fact date the beginnings of the global age to the late 1960s or early 1970s, the first time at which an effective satellite system was sent up above the earth, making possible instantaneous communication from any one point in the world to any other. The generalization of the Internet, which dates only from the late 1990s, has added to this process. Many aspects of social and economic life in the EU countries – as elsewhere – have been changed by these developments. Migration, for instance, arguably changes its nature, as migrants can now keep in touch with those in their countries of origin whenever they wish.

'The EU must respond to globalization', it is often said. Well, yes, but globalization is a two-way set of processes. The EU cannot just 'respond' to globalization, since today it is both an instrument and an expression of it. Globalization – in its diverse forms – doesn't just come from the outside. Every time I switch on a computer, send an email, look at information on the Internet, put on the television or radio, I actively contribute to globalization at the same time as I make use of it.

Talk of 'countering globalization' or creating 'globalization with a human face' makes no sense in such a context. Some aspects of globalization need to be managed, often at local, national and transnational levels. But globalization, often increasing globalization, is usually the means of doing so. This observation is as true of the world marketplace as it is of climate change, new-style terrorism, money laundering or organized crime.

Competitiveness in global markets is essential to Europe's future, and to the survival of the social model too. The rise of India and China and other countries in the less developed world shows

---

[9] Martin Wolf, *Why Globalization Works*. New Haven, CT: Yale University Press, 2004, p. 14.

definitively that globalization is not just a means for the West to dominate the rest. Yet we have to consider many other ways in which globalization affects, and is affected by, the EU. The economic advances made by China, for example, have a direct impact on geopolitics – and from there to other areas. China's need for oil, for example, has caused it to have close ties with Iran. Iran looks bent on acquiring nuclear weapons. Largely because of its oil dependency, China is not likely to join other nations in imposing effective sanctions on the country. A nuclear Iran would represent a new power, and perhaps a highly dangerous one, standing close to many of the sources of energy supply to Europe, from the Middle East and central Asia. Individual nations cannot hope to cope with these problems.

Types of social model

It is obvious that there is no single social model in Europe. Many attempts have been made to classify welfare states in Europe into different types, but by far the most widely used is that offered by the Danish social scientist Gøsta Esping-Andersen. He distinguishes three main types of 'welfare capitalism'.[10] These are the Nordic type, based upon high taxation and extensive job opportunities provided within the welfare state itself; the conservative or corporatist type (Germany, France, Italy), based mainly on payroll contributions; and the liberal or Anglo-Saxon type, represented by the UK and Ireland, a more 'residual' form of welfare system, having a lower taxation base and using more targeted policies. Others have added a fourth type alongside the three Esping-Andersen originally recognized – the Mediterranean one (Spain, Portugal, Greece), which also has a fairly low tax base and depends heavily upon provision from the family.[11] Today we would have to include a fifth type too, the post-Communist one, referring to the countries of former Eastern Europe, struggling to develop Western-style welfare states.

[10] Gøsta Esping-Andersen, *The Three Worlds of Welfare Capitalism*. Cambridge: Polity, 1990 .
[11] Maurizio Ferrera seems to have been the first to identify the fourth type, in his *Le trappole del welfare*. Bologna: Il Mulino, 1998.

In developing his typology, Esping-Andersen made much of the 'service economy trilemma' – a notion originally formulated by Torben Iversen and Anne Wren.[12] This 'trilemma' is the main reason why Esping-Andersen believes the three types of welfare system he sets out have diverged, since it limits the degree to which common policies can be applied across them. The idea is that it is impossible in a modern economy simultaneously to have balanced budgets, low levels of economic inequality and high levels of employment. Two of these goals can be successfully pursued by governments at any one time, but not all three. The different types of system are distinguished partly because they have chosen varying combinations.

In the Nordic countries, Esping-Andersen says, the welfare state acts as employer, providing a large number of public-sector service jobs, hence helping to lower unemployment. Taxation is high, however, and this situation puts a continual strain on borrowing levels. The Anglo-Saxon countries, such as the UK and, outside the EU, Australia and Canada, have generated large numbers of private-sector jobs, and have maintained fiscal discipline, but are marked by high levels of poverty. In the corporatist type, such as Germany or France, by contrast, there is a commitment to limiting inequality and (at least until recently) to budgetary constraint. However, these countries are dogged by low levels of job growth.

But is the 'trilemma' real? Anton Hemerijck and his colleagues have argued persuasively that the empirical evidence for it is 'surprisingly shaky'.[13] The recent history of Scandinavia shows that it is in fact possible to have sound public finances, low inequality and high levels of employment at the same time. *Per contra*, it also seems possible to have only one of the three. Germany, for example, now has high levels of unemployment and a burgeoning public debt. Moreover, the various 'types' are themselves not very clear-cut. Thus Nordic states in some ways differ from one another

[12] Torben Iversen and Anne Wren, 'Equality, employment and budgetary restraint: the trilemma of the service economy', *World Politics*, 50 (1998).
[13] Anton Hemerijck, 'The self-transformation of the European social model(s)', in Gøsta Esping-Andersen (ed.), *Why We Need a New Welfare State*. Oxford: Oxford University Press, 2002.

significantly. It is not obvious that Germany and France belong to a single type. The UK is supposed to be a 'residual' welfare state, dominated by markets, but its net taxation levels are now about the same as Germany's. In the shape of the NHS, moreover, it has the most 'socialized' system of medicine in Europe.[14] Hemerijck concludes that the welfare states which have adapted best to changing conditions have created 'hybrid models', borrowed in some part from elsewhere. It is a case I find convincing, and I shall suggest below that a great deal of mutual learning is possible. Esping-Andersen's typology remains useful (as will be shown in what follows) – and was only supposed to be a series of ideal types in the first place – but the boundaries between the types are in practice porous and becoming increasingly so.

Good performers, poor performers

Since the early to mid-1990s, some EU states have performed much better than others, both in economic and social terms. It is actually a mistake to say that the welfare state everywhere is failing. Comparison of the good performers with those that have fared less well yields some interesting results. As measured in terms of economic criteria such as levels of GDP growth, inflation and economic sustainability, the most impressive countries in the EU over that period have been Denmark, Finland and Sweden, all of which have developed welfare states. The three least effective have been the large Continental economies, Germany, France and Italy. A detailed comparison between these two groups has been made by the Austrian economist Karl Aiginger.[15]

Average growth rates in the 1990s and early 2000s in the three Nordic states, Aiginger points out, were 2.9 per cent, very close to

---

[14] Katinka Barysch, 'Liberal versus social Europe', *Centre for European Reform Bulletin*, August/September 2005.

[15] Karl Aiginger, 'Towards a new European model of a reformed welfare state', *United Nations Economic Survey of Europe*, 1 (2005). For another important contribution, see Joakim Palme, 'Why the Scandinavian experience is relevant for the reform of the ESM'; available online at <http://www.progressive-governance.net/php/article.php?aid=501&sid=7>.

the US level. Germany, France and Italy managed an average of only 1.6 per cent. In the Nordic countries over the 1990s productivity increased by 2.4 per cent, compared to 0.5 per cent in Germany, France and Italy. Their employment rate in 2002 averaged 71 per cent compared to 62 per cent in the other group. Budgets have been balanced or in surplus, while the three Continental countries have been running big deficits. In contrast to larger states, the Nordic countries are highly open and market-oriented. Finland and Denmark have regularly topped lists of the most business-friendly countries produced by the World Economic Forum and similar organizations.

A variety of factors seem to have influenced their success. The prime one, however, is the patterns of social investment that the countries have followed. All three countries have invested heavily in innovative forms of technology and education. The Danish strategy involves diffusing IT widely and building successful technology clusters. Finland makes even more extensive use of IT, both in economic restructuring and in government. The country has a higher degree of IT penetration than the US.

Expenditures on R&D in Scandinavia[16] are twice as high as in the three Continental countries. Spending on education in general, and higher education in particular, is considerably greater. The Scandinavian countries are also rated very highly in international rankings of educational attainment.[17]

The Nordic states have the lowest levels of economic inequality in the world and levels of child poverty are very low. They also fare well on most other indicators of well-being and health. These achievements have come not from *refusing* reform, but from *embracing* it. All three societies have restructured their labour markets – 'flexicurity' (flexibility plus security) has its origins in Sweden but, in somewhat varying guises, has been adopted by Denmark and Finland too. If job search is unsuccessful after a certain period, the unemployed are obliged to undertake retraining and to accept jobs that they are offered.

[16] I shall use 'Nordic' and 'Scandinavian' interchangeably, although technically 'Scandinavia' and 'Scandinavian' are more restricted terms – Denmark is not on the Scandinavian peninsula.
[17] Aiginger, 'Towards a new European model'.

To achieve balanced budgets, cut-backs were made in state expenditure in the early 1990s, but without creating major increases either in poverty or overall economic inequality. A crucial part of the Nordic adaptation to change has been the promotion of family-friendly policies. Their experience shows that business- and family-friendly policies are not incompatible, especially as long as part-time work preserves much of the status and privileges of full-time work. Although the level of gender segregation in Scandinavia is high, partly because many women work for the state, in general both women and children fare particularly well.

Work has been made a priority – in order to have a high employment rate, but also because having a decent job is the best route out of poverty. This precept applies to women as well as men; in Denmark, for example, 90 per cent of single mothers are in work. Post-school education and training have become extremely widespread. So far as public (state-based) services are concerned, the Nordic states have been not only reformist but also experimental – considerably more so than the poorly performing societies. (Many of the policies involved were initially highly controversial.) Education and health care have been radically decentralized and incentives introduced to improve efficiency. Foundation hospitals – non-profit organizations having a high degree of control over their budgets and their programmes of health care – were pioneered in Denmark and Sweden.

The egalitarian nature of the Nordic countries, Aiginger points out, comes less from direct redistribution as such than from the social investment made in children and in improving the position of women. Patriarchal power has not disappeared, but is more muted than in most other countries. As a consequence – and together with welfare reforms – women and children are less dependent upon a male breadwinner's wage than anywhere else in Europe. Single mothers or divorced women lose less of their income relative to men than happens elsewhere.

Birth rates remain quite high in Scandinavia, certainly by EU standards. Of the three big Continental countries, only France has a comparable birth rate. France has invested in child care, and has a benefit system that supports mothers regardless of whether they are married or in a relationship (it has not done nearly as well at getting them into or keeping them in work). The system in Germany and Italy, by contrast, depends heavily on the traditional family, which supposedly will pick up the pieces when financial hardship or other problems loom. Yet the traditional family, with its clear division of labour between the sexes, and its various forms of mutuality, is disappearing everywhere. In any case it provided no real place for unmarried mothers or divorced women.

The Scandinavian countries have reformed their pensions systems to make them sustainable in the longer term. They have also instituted measures to encourage older people either to continue working or to come back into the labour force. Sweden, for example, carried out basic pensions reforms in the 1990s. The old earnings-related benefit system was replaced by one of fixed contributions. There is a universal guaranteed pension, but the size of the guaranteed element is fixed in relation to the level of income. The system provides very effective cost controls, while the tie to lifetime earnings creates savings incentives.[18]

A basic move in Sweden, followed to some degree by Denmark, has been the introduction of choice into the state school system. In policies introduced in Sweden in 1992, independent profit-making and non-profit-making schools were set up alongside orthodox state schools, founded on equal per pupil financial terms. Vouchers are available to parents to select the school of their choice. Studies indicate that the programme has been successful – although it remains controversial. Overall performance in the school system has improved, with fewer pupils leaving without qualifications.[19]

The Scandinavian countries are not the only European nations to have done well over the past decade and a half. Others include Ireland, the UK, the Netherlands and Spain. They all share some elements in common: an overall orientation to reform, high levels of structural investment, and the liberalization of labour markets. I shall have more to say about these countries in what follows later.

Some have suggested there is little for the rest of Europe to learn from the Nordic states. They are all small – smaller countries might

[18] Palme, 'Why the Scandinavian experience is relevant for reform of the ESM'.
[19] For an analysis, see the Swedish National Institute for Education, *Schools like any Other?* Stockholm, 2005; and idem, *Equity Trends in the Swedish School System*, Stockholm, 2005.

be different from larger ones generically, and in any case are easier to change. Tax revenues are higher than in other EU countries. These points are important, but no one would suggest exporting the 'Nordic model' en bloc. The point is to identify policies that can be implemented elsewhere.

Today's success can become tomorrow's failure, so the lessons of current best practice should be treated with some caution. After all, it was not long ago that Germany's 'consensus capitalism' was widely perceived to be a way forward for Europe as a whole; now it is at the other end of the scale. However, it would be perverse indeed to say that there are no lessons to be learned by others from the countries that are faring best. Not just the policies, but some of the mechanics of change may be relevant. The union movement in the Nordic countries has played an important role in facilitating change and reform. When the social partners (employers as well as unions) do in fact act as social partners, looking for constructive reform rather than seeking to defend sectional interests, the results can be positive for the labour force.

Lisbon and After

We don't lack for reports suggesting what should be done to get the underperforming parts of the EU back on their feet again, and generally to make the EU states more competitive. Most centre upon the Lisbon Agenda, to which European leaders committed themselves in March 2000. The EU at that point set itself a number of strategic goals for the next decade: 'to become the most dynamic and competitive knowledge-based economy in the world, capable of sustainable economic growth with more and better jobs and greater social cohesion and respect for the environment'. Average growth was to reach 3 per cent per annum and employment an average of 70 per cent by 2010. To reach these declared goals, it was argued, member states would have to act in concert with one another. The 'open method of coordination' (OMC), essentially a benchmarking exercise, was invented because the EU lacks power to intervene directly in producing most of the reforms deemed necessary. Under the OMC, member states agreed voluntarily to pursue a designated range of targets, customized to suit their specific needs in the relation to the knowledge economy.

The results so far have fallen well short of expectations – so much so that the ambition of becoming the world's most competitive economy by 2010 has been widely lampooned. The announcement of the Lisbon Agenda was almost immediately followed by two years of recession in the world economy, in which the US was affected, but the EU suffered even more. By and large, the states that took most notice of the Lisbon Agenda were those that least needed it – the 'best performers' noted above. In the larger Continental countries it was more or less ignored, at least until quite recently.

Average GDP per head in the EU15 in 2005 was 27 per cent below that of the US – exactly the same as was the case in 2000. Moreover, productivity growth in the US was 1 per cent higher than that of the EU in each of the years 1995–2005.[20] Of the EU25 countries, twelve currently have budget deficits at or above the 3 per cent limit set in the 1997 Growth and Stability Pact. In other words, they have little or no money to invest in the areas covered by the Lisbon Agenda.

Some progress has been made since 2000. The average employment rate rose from 62.5 per cent in 1999 to 63.3 per cent in 2004 in the EU15 countries. In the same year, 41 per cent of 55–64-year-olds were in employment, compared to 36.6 per cent in 2000. The female participation rate has grown substantially, reaching 55.7 per cent. These averages conceal large variations between different countries. For instance, only 45 per cent of women are in work in Greece and Italy, and just 33 per cent in Malta. Enlargement means that the targets, at least for the time being, have become even more difficult to meet – although this situation may be compensated for by higher growth rates in the new entrant states. At the point of enlargement, the average employment rate for the EU dropped by 1.5 per cent.

In the light of its slow progress, and Europe's economic weaknesses more generally, the Lisbon Agenda has been subject to a series of revisions; and has been monitored and criticized in an almost endless range of reports. The most important are those

[20] Aurore Wanlin, *The Lisbon Scorecard VI*. London: Centre for European Reform, 2006.

produced by two 'high-level groups', one chaired by Wim Kok (Dutch prime minister from 1994 to 2002), the other by the Belgian economist André Sapir.

The Kok Report endorsed the goals of the Lisbon Agenda, and defended the possibility of achieving them by 2010. However, it offered a range of criticisms. The original strategy was too broad, with responsibilities for change too inadequately pinned down. In a much-quoted statement, the Kok Report observed that 'Lisbon is about everything and thus about nothing. Everybody is responsible and thus no one.'[21] The report strongly emphasized the need to complete the Single Market. Continuing to open the market in Europe to goods and services, while resisting protectionist pressures, is fundamental to Europe's economic prospects. In supposedly liberalized sectors such as utilities, the report points out, national operators are still often accorded a privileged place. Electricity and gas markets are due to be wholly opened by July 2007, and it is expected that member states comply with this obligation, although the prospect looks distinctly unlikely.

The Sapir Report, published slightly earlier, reaches similar conclusions. Growth in Europe overall has been disappointing, likewise job creation – 'it is as if Europe has become stuck in a rut'.[22] The report is a very thorough one, the best that has been produced in recent years concerning the economic prospects of the EU and what can be done to improve them. It concentrates on a six-point agenda for change:

1 Make the Single Market more dynamic. Services must be opened up to competition, regulation relaxed and competition policy altered to give better market access to new enterprises. A proactive strategy towards mobility of labour in Europe is needed.

2 Boost investment in knowledge: increase national and EU spending on research and postgraduate education and introduce tax credits to encourage private-sector R&D.

[21] Wim Kok, *Facing the Challenge*. Report of the High Level Group, November 2004, p. 16.
[22] Sapir, *An Agenda for a Growing Europe*.

3 Improve the macroeconomic framework for Economic and Monetary Union (EMU) – basically, create incentives for countries to build up surpluses in good times and provide more flexibility in more difficult ones.

4 Redesign policies for convergence and restructuring. Convergence funds given to lower-income countries should focus upon institution-building and investment in human and physical capital. There should be EU restructuring support for workers who lose their jobs and need to retrain, as an adjunct to national policies.

5 Achieve more effective decision-making and regulation by having a clearer definition of the relations between EU and national decision-processes, strengthening the purchase of the OMC.

6 Refocus the EU budget away from agricultural spending by devolving rural financing to the member states. Spend the budget primarily on growth, convergence and restructuring funds.

A review of the Lisbon Agenda was made by the European Council in March 2005, the halfway point in its development. In accordance with recommendations of the Kok Report, the programme was streamlined and clarified, with the dominant emphasis being placed upon growth and jobs. Other goals, including those of improving social cohesion and reducing social exclusion, were not discarded, but along with environmental goals were given lower priority. Since these aims demand investment, it was reasoned, growth and jobs must come first. The Commission set out new guidelines to make sure that funds allocated to lower-income nations and regions are spent pursuing Lisbon goals.

The budget deal concluded in December 2005, however, incorporated virtually none of these prescriptions, although a thorough review of expenditure was promised for 2008. The budget as it stands means that less than 10 per cent of EU spending over the period 2007–2013 will be on Lisbon priorities. Some of the difficulties of the EU were fully on display in the budget negotiations. Leaders play to their national audiences and defend first and foremost their national interests. There seems little notion of making sacrifices for the collective good; on the contrary, such an attitude tends to be interpreted as a sign of weakness.

It isn't surprising that Lisbon 'league tables' closely match the track records of the various EU nations. Denmark, Sweden, Austria and the UK occupy the top four places in those tables. France is in eighth place, Germany tenth, and Italy a lowly twenty-third. The new entrant states are down near the bottom and have a lot of work to do to catch up.

There are two quite distinct views held across Europe about the reasons for the EU's poor overall record on job creation and economic growth. The approach of the Lisbon Agenda (and of this book) is that lack of structural reforms, particularly in certain key countries, is the main explanation. Innovation and reform, much of which has to happen at national level, are essential.

The other view is that Europe's poor performance can best be explained in terms of deficiencies in macroeconomic policy – and that this is the level on which they need to be remedied. The European Central Bank, it is said, has placed too much emphasis upon price stability and not enough upon stimulating growth. Those who take this view argue that Keynesian policies can still work at a European level even though they no longer apply at a national one. Thus there could be a Europe of '*grands projets*' – for example, large-scale investments in new transport links – which could help generate jobs and restore higher levels of growth. Proponents of this idea also tend to argue that social justice can also be most effectively created by EU-level policies. For instance, the idea of a Europe-wide minimum wage has been widely promoted.[23]

A Europe of '*grands projets*' may very well be worthwhile if appropriate sources of finance could be found. But as a way of generating jobs and restoring growth it would fail for the same reasons as Keynesian policies have failed at the national level. Investors today factor in the anticipated consequences of new projects, and hence negate their impact on demand. A European minimum wage

23 European Foundation for the Improvement of Living and Working Conditions, 'Minimum wages in Europe', July 2005; available online at <http://www.eiro. eurofound.ie/2005/07/study/tn0507101s.html>.

is not a serious option, since the levels of prosperity of member states are so different. It could at most be a formula applied as a proportion of the income levels of member states; but the divergences would be so great as to make it largely meaningless.

The current Eurozone banking rules were set up to prevent political interference with the European Central Bank's decisions, as well as to establish the credibility of the single currency. The EU fiscal discipline framework can certainly be questioned. However, any reform of this framework has to accept that fiscal responsibility is an essential quality of monetary union. The two positions are only mutually exclusive if radicalized, which is surely a mistake. Macroeconomic policy could be oriented more towards helping create the conditions within nations known to be relevant to productivity and growth. It is just such a position that is in fact suggested in the Sapir Report.[24] I shall return to some of these issues in chapter 6.

Some implications

Let me at this point summarize the implications of the material discussed so far. The experience of the good performers in Europe, and the contrasts with those that have fared poorly, gives us a framework for policy capable of wide application. The following comments set out some of the policy orientations stemming from this analysis.

First, an effective social model has to put growth and jobs at the forefront, just as the best performers have done, although certainly not to the exclusion of all else. A high level of employment, above a decent minimum wage, is desirable for more than one reason. The greater the proportion of people in jobs, the more money is available – other things being equal – to spend on social investment and social protection. Having a job is also the best route out of poverty. The Lisbon aim of getting an average of 70 per cent or more of the workforce into jobs is not in principle unrealistic. But all depends on the will to reform in those countries where the

---

[24] Jean Pisani-Ferry, 'Growth policies for Europe', in Policy Network, *Where Now for European Social Democracy?* London, 2004; Sapir, *An Agenda for a Growing Europe.*

employment ratio is well below this figure. Many factors, of course, go into creating more net jobs. However, it cannot be accidental that all the countries that have employment ratios of over 70 per cent in Europe have active labour market policies.

Second, those on the right of the political spectrum argue that only low-tax economies can prosper in a world of intensifying competition. Yet the evidence to the contrary seems unequivocal. There is no direct relationship between taxation as a proportion of GDP and either economic growth or job creation. There probably is an upper limit, as is indicated by the case of Sweden, which has for some while had the highest tax rate among the industrial countries, but saw its level of income per head slip markedly in relative terms. However, more important than the size of the state is how effective the state institutions are and the nature of economic and social policies pursued.

Third, flexibility in labour markets is an essential part of the policy framework of the successful states. It does not mean American-style hire and fire. In an era of accelerating technological change, 'employability' – being willing and able to move on – becomes of prime importance. 'Protect the worker, not the job', the slogan of labour market reform in Denmark, is the core principle in a world of economic uncertainty. 'Moving on' often has to happen within the same job, because of the importance of technological change. It has been estimated that in the EU15 economies, 80 per cent of the technology in use over the period 1995–2005 is less than ten years old. However, 80 per cent of the workforce was trained more than ten years ago.

Flexibility has a bad name, especially among some on the left. For them, it means sacrificing the needs of the workforce to the demands of capitalistic competition. But the nature of labour market regulation is at least as important as its extent. Many labour rights can and should remain. They include rights of representation and consultation, the regulation of working conditions, laws against discrimination, and so forth. Ireland has enjoyed phenomenal growth while implementing all relevant EU labour legislation of this sort.[25]

[25] James Wickham, *The End of the European Social Model Before it Began?* Dublin: Irish Congress of Trade Unions, 2004.

Many employees in fact want flexible working, and part-time work, in order to accommodate family demands. Flexibility also meshes to a considerable degree with wider trends in everyday life in modern societies. Most citizens are accustomed to a much wider range of lifestyle choices than a generation ago, including, if it is feasible for them, when and where to work and what type of work to do (much more on this point later).

Fourth, the much-touted 'knowledge economy' is not just an empty term, an invention of the Lisbon Agenda that lost its relevance when the dot.com bubble burst. It should more accurately be called a knowledge and service economy, because by no means all services demand high levels of training. Only 16 per cent of the labour force on average in the EU15 countries now work in manufacturing, and that proportion is still falling. To put it the other way around, over 80 per cent of people must now get their living from knowledge-based or service jobs.

Full or near-full employment is possible in the knowledge/service economy – it has been attained in some of the better-performing European economies mentioned above. But there is a price to be paid. More than two-thirds of the jobs created in the knowledge economy are skilled – and they are becoming more plentiful. Over the period 1995–2004, the proportion of jobs in the EU15 needing advanced qualifications went up from 20 to 24 per cent.

Low-skilled jobs fell from 34 to 25 per cent. But a lot of people must still work in such jobs – serving in shops, supermarkets, petrol stations or coffee shops. The minimum wage cannot be set so high as to exclude these jobs, or we also lose the more skilled jobs that come along with them. We have to try to ensure that, in any given national context, it is set at the right level so that there are no working poor; and to make sure that as far as possible people don't get stuck in those jobs when they would like to move on.

Fifth, investment in education, the expansion of universities and the diffusion of ICT are crucial parts of the modernization of the ESM. Finland is an interesting example of a society in the vanguard of ICT and also with a strong welfare system. As Manuel Castells and Pekka Himanen point out, the country shows that the thesis that a high-tech economy must be modelled after Silicon Valley – a deregulated business environment – is mistaken.[26] Finland has a greater degree of IT penetration than the US. Its growth rate in 1996–2000 was 5.1 per cent. It also ranks near the top of all developed countries in terms of measures of social justice and has a high tax base. The success of the country, Castells concludes, offers hope for others. Only four or five generations ago, Finland was a poor, heavily rural society.

An analysis of Eurobarometer data carried out by the Institute for Futures Studies in Sweden showed clear differences between the Scandinavian countries and most other states in Europe as regards skills and attitudes to skills acquisition.[27] The Scandinavian countries are distinctive in showing:

- a small 'skills gap': a low proportion of people who say they do not have the skills important for them in working life;
- a small 'credentials gap': those who say they have skills important in working life have the credentials to back up that claim;
- a high proportion of people have recently taken part in study or training;
- a high proportion affirm that there were no barriers preventing them from taking part in such training;
- only a small percentage of individuals say there is nothing to motivate them to take up further education or training.

Sixth, income inequality has grown in most industrial countries over the past thirty years, but there are signs that this process is now levelling off. Some societies have managed to stay remarkably egalitarian, with the Scandinavian countries once more being in the lead.[28] The lesson is that in reforming the ESM elsewhere, we must promote values of equality and inclusiveness. We do not have to have highly elevated tax rates to do so. Among other policies, we

[26] Manuel Castells and Pekka Himanen, *The Information Society and the Welfare State*. Oxford: Oxford University Press, 2002.
[27] Palme, 'Why the Scandinavian experience is relevant for the reform of the ESM'.
[28] Andre Sapir, 'Globalization and the reform of European social models', Background document for ECOFIN meeting, Manchester, 9 September 2005; available online at <www.bruegel.org>.

have to invest heavily in education in the early years since so many capabilities are laid down then. Investment in early education and child care is a key element in reducing levels of child poverty.

Seventh, pensions reform is essential. Yet again the Nordic countries are in the lead here. Sweden, Denmark and Finland have all reformed their pensions systems to make them sustainable in the longer term. Younger people have to be persuaded to save more. The state should help provide people with incentives to have more children, and make sure the right type of welfare measures are in place.

No matter what innovations are made to help or force people to save, there is only one main way to solve the issue of unaffordable pensions commitments. We have to persuade or motivate older people to stay in work longer. Such a goal is surely not just a negative one. We have to contest ageism both inside and outside the workplace. If it means people over 55, over 65 or indeed over 70, 'old age' is no longer the incapacitating factor it once was.

Finally, continuing reform of the state itself, and of public services, is just as important to the future of the ESM as any of the factors noted above. Where needed, decentralization and diversification are the order of the day. Plainly, there has to be a balance between these and integration. Public services should become just as responsive (in some ways, more responsive) to the needs of those they serve as commercial organizations are.

Beyond Best Practice

Best practice can only take us so far and not only because of the point made earlier about the rise and fall of countries held to be the ones to emulate. There are issues and problems that even the Nordic states and other currently successful countries do not deal with adequately. We need to think well beyond what exists anywhere at present, as I shall argue in detail in the rest of the book.

- Even nations that have high levels of employment have not fully overcome under-employment, if that term is understood to mean that everyone who can work has a job. Most have experienced increasing rates of long-term sickness and disability. By

2004, absence from work from these causes in Sweden, for example, had doubled since 1999. The reverse trend would in fact have been expected, because the decline of manufacture and industries like mining should have reduced accidents with machinery, or the physical exhaustion coming from a life of manual toil. It is not known how far the rise in sickness and disability is 'real' or how far it is a masked form of unemployment. In the case of disability, however, it is clear that disabled people able to work should be provided with adequate resources to make it possible for them to enter or re-enter the labour market.

- Flexicurity is highly important as a means of reconciling social protection and adaptability to change. However, on its own it is not enough. The main problem with it is that it comes into play only when a person loses his or her job. We should be looking also for policies that help people even before job loss occurs.

- A successful economy and a well-functioning welfare system do not guarantee the ready assimilation of immigrants or ethnic minorities. Right-wing populism and anti-immigrant sentiments have gathered strength in Denmark and Finland (although less so in Sweden). The Netherlands saw the rise of the movement led by the Dutch politician Pym Fortuyn (murdered in 2002), with its catchphrase, 'the Netherlands is full'. Following the murder in 2004 of the filmmaker Theo van Gogh, the reputation of the country for social peace and for tolerance has been shattered. These happenings, and the broader fears and anxieties they reflect and have helped produce, clearly influenced the outcome of the Dutch referendum on the EU constitution in 2005.

- Welfare systems built mainly on supply-side policies – as those of the current best-performers are – are potentially vulnerable. How well protected are these societies against times of recession, when there aren't enough jobs to go round? Moreover, according too much primacy to work could arguably bring other problems in its train. Rising rates of absence through sickness, for instance, might in some part reflect the psychological strains of a life built around work. No country could be said fully to have resolved issues of work–life balance.

There is evidence that some forms of mental illness have increased significantly over recent decades.[29]

- Social mobility in the post-war period has been based upon structural change. In other words, opportunities for self-betterment have come mainly from shifts in the distribution of jobs. That period has seen a more or less continuous expansion of white-collar and professional occupations at the expense of agricultural and industrial ones. Thus many people coming from manual or blue-collar class backgrounds have been able to move into higher-level occupations. However, the proportion of the workforce in manufacturing jobs has now become so reduced that it cannot go very much lower. The structural sources of opportunity are decreasing and look like continuing to do so, unless as yet unforeseen new dynamics appear in labour markets. There is likely to be more 'directionless' fluidity in our societies than there was before.

- New issues have arisen with the entry of the ten new member states into the Union. Anxieties about their likely impact on the richer countries have been widely expressed – and once more influenced the results of the constitutional referendums. Workers from these countries, including highly skilled workers, are willing to work for lower wages than their counterparts in the established EU states. Will their presence, especially as they move around Europe, have a damaging effect on wages? Will industries migrate from the richer countries to the new member states, taking jobs with them?

- The rising intensity of international competition carries threats to all EU countries, no matter how successful they have been in the recent past. This is one area where smaller countries may be more vulnerable than larger ones. A country like Finland, for example, which has built part of its success around high-tech industries, could suffer if new competitors were either able to undercut prices or if technological change suddenly undermined its markets.

[29] BBC, 'Mental health linked to diet', BBC News; available online at <http://news.bbc.co.uk/2/hi/health/4610070.stm>.

In the following chapters I shall suggest approaches for dealing with these various points. The main arguments I shall stress are:

1 The Lisbon Agenda (quite correctly) emphasized the extraordinary transformations sweeping through the economies of the advanced societies. A few years ago it was controversial to assert the existence of the knowledge/service economy. Now it has become generally accepted that the new economy is a reality, and that it is here to stay. But little analysis was provided of the *social transformations* that went along with these radical changes. The wider society, and with it people's everyday lives, are changing just as dramatically as the economic order. We have to identify these changes and ponder their implications for policy.

2 We must introduce the concept of *social justice* into the core of the debate about Lisbon. It is not enough to make airy statements about reducing social exclusion, as so much of the EU official literature does. Lack of a developed analysis of the changing forms of social justice is one of the main reasons the Lisbon Agenda has proved so hard to implement. Those who have opposed it on a national level have often done so on the grounds that it promotes markets at the expense of the less well-off. We have actively to make the case – with evidence – that reform promotes social justice, not undermines it.

3 The Lisbon Agenda recognized that welfare risks are changing. For instance, there has been a rise in poverty among children in many countries. However, this rethinking has not been far-reaching enough. We have to transform the very idea of welfare and with it some of our preconceptions about the welfare state too. Welfare is not just about the avoidance of risk. Increasingly it is about positive lifestyle change. To deal with this question we need a notion of *positive welfare*.

4 The issue of *cultural diversity* has to be brought into the centre of welfare debates. It is a basic element involved in reform of the social model. However, the idea of multiculturalism, I shall try to show, together with its policy consequences, has been widely misunderstood. It does not, or should not, imply

27

leaving immigrants or minorities alone to get on with their own lives as they see fit. Almost the opposite: multicultural-ism means looking for ways of directly relating diversity to mainstream values.

All these issues bear very directly upon what the EU is and what it should become. Europe's 11:9 was not just another enlargement, but placed the EU in a qualitatively different position from the past.

Conclusion: The Best of All Worlds?

The question is often asked: Can Europe afford its social model? But perhaps we should turn it the other way around: Can Europe afford *not* to have its social model? The levels of inequality that exist in the United States could cause that country immense prob-lems in the years that lie ahead. The US, for example, may have the best universities in the world, but it also has the highest illiteracy rate among the industrial countries. According to the Programme for International Assessment, 15-year-olds in the US rank no higher than twenty-fourth out of twenty-nine nations compared; and only twenty-fourth in tests of problem-solving skills. At a time when the knowledge economy is itself becoming globalized, a reformed European social model might mean that Europe may be better placed than the US.

A Europe to take on the world would have:

Finnish levels of ICT penetration
German industrial productivity
Swedish levels of equality
Danish levels of employment
Irish economic growth
Italian cooking, washed down with Hungarian wine (drunk sparingly)
Czech levels of literary culture
French levels of health care
Luxembourg level of GDP per head

Norwegian levels of education (although the country is not – yet
  – in the EU)
British cosmopolitanism
Cypriot weather

I offer apologies to countries excluded from this somewhat arbitrary list! And I don't mean it to be taken too seriously. We will not be able to integrate all these elements, of course. Some are no doubt incompatible with others anyway. Yet apart from the weather, mutual learning is possible on all these dimensions and the list at least brings home just how many rich qualities Europe has.

One of Europe's main problems is how to coordinate its diverse attributes without undermining them. Pro-Europeans should be ambitious for the EU, but ambition must be tempered with sobriety. I shall call this attitude *eurorealism* – Europe can be a major force in the world, but it is very unlikely ever again going to be *the* major force in it.

2

Change and Innovation in Europe

Achieving further reforms in the European social model will not be easy. Most of the innovations needed have to be introduced at the national level. Some nations matter more than others, not just because of the past history of the Union, but because of their size and their overall economic contribution. With the exception of the UK and Spain, all the countries that have done well recently are small. As I have argued, this fact does not imply that others cannot learn from their policies. It does mean that their impact upon the overall economic health of the EU has been limited. Some two-thirds of the unemployment in the EU is in Germany, France and Italy – and is indeed concentrated heavily in regions of those countries: in the east of Germany, in northern France and southern Italy.

The post-war history of Europe suggests that far-reaching structural reform in nations usually takes place only after there is a mounting sense of crisis. The innovations in the Scandinavian countries took place against the backdrop of severe economic difficulties, first of all in the late 1980s and early 1990s. Reforms in Britain only followed a lengthy period during which the UK was the 'sick man of Europe'. Much the same was true of the Netherlands, whose economy was in a parlous state for a long while.

A major question for current times is whether there exists an acute enough sense of crisis in the big underperforming EU economies to generate the impetus to change. The events of recent years suggest that there may be. The 'no' vote in the French referendum on the European constitution in a certain sense was a vote for the status quo – 'no more dilution of the European social model!' – but it was also plainly a cry of frustration. The riots in French cities late in 2005 were an even more acute expression of such sentiments.

Political upheaval in Germany didn't lead to a clear direction for government, but there is probably a greater appetite for innovation than there has been for a long time. It is not at all clear whether the same is true of Italy, which as of 2006 has some of the worst economic indicators of the EU15.

Defence of the European social model in these countries cannot possibly mean endorsing the existing order of things, no matter what the emotional reactions of some may be. Here one must repeat the point about globalization. Events in the outside world are only one source of the difficulties these societies face. What was effective a generation ago is in some part actively dysfunctional today.

The 'three large underperformers' can't be blamed for everything. Plenty of difficulties remain in other core European states. Since the early 1990s, individual prosperity as measured by purchasing power parity has risen by 33 per cent in the UK, but only by 20 per cent in France, 17 per cent in Italy and 16 per cent in Germany. In spite of its successes, the UK has plenty of problems. Fully a quarter of the population leaves school with rudimentary educational qualifications. Improvements have been made in reducing levels of child poverty, but the country still only ranks eleventh out of the EU15 states in respect of this crucial indicator. Economic productivity remains stubbornly below that of either Germany or France, let alone the United States.

Spain has made extraordinary progress, political and cultural as well as economic, since joining the EU – indeed, in some large part as a result of joining the Union. Yet although reduced significantly, unemployment remains high and the level of employment relatively low. There are serious problems in the educational system, while labour market reforms have not progressed sufficiently to prevent insider/outsider divisions. Spain ranks low down in terms of Lisbon-style reforms.

In the opening part of this chapter I shall consider what the possibilities are for reform in Germany, France and Italy. Germany is a key country for the whole of Europe, since it has, by some distance, the largest economy. Probably, however, a breakthrough is needed in at least two of the three countries in a relatively short space of time if the EU economy as a whole is to be put back on track.

I will then move on to consider the position of the new member states from former Eastern Europe (now widely called Central and Eastern Europe), since their accession has contributed to some of the anxieties widely felt in the established EU nations. These anxieties merge with those felt about new forms of global competition more widely, and this crucial issue needs looking at. Finally, I shall consider how far such anxieties are justified by looking at a debate that bears directly upon them – the controversy over the attempt to extend the Single Market to service industries.

Blocked Societies

Germany, France and Italy have a combined population of about 200 million people, some 40 per cent of the total in the EU. The first two, of course, were for many years the prime drivers of EU integration. Germany in the past has been regarded as a 'miracle economy', a success story for others to emulate as far as they could. Today the three countries appear as the prime examples in Europe of *blocked societies*.[1] I define a blocked society as one in which the need for change is apparent, not only to many of its citizens, but to most informed observers – yet where either natural conservatism, vested interests, or both, prevent needed reforms from occurring. The bigger the blocks, the more profound the sense of crisis needed before major reform is likely to happen.

Germany

A blocked society is not one that is unchanging. In all three societies there are significant changes going on. German companies,

---

[1] See Wolfgang Merkel, 'How the welfare state can tackle new inequalities', in Patrick Diamond and Matt Browne (eds.), *Rethinking Social Democracy.* London: Policy Network, 2004.

especially the large firms, are proving much more adaptable than seemed possible a few years ago. Financial companies have moved on from their old role of servicing manufacturing companies to larger investment strategies. As Deutsche Bank has restructured to take on a more global profile, 50 per cent of its employees now live outside Germany. By 2000 a third of the largest 100 companies in Germany were listed on international stock exchanges, and that proportion has since climbed higher.[2]

The union movement in the mid-1990s was one of the main sources of resistance to reform, but its influence has waned, and it has become less intransigent. Plant-level bargaining now happens in most big manufacturing firms, while more flexible working practices have spread through much of the economy. The 35-hour week, once the pride of German unionism, is now honoured in its absence. The large engineering union, I. G. Metall, for instance, now negotiates a two-year agreement with employers, whereby the 35-hour week is averaged over two years. But most German employees are simply working longer – the majority of white-collar employees now work a 40-hour week.

The labour market reform package, Agenda 2010, was introduced too late to save Gerhard Schröder's government, but the coalition led by Chancellor Angela Merkel, in power at the time of writing, should profit from it. Agenda 2010 involves a substantial range of reforms, but is essentially flexicurity tailored to German circumstances. In the German context, it represents a radical turnaround from pre-existing policy. Unemployment benefits are now conditional and are designed to create personal responsibility for active job search. The crucial element in the traditional social security system, the linking of unemployment benefits to previous earnings, has been discarded. Non-wage labour costs, which have inhibited job creation, have finally been reduced, in conjunction with increases in consumption taxes. Pensions reform is seriously on the agenda. Reform proposals include a gradual increase in the retirement age by one month a year from 2011 onwards, rising eventually to age 67. Policies designed to attract older people into

---

[2] Anke Hassel and Hugh Williamson, *The Evolution of the German Model.* London: Anglo-German Foundation, 2004.

the labour market, or keep them there, are being considered – plus extensive reforms to health care to contain costs, although the problems here are acute.

Do these reforms add up to a significant modernization of the German social model? Yes, in principle they do, although for their further implementation a great deal will depend upon overall political leadership, and upon targeted reforms in East Germany. When a blocked society does start to reform, change can happen fast, because of pent-up pressures for innovation. The grand coalition has been labelled by its supporters a 'companionship of destiny', but at the current time its effectiveness and durability are unknown.

Fundamental welfare reforms need to be made that as yet do not figure centrally in the German debate. Germany spends too much on the old and not enough on the young – the proposed pensions reforms are not sufficiently far-reaching to alter this situation. Only a low proportion of women are in the labour force compared to other EU15 countries. The German welfare system still depends substantially upon the traditional family, even though the traditional family, with its clear division of male and female roles, is ceasing to exist.

After its initial problems, Germany seems to have benefited from monetary union. The secret has been moderation. In 1996 labour costs were estimated to be overvalued by about 20 per cent. However, since then, wage inflation in Germany has been kept under the EU average, greatly helping competitiveness. The rest of Europe watches and waits anxiously. Without a return to growth and a much higher level of job generation in Germany, there isn't much prospect of a leap forward in the overall economic situation of Europe.

France

France has at least one major circumstance in common with Germany – the success of its large companies. France is often thought of as the home of economic nationalism. So far as its leading companies are concerned, however, it is very much at home with globalization. Danone, for example, is the largest distributor of dairy products and bottled water in the world, with sales in 120 countries and a turnover of some €14 billion.[3] In the ranking of the world's best-managed big companies carried out by *Forbes* magazine in 2003, France was number two, behind the US but ahead of Japan, the UK and Germany.

One in every seven employees in France works for a subsidiary of a foreign firm, a number which almost doubled between 1994 and 2003. This figure is now equivalent to 16 per cent of the labour force in the non-state sectors – a higher proportion than in either the UK or the US. Foreign companies have a majority holding in 42 per cent of the larger firms listed on the Paris stock exchange – compared to 33 per cent in the UK. France is the third most popular destination for foreign direct investment in the world, just behind the US and China.

Like Germany, the embrace of globalization has happened largely 'by stealth'. In France, unlike Germany, globalization is very generally equated with Americanization, and criticizing globalization is an attractive political message.[4] The anti-globalization movement has had prominent champions in France, creating a political atmosphere different from almost any other European country. These differences are reflected in opinion polls. A poll held in 2002 revealed that 63 per cent of the French population felt 'worried' about globalization. Only 10 per cent expressed themselves as 'confident' and a mere 2 per cent were 'enthusiastic' about globalization. France is hence at best schizophrenic about globalization, and at worst in denial. Much the same applies to its cultural diversity – or did so until the riots in French cities in 2005. France is home to the largest Islamic minorities in Europe, and to diverse other minority groups and immigrant groups. Yet it has seen itself as a monocultural society. Like globalization, multiculturalism is associated with the 'Anglo-Saxon' world.[5]

[3] Sophie Meunier, 'France and globalization in 2003'. US–France Analysis series, Brookings Institution, May 2003.

[4] Philip H. Gordon and Sophie Meunier, *The French Challenge: Adapting to Globalization*. Washington: Brookings Institution Press, 2001.

[5] Jeremy Jennings, 'Citizenship, republicanism and multiculturalism in contemporary France', *British Journal of Political Studies*, 30 (2000).

In some areas, France has excellent welfare services. For example, child care facilities are far superior to those available in Germany – one of the main reasons, as already mentioned, why the birth rate is so much higher. Standards of health care are excellent although, as in Germany, the health care system is not affordable in its current form. Higher education, however, is largely unreformed (as is also true in Germany). Unemployment in France rivals that of Germany; a relatively high proportion of those out of work in France are long-term unemployed. The level of employment is relatively low – well under the Lisbon target of 70 per cent of the labour force in work. France's main problems are divisions in the labour market coupled to very high youth unemployment, most pronounced among minorities.

France spends virtually as much as Sweden does on social policy, but has three to four times as much poverty. In his book *France in Crisis*, Timothy Smith shows that French social policy is not redistributive – most social spending actually serves to increase existing inequalities.[6]

Unemployment rose to 10 per cent in 1983 and has hovered around that level ever since. In spite of this situation, a succession of legal interventions designed to protect jobs have been made into the labour market. Up to 25 per cent of lay-offs now go to court. To avoid court proceedings, employers often pay higher severance payments than they are obliged to do by law. The main consequences have been to entrench further the divided labour market and help drive up overall economic inequality. Many young people, if they get work at all, find themselves in jobs with fixed-term contracts – or are working in the secondary economy. Of new hires overall, 70 per cent are now in fixed-term contract jobs; spells of unemployment last an average of 13 months.

The reforms introduced – albeit briefly – in early 2006 were a significant break with the past. The 'New Hiring Contract' (CNE) was for small firms; the 'First Hiring Contract' (CPE) for larger ones. They effectively abrogated the whole framework of existing labour law for the first two years of a job hire for a young person.

---

[6]   Timothy Smith, *France in Crisis: Welfare, Inequality and Globalization Since 1980*. Cambridge: Cambridge University Press, 2004.

Employers would have been able to lay off workers at will during their first two years in a job. Only two weeks' advance notice had to be given. An example given by government was Spain, where temporary contracts are widely used and have played a part in elevating employment levels.

The very people who were supposed to gain from the changes, young people, took to the streets in large numbers to protest against them. The protestors were not persuaded that the proposals would bring the promised returns in terms of opportunities. And perhaps they were right, since the reforms did nothing about the privileges of the insiders – workers who hold secure and protected contracts, mainly state employees or those working in large companies. France needs its own version of Agenda 2010, focused on the labour market as a whole and providing resources for job search retraining. Yet creating a political climate where such reforms can be seriously contemplated looks much more difficult even than it was in Germany.

Italy

Serious though the problems of Germany and France are, they are outweighed by those of Italy – *the* blocked society of blocked societies in Europe. In 1987, Italy officially announced that its GDP had overtaken that of Britain. Over the years since then, Italy's growth rate has been the lowest in the EU, behind that of both Germany and France. Even if the sizeable secondary economy is included, the Italian economy is now only about 80 per cent the size of the UK. In 2005 its growth was close to zero.

Public debt stands at more than 100 per cent of GDP; the country spends 4.5 per cent of its revenues each year on paying off the interest. Italy's prosperity was built on industries vulnerable to competition from abroad, such as textiles, clothing and furniture. It lags behind in terms of most Lisbon criteria, including education and investment in IT. Very few people over the age of 55 are in work. An analysis carried out by the European Commission in 2003, which looked at eight structural indicators, ranked Italy at the bottom of the member states. Its underlying competitiveness was judged lower than that of Portugal and Greece, other laggards in this respect.

Unlike in the case of Germany, wage costs have not been reduced or even contained. Unit labour costs in Spain have fallen by 15 per cent since 1995; in Italy they have grown by 40 per cent. Italy does not possess the avant-garde of progressive big business found in Germany and France. The country got by for a long while by means of currency devaluations (as in the UK in an earlier period). These created a temporary return to competitiveness, but meant that needed reforms were simply deferred indefinitely. Only after Italy entered the single currency did its underlying structural weaknesses become fully apparent.

The Italian welfare system is an extreme case of dependency on the traditional family which, as in other developed countries, is faltering. Only a relatively small proportion of women are in the labour market. The birth rate in Italy is one of the lowest in the world, at 1.2 per 1,000 (compared to 2.7 in the 1960s). The stay-at-home son is a common figure in Italian households. More than 80 per cent of men aged between 18 and 30 still live with their parents. The average Italian man is 33 years old when his first child is born.

Business start-ups are difficult in Italy because of arcane regulations. Anyone who wants to start a business needs to go through sixteen steps, which take sixty-two working days. It needs fifty-three days in France to do the same, forty-five in Germany – and only three in Denmark. The labour market is as divided as any in Europe, with the insiders well protected. All net job creation is taking place in the unprotected sectors and in the sizeable secondary economy. It is the secondary economy that gives the society a robustness belied by the official statistics – and greater flexibility and adaptability.

As in France, Italy has large numbers of workers in temporary contract jobs. There is no comprehensive system of unemployment insurance. The pay-outs given by government are decided on a case-by-case basis, and do not generally cover small companies – and such companies create 70 per cent of GDP in Italy. The incoming centre-left government proposes a scheme that would give increasing protection for a worker the longer he or she is in a job, instead of creating a new labour contract as was tried in France.

The formal age of retirement in Italy is 65 years for men and 60 for women. But the real average retirement age for both sexes is 57.

The Berlusconi government introduced plans to bring the average real retirement age up to 60 by 2010, by reducing pensions for those who retire early. However, the eventual reforms made were even less ambitious than this.

Italy's universities are over-crowded to the point of exhaustion, with few effective reforms having been made, and expenditure on R&D is low too. Without structural change, the country has nothing to invest. Because of the size of the secondary economy – much of which is concentrated in the south, with Naples as its 'capital' – something close to €100 billion is evaded in taxes every year. Italy has been likened to a frog put in cold water. 'The fire has been turned on and eventually the frog will die, nicely, without realizing.'[7] There is a certain truth to the observation. The sense of crisis so visible in Germany and France does not seem to exist in Italy. It is a country perhaps too accustomed to crises, and the rise and fall of governments, to take the current impasse too seriously.

Yet by any definition the country does face extremely pressing difficulties. Its way of life is becoming unaffordable, even in the relatively short term. Since the traditional quick fix of devaluation can no longer be used, there is no option but structural reform of a quite profound kind. Yet the country's political system, with its complex coalitions and embedded vested interests, seems ill-equipped to deliver the necessary political leverage. In current circumstances, this problem seems even greater, given the wafer-thin margin of victory of the government elected in April 2006.

Without a dynamic reform programme, Italy's plight could directly affect the rest of the European Union. Membership of EMU in principle forces the country to face up to its difficulties and take active steps to resolve them. But will it be able to do so? The cost of continued inaction could be withdrawal from EMU, and that of course would have ramifications for the status of monetary integration as a whole.

When we look at societies that have managed to reform, we see that the nature of their political systems, as one would expect, is a key element. Arguably, those political systems that permit or facilitate

---

[7] Francesco Giavazzi, 'Italy: the frog in cold water', *Telos-EU* (1 April 2006), p. 2.

reform are of two types. One type is where reform is achieved through consensus politics, even in the face of divisive issues. In these societies there is typically a strong labour movement, but one accustomed to working both with government and business.[8] There may be charged debates, and quite severe divisions, but there is enough give and take to get an overall consensus for change. The Nordic countries, the Netherlands and some other small states seem to be able to change in this way – although at the current time there are big schisms in several of them around minorities and migration.

In larger countries a consensual system can operate effectively – for example, West Germany in the 1960s and 1970s – but can also translate into a structural conservatism. It is difficult to produce effective leadership when consensus breaks down. The West German 'Bonn model' was a success, but its cohesion was in some part the result of the country's Cold War status as a 'front-line' Western state. Federalism worked well then, but it is not clear that it has done so after reunification. As of the 1990s, 60 per cent of federal legislation required approval of the second chamber, which has the power of absolute veto. Reforms in play in early 2006 are set to reduce this proportion to 35–40 per cent, but in some respects could make decision-making even more difficult.

In other countries, the blocking mechanisms are quite different. These are states where the level of union membership is low, but where the unions have influence in the state sector and have traditions of radicalism. The ability of government leaders to lead is limited by 'street veto power' – the capability of sectional groups to mobilize direct action to block reform measures. France, Italy and Greece are the prime examples in Europe. The short life of the CPE in France in 2006 shows just how forceful street veto power can be.

Former Eastern Europe

The problems of the ex-Communist states are different again. For many in what was Western Europe, the new member states have

---

[8] See the classic work by Geoffrey Ingham, *Strikes and Industrial Conflict: Britain and Scandinavia*. London: Macmillan, 1974.

become associated with low taxes and unfair competition – issues that figured so strongly in the constitutional referendums. Yet such views are in fact largely inaccurate. Four erstwhile East European states in the EU – Latvia, Lithuania, Slovenia and Slovakia – have introduced flat income taxes. The logic behind the introduction of such taxes, however, is not to tax less but to tax more. Flat income taxes have been set up in countries, inside and outside the EU, where levels of tax evasion have historically been high. In any case, average taxation rates in the ten accession countries are not in fact much lower than the average for Western Europe. Their average rate of taxation in 2003 was 36 per cent of GDP, compared to just over 40 per cent for the established EU15 states.

The largest ex-Communist EU members, Hungary and Poland, have overall levels of taxation quite close to the average of the EU15. The difficulties they face are actually more severe than any of the EU15 countries, save perhaps for Italy, because they combine the need for extensive welfare reform with a low level of industrial competitiveness. Poland, the largest of the new member states, currently has the lowest employment rate in the EU, at 51 per cent of the workforce. Very few businesses are internationally competitive and the transition to a market economy has meant that many state-owned enterprises have collapsed. Unemployment stands at over 30 per cent in some regions, while fully 45 per cent of young people under the age of 25 are out of work. The welfare system is consequently under great strain, and in spite of reforms doesn't really reflect need. Social welfare recipients are heavily weighted towards older people and traditional unemployment benefits.

In Communist times, the welfare system in Eastern Europe was geared to the objective of 'creating socialism' through the centralized wage system, the guarantee of employment and policies linked to the state-controlled enterprises. Participation in the labour force was the prime basis of entitlement. In the more advanced countries, such as Hungary, this system began to be changed well ahead of the transformations of 1989–90. The traditional welfare policies were supplanted by means-tested measures.

Determined attempts at modernization continue in Hungary, but in a situation where many look back in a rose-tinted way to times past. The present government lays considerable emphasis upon dialogue with civil society groups, a big difference from the Communist period when, in spite of much talk of partnerships, most welfare measures were imposed from the top down. The aims of the government in continuing the reform process are explicitly geared to the goals of reform in the EU15. The stated goal is to pursue the objectives of the Lisbon strategy, including the ambition of increasing social cohesion.[9]

Those in the established EU states should be conscious of the problems faced by the new entrants. Many in former Eastern Europe, including political leaders and citizens, have become disillusioned both with change post-1989 and with the effects of entry to the EU. As Janos Kornai has said, what was once 'a hopeless daydream' – that their societies would become freed from the yoke of the Soviet Union and become democratic market economies – 'has become a reality'. Having got what once seemed impossible, however, 'many are disappointed and bitter'.[10]

The economic background in and of itself is actually encouraging. Kornai studied eight countries intensively: the Czech Republic, Estonia, Poland, Latvia, Lithuania, Hungary, Slovakia and Slovenia. In six of them the growth rate was markedly higher over the period 1990–2000 than it had been during the ten years before 1990. Since 1995, per capita GDP and labour productivity increased much more rapidly than in the EU15 states. Labour productivity has grown at four times the pace of the older-established EU countries.

However, the transition process has not been at all pain-free. Before 1990, considerable proportions of the population lived in poverty, and some have now become even further impoverished. Others have suffered a deterioration in their incomes.[11] Overall levels of economic inequality have increased. Perhaps most important, the economic security that used to exist – 'we pretend to work and you pretend to pay us' – has disappeared. Chronic shortages, and waiting lists even for basic goods, were commonplace during

---

[9] 'The wild East', *New York Times*, 13 December 2005.
[10] Janos Kornai, 'The great transformation of Central Eastern Europe'. Presidential address, 14th World Congress of the IEA, August 2005.
[11] Ibid, pp. 26–8.

the Communist period. But there was job security for everyone. Unemployment is now open rather than masked, as it was in the old regime.

The disappearance of taken-for-granted job tenure has gone along with new insecurities on several fronts. Some are the same as elsewhere, but to people accustomed to a different order of things, they are more unsettling. For example, once upon a time prices in the shops were fixed for lengthy periods, but today they are constantly changing. State-controlled corporations were fixed entities in the landscape – now companies come and go. Corruption used to be institutional and hidden from public view; today it exists in a whole variety of transactions, from an individual to a governmental level.

There are other resentments too, some of which have become turned towards the European Union – including the empty feeling that accession can bring when it is completed. After all, a very large range of changes have to be made before accession, which then seems to offer little once achieved. Many look forward to immediate benefits that do not come. Finally, there is the phenomenon of relative deprivation. How people feel about their lives depends in large degree upon whom they compare themselves to. In previous times, citizens in Eastern Europe contrasted their life circumstances favourably with those pertaining in the Soviet Union. But now their point of reference has shifted to countries such as Sweden or Austria, where most people are much better off than they are.[12]

Social Dumping

Care must be taken to ensure that the very division of Europe that enlargement was intended to overcome isn't opened up again. Only the UK, Sweden and Ireland permitted immediate freedom of movement for citizens from the new member states on accession in 2004. 'Social dumping' has emerged as a major issue across Europe, seemingly setting the interests of the older EU states against those of the new ones. It is an emotive term, meaning

[12] Ibid, pp. 30–1.

several different things. One is that the availability of cheap labour power from Eastern Europe will create downward pressure on wages in the richer countries. Another is that low taxes in the new member states will give them unfair competitive advantage over those with higher overall tax levels. Yet another is that industry will migrate to the new member states because they can cut costs that way. To these issues we should add fears about low-cost competition coming from developing countries outside Europe. Anxieties on this count can merge in people's minds with those felt about enlargement, even though the two have nothing directly to do with one another.

The now celebrated Polish plumber played a major role in the French referendum – in his absence, of course, since there are in fact very few Polish plumbers in France. Anxieties about 'social dumping' are felt not only at the level of the lay public, but also by political leaders too. They underlie calls for the harmonization of taxes and worries about the Services Directive that the Commission initiated in January 2004 (see below).

It is crucial, however, to separate well-founded anxieties from false ones, bracketing off for a moment the political problems, and populist pressures, involved. How far are living standards in the richer EU countries really threatened by entry of the poorer ones? Could a 'race to the bottom' within the EU be initiated as a result? A relatively new, but related, question has come to the fore more recently, although it has not as yet received as much attention in Europe as in the US – the outsourcing of knowledge-based and service jobs to poorer countries, where workers are paid much lower wages than in the West.

Fears about a potential race to the bottom with enlargement may be widely felt, but they are not well founded. Such worries have been expressed before in two contexts. One was in relation to intensifying global competition generally, the other concerned earlier EU expansions, when Greece, Spain and Portugal were accepted as members (Greece in 1981; Spain and Portugal in 1986). The anxieties expressed by many some years ago that economic globalization would force cut-backs in European welfare states have proved to be almost wholly unfounded. Taxation revenue as a proportion of GDP has remained stable in virtually all the industrial countries, although with a few exceptions, such as the UK, it is no longer climbing. Some of the most important difficulties facing the European social model, as mentioned earlier, are in any case primarily internal rather than external in their origins.

Studies of the economic impact of Portugal, Spain and Greece after their accession show positive rather than negative effects on the pre-existing EU countries. There was no reining in of the development of welfare programmes within the three states to put them in a more favourable competitive position. On the contrary, the welfare systems developed since the 1980s have been marked by strong expansionary trends.[13] At the time of the accession of the three Mediterranean countries many thought that further divisions would develop between the nations in the EU – the rich states would get even wealthier, while the new entrants would get relatively poorer. Such proved not to be the case.[14] Of course it could be argued that in the current round of enlargement the incoming states are poorer in relative terms than Portugal, Spain or Greece were, and have adopted more aggressive tax policies. Yet the gap is not nearly as great as that between the developed countries and poorer countries on a world level.

There are further important misconceptions to be corrected.[15] In the first place, de facto enlargement to the East has been taking place for quite a number of years. Trade barriers were initially dismantled early in the 1990s. By the turn of the new century tariffs and quotas for trade in manufactured goods had disappeared. It was this very lifting of barriers that helped the East European economies to recovery. At that point the larger East European countries were already exporting more than 60 per cent of their goods to the EU, one or two as many as 75 per cent. Investment by companies in these countries also came well before actual accession. The lowering of trade barriers, plus the fact that the East

---

[13] Ana M. Guillen and Manos Matsaganis, 'Testing the "social dumping" hypothesis in Southern Europe', *Journal of European Social Policy*, 10 (2000).

[14] Loukas Tsoukalis, *What Kind of Europe?* Oxford: Oxford University Press, 2005, p. 55.

[15] Katinka Barysch, 'East versus West? The European economic and social model after enlargement', in Anthony Giddens, Patrick Diamond and Roger Liddle (eds.), *Global Europe, Social Europe*. Cambridge: Polity, 2006.

European nations would soon become members of the EU, were enough to persuade firms to move production facilities there. About €150 billion was invested by companies in the ten 2004 accession countries prior to their formal entry.

Since the late 1990s growth rates in the East European countries have substantially outstripped the EU average. Have these achievements been at the expense of jobs in the West European states? The short answer is that they have not. From the point at which serious trade was resumed between Western and Eastern Europe, the West has run a trade surplus. According to one study, mutual trading created a net gain of more than 100,000 jobs in the EU15 by the year 2000.[16] Companies that have transferred plant to the East have produced job losses where offices and factories in Western Europe have closed down. However, unless companies have moved en bloc to the East, which is very rare, more jobs have probably been protected in the established EU states than lost there. The reason is that some or most of the companies would not have prospered or even survived without shifting some of their production.

Established EU states that have failed sufficiently to reform, and have high unemployment, have been the ones where governments and citizens are most anxious about 'social dumping'. Germany and France have been in the lead in the moves to demand a long transition period before freedom of movement is allowed to happen. Many workers have come to the three countries that have opened their borders. These countries have in fact gained from the process, especially since many of those who have come are skilled. In Ireland, for example, 85,000 people arrived in the first year after enlargement, the largest proportion relative to population size. However, the Irish are actively recruiting more, because of labour and skill shortages. In the UK, 175,000 people from the new member states registered for work between May 2004 and March 2005, of whom 40 per cent had been in the country previously anyway. They have been readily absorbed into the labour force and labour shortages remain.

The overall effect of enlargement is bound, in fact, to be quite small overall so far as the bulk of the EU is concerned. The GDP

[16] Ibid.

of the new member states is only 5 per cent of the EU total. But it is in the interests of the EU as a whole that they should prosper and have a period of rapid economic growth. Such a scenario would cause no serious problems for the established EU states if they themselves are able to reform. The danger is that mutual misunderstanding and resentment might produce an opposite effect. Those in the new member states continue to feel like second-class citizens, while the threats they supposedly pose block needed reforms in the richer EU countries.

Globalization, China and India

Economic globalization in its earlier phases may not have produced the race to the bottom that was widely feared, but what about newer developments in off-shoring and outsourcing? Coupled to the rapid emergence of China as the world's manufacturing centre and of India as a focus of the outsourcing services, what will the effects on Europe be? As with enlargement, the ideological impact has already been considerable. Protectionism has made a comeback, both in the EU and the US. It is one thing, it seems, to proclaim the value of free trade to others, another when it seems to react back on the prospects of the affluent countries. In general terms, the growing economic importance of China, India and other developing economies is to be applauded. In terms of overall world welfare – if one excludes environmental issues: a big 'if' – the net gain in wealth on a global level is large. Moreover, it is obvious that in principle there are new export markets for Western goods.

When developing countries first enter the world economy on a significant scale, they do so either with agricultural products or with labour-intensive manufactured goods such as clothing and textiles. During this stage, tensions are caused within the economy of the country. As markets are opened up, indigenous industries come under pressure from products from more developed countries whose higher costs are compensated for by being of better quality than local goods. Consequently, it is difficult to progress beyond this phase, and some developing countries fail to do so.

47

China and India have become so successful because they have now made this advance. In other words, they are no longer competing on the basis of cheaper wages, but, increasingly, on the level of quality and technology. A growing number of indigenous companies in China and India are at or close to the frontier of global best practice.[17] China's market share in imported electronic goods in the EU increased from 5 per cent to 10 per cent between 1995 and 2000, and then doubled again to 20 per cent by 2003. Consumer electronics, like TVs or computer games, made up 80 per cent of China's electronics exports to the EU in 1998, but accounted for only 20 per cent of those exports by 2003. All the rest now comprises higher-level goods such as office computers and telecommunications equipment.

High-tech clusters are appearing around not just the main but even the secondary metropolitan areas in India.[18] There are well-established universities and institutes in India, but the growing second tier of new institutions may in the medium term have more impact. In China there are similar initiatives, some of them extremely bold. For instance, a major science park in Beijing includes 56 universities and 232 research institutes coordinated by the Chinese Academy of Sciences. Some of the initiatives in play are joint ventures with foreign universities and companies. Western companies have outsourced activities in areas including pharmaceuticals, biotechnology and computer hardware and software – and not only to India and China. For instance, Intel owns labs carrying out cutting-edge work in microprocessor design in Novosibirsk and St Petersburg in Russia.

How can the European economies – and companies – cope with this type of direct competition? We can get an indication from a study by Schott and Bernard in the US, where high-level competition from China came earlier than in Europe.[19] Schott and Bernard compared firms that survived with those that failed in the US over

---

[17] John Sutton, 'Globalization: a European perspective', in Anthony Giddens, Patrick Diamond and Roger Liddle (eds.), *Global Europe, Social Europe*. Cambridge: Polity, 2006.

[18] A. D. Bardhan and Dwight Jaffee, *Innovation, R&D and Offshoring*. Fisher Centre for Real Estate and Urban Economics, Fall, 2005.

[19] Quoted in Sutton, 'Globalization: a European perspective'.

the period since the early 1990s. Firms that succeeded, they showed, managed to run ahead of the game. That is to say, they were adaptable enough to shift their product range from sectors where overseas competition became intense to new products or adjacent industries. Flexibility in the labour market conjoins with creativity of management to produce success. Even in an American context, however, flexibility means training and retraining, not simply insecure labour. The companies that do well help their employees adapt.

Those most directly affected by the transfer of manufacturing plant overseas, both in the US and the EU, have until recently been the less well-off – mainly manual workers. The new forms of outsourcing, in which India rather than China is in the lead, affect different groups. They concern exactly that area upon which advanced economies are now wholly dependent for job creation – the large range of service industries. Professionals, such as medical specialists, computer software engineers, accountants or journalists, did not in the past worry about their jobs going abroad; indeed, they gained from the cheaper goods that open trading and improvements in manufacture made possible.[20] They have to worry now. Surveys in the US show that the proportion of professionals who support free trade, which used to be very high, has dipped sharply as their own jobs enter the firing line.

Reactions to the advent of international outsourcing vary widely. The press in the US has been full of scare stories. For instance, *Fortune* magazine in August 2005 had as its cover story, ' "Can America compete?" is the nation's no 1 anxiety'.[21] *New York Times* journalist Thomas Friedman has argued that we entered a new era in 2000 – not so much the turn of the millennium as the point at which 'the world became flat', 'as flat as the screen on which a [business leader] can host a meeting of his whole global supply chain'.[22] Developments in communications technology, and

---

[20] Mary Amiti and Shang-Jin Wei, 'Fears of service outsourcing', *Economic Policy*, April 2005.

[21] 'America isn't ready', *Fortune*, 8 August 2005.

[22] Thomas Friedman, *The World is Flat: A Brief History of the Twenty-First Century*. New York: Allen Lane, 2005, p. 7.

especially the cheapening of that technology, are empowering individuals and groups across the world – not just the large corporations. Small providers can enter the world market in a direct way.

More than 50 per cent of manufactured goods are currently traded globally, compared to only 10 per cent of services. The volume of service trading is bound to rise further, perhaps even quite steeply. Trade in economic theory is supposed to bring mutual benefits. The new international division of labour should not in principle be any different. Outsourcing should allow companies to reduce prices, helping consumers and also generating revenue for further investment. Lower prices should renew demand, in turn creating new employment. A recent study in the US showed such a cycle in operation. The researchers analysed the outsourcing of software production in American IT and telecommunications companies in the 1990s. As a result of this process, the prices of computers and other IT goods were reduced by between 10 and 30 per cent over a ten-year period. Lower prices then fuelled an investment boom in IT, as well as elevating productivity in industries making use of the technology. American economic growth rose by 0.3 per cent as a direct result, producing a rapid expansion of IT jobs in the US.[23]

However, in all such processes there are workers who lose their jobs and are forced to relocate. Losing a job is almost always a traumatic affair for those involved. There is an overall net benefit to the economy only if those whose jobs disappear find new jobs quickly, and at approximately the same level as those they have lost. A McKinsey study showed significant differences between the US and EU. For every $1 of business services outsourced to India, the net benefit to the US economy was $1.14, coupled to a benefit of $0.33 for the Indian economy. In contrast to the US, the German economy is likely to lose €0.15 for every €1 of services outsourced.[24] The reason is the lower proportion of the workforce who will find new jobs.

---

[23] Simon Commander, Axel Heitmueller and Laura Tyson, 'Migrating workers and jobs: a challenge to the European social model?', in Anthony Giddens, Patrick Diamond and Roger Liddle (eds.), *Global Europe, Social Europe*. Cambridge: Polity, 2006.

[24] McKinsey & Co., 'How offshoring of services could benefit France'. McKinsey Global Institute, June 2005.

For there to be mutual trading gain from outsourcing in the EU, labour market reform is needed, but it does not have to be in the direction of American-style deregulation. Instead, the European countries should tailor deregulation schemes to workers affected, with the aim of sustaining jobs and income levels. Retraining will be important, but more specific programmes may be required for those individuals with higher-level skills – much depends upon how generalizable or adaptable the skills they possess are (more on these issues in chapter 3). Outsourcing is still in its early stages, and so far has had little impact on Western economies – it could have far more influence in the future, and it is as well to prepare for such a scenario.

It is not certain, of course, that the rise of China and India will continue – in common with most other developing countries, both have major structural difficulties to resolve. India is currently surging ahead economically, but has a chaotic transport infrastructure, as well as yawning inequalities on a household as well as a regional level. Economic inequalities in China have become almost as large, while the continuing dominance of the party cadres could at some point become a fundamental handicap. China has achieved great success in export markets, but domestic economic efficiency is low. Unless the majority of state-controlled companies are further liberalized, it is possible that the Chinese miracle – like so many 'economic miracles' before it – will turn sour.

It is said that only 1 per cent of companies in China submit themselves to independent auditing. China's banking system is insolvent to the tune of US$500 billion. Chinese banks are not capable of putting their own house in order, since they only generate an average of 0.2 per cent return on their assets. The reason is that, until recently, banks met government policy demands by financing the state-owned enterprises, regardless of profitability or risk.

In addition, the country is struggling under the weight of an accelerating environmental crisis – one of great consequence for the wider world, but which within China is threatening the very process of economic development. More than eight million Chinese peasants are moving into cities every year. China now has ninety urban centres with more than a million inhabitants, most of them choking with the pollution produced by old-style factories, coal-fired power stations and streets crowded with motor vehicles. Chongqing is the biggest city in the world, with more than thirty million inhabitants. Sixteen of the world's biggest polluting and polluted cities are in China: Chongqing tops the league. It is surrounded by gigantic waste pits. The biggest is more than 30 metres deep and covers an area of 350,000 square metres; none of the rubbish is recycled.[25]

The Services Directive

Many of the issues discussed so far in this chapter reappear in emblematic form in the controversy surrounding the Services Directive. In a service/knowledge economy it is obvious that the Single Market must include the service industries, since the vast majority of the labour force now works in them. Progress in the Single Market so far has brought clear benefits to member states. Since the completion of the first Single Market programme in 1993, 2.5 million net new jobs have been generated in the EU15 as a result of the dissolution of barriers to competition and exchange. The increase in wealth attributable to the same source over that period is €900 billion, equivalent to about €6,000 per family in the EU. However, most of these benefits have accrued in markets for goods. The report produced by the Commission on the internal market for services, published in July 2002, concluded that there was a huge gap between the vision of an integrated EU economy and the segmented nature of service industries, most of which should be opened to competition.

The Services Directive was the response to this diagnosis. In its original form, it covered a large variety of services, including finance and business services (such as management consultancy and recruitment), trade (legal advice and distributive trades), consumer affairs/leisure, travel and some health and welfare services. If fully implemented, the Directive would reduce prices, encourage productivity gains and provide a major overall stimulus to the EU economy. A major study on the issues concluded that a net benefit

[25] Jonathan Watts, 'Invisible city'. *Guardian*, 15 March 2006.

of 600,000 jobs would be created across the Union, other conditions being equal.[26] The estimate of 600,000 net new jobs is a
minimal one, since the analysis uses conservative assumptions, and
includes only three service sectors – regulated professions, distributive trade and business services.[27] The true level of net job generation could be twice that figure or more.

According to the Directive as first drafted, formalities for establishing new services would be simplified from those in use between
member states at the moment. All procedures would be able to be
completed at a 'single point of contact', using electronic means. It
would be open to firms to supply services in any member state and
for an initial period be subject only to the regulations of the
country where the company is established – the so-called 'country
of origin principle'.

The launching of the Directive achieved a sympathetic reception
in some quarters, but provoked a furious response from others.
Some union organizations, and other critics, demanded radical
changes in the programme, or even its complete dissolution. Thus
the union organization Unison in the UK set out three 'key
demands' in its reaction to the Directive. One was to remove
public services from the Directive altogether, on the grounds that
'the Directive threatens public services with liberalisation and pri-
vatisation, undermining the key role they play in ensuring access
to quality public services for everyone, not just those that can
afford them'.[28] The second was that there should be no weaken-
ing of employment law or the rights of collective bargaining. As it
stood, Unison argued, the Directive would do just that. Workers
who move across national boundaries as service firms do – so-
called 'posted workers' – would only be covered by the labour
laws of the country to which they go. The state from which they
come would lose its capacity to enforce national laws covering
their rights.

---

[26] Copenhagen Economics, *Economic Assessment of the Barriers to the Internal Market for Services*. Final Report, Copenhagen, 2005.
[27] Anders Sejeroe et al., 'The Copenhagen Economics study on the economic impact of the Services Directive', *Intereconomics*, May/June 2005.
[28] Unison, 'Defending public services in Europe: stop the Services Directive', *Unison International*, 5 November 2005.

Finally, Unison strongly opposed the country of origin principle. If the principle were accepted, the union claimed, there would be a race to the bottom within Europe, as firms compete with one another to move their headquarters to the countries that have the lowest level of regulations, in order to cut costs. Not only would such a development depress wages; it would also have major implications for health, safety and environmental protection. Other critics have gone much further: the proposals have been labelled 'the Directive from Hell'.

Early in 2005 EU political leaders asked the Commission to look at the Directive again because of worries about whether it might adversely affect the social model. Even the leaders of countries normally sympathetic to the liberalization of markets, such as Sweden, voiced their hesitation. Thus Thomas Östros, a trade minister, said that his government wanted to see an outcome 'in line with the values for society and working life that we in Sweden abide by'. Sweden, he accepted, has an enormous amount to gain by the creation of a more efficient services sector in Europe. Probably more than any other country in Europe, Sweden has opened up to the world in terms of trade. However, he went on to emphasize, the Swedish welfare system must not be weakened by the changes that are introduced.[29] What would happen if welfare services were provided at levels of regulation well below those insisted upon by the Swedish state?

The Services Directive was approved by the European Parliament in February 2006, but with major changes. The country of origin principle was deleted – service providers are to be governed by the regulations of the country in which the service is being offered. In place of the country of origin principle, some minor advantages for small firms have been put in place. Thus providers will not have to establish an office in the receiving country. A range of sectors are excluded, including health care. Member states can still regulate markets in the areas of health, public safety and environment; and they can also apply national local labour law.

[29] Thomas Östros, 'The EU Services Directive must be adapted to the Swedish context', Government Office of Sweden, 25 November 2004; available online at <www.sweden.gov.se/sb/d/3212/a/34984>.

There is still some way to go with final ratification, but the outcome looks unsatisfactory. It symbolizes the deficient nature of much of the wider debate in Europe about social justice and the role of markets. Advocates of extended competition in services mainly emphasize economic advantages, and appear indifferent to the social consequences that might ensue. Those who would restrict the reorganization of markets, and continue with a cosy protectionism, pose as the defenders of the social model. The result is a weak compromise that satisfies no one – and, crucially, does little to help resolve the problems that Europe faces. As the American author Gene Sperling has written, 'protectionists have no vision for the future and free traders have no vision for the present'.[30]

The relation between competitiveness and social justice is far more complex than this stand-off suggests:

1 Fears of social dumping, for reasons already given, are vastly exaggerated. The country of origin principle would not have seriously threatened local producers, save in terms of competition. 'Social dumping' has largely become an accusation used to justify protectionism. Why should the Services Directive not initiate a race to the top rather than one to the bottom? In the EU societies, competition on the grounds of quality, efficiency and customer service is likely to be far more important than competition solely on the grounds of cost. Moreover, EU-wide rules on consumer protection, health, safety and minimum rest periods are already at quite a high level.
2 Where protectionism continues in place, the result will often be to reinforce divided labour markets, resulting in less social justice, not more.
3 The country of origin principle was the basis of opening a front against monopolies, both state-based and market-based. The point of the principle was not to lower standards, since it only applied to the initial point of entry of a provider. Opponents have concentrated their arguments upon the point

---

[30] Gene Sperling, *The Pro-Growth Progressive: An Economic Strategy for Shared Prosperity*. New York: Simon & Schuster, 2005, p. 73.

of final consumption (Polish plumbers in France) or the down-grading of public services (Latvian carers in Sweden). Yet the Directive in its more radical form would have affected mainly small and medium-sized enterprises. The natural costs of hiring individual Polish plumbers are huge, save in direct border regions. The larger companies whose attentions might have implications for state-based services have mostly been able to build networks of service providers anyway.[31]

4 Increased competition in some areas now excluded from the Directive would have helped some key categories of people. For example, where the costs of child care services, domestic services or care services for the infirm are kept artificially high, the chances of women reconciling work and home are affected.

5 As previously discussed, manufacturers have been locating in the former East European countries, bringing cost advantages to their products when sold elsewhere in Europe. But where such a process happens in reverse, as it would to some degree under the original Directive, this competitive advantage has been blocked off. No wonder East European political leaders protested so vociferously about the watering-down of the original version.

6 Social justice means caring about the unemployed, not just those in work. Increased competition will create more net new jobs. It is a myth to suppose that all new jobs mean the destruction of old ones, or that competition always drives down wages. The virtuous circle described earlier applies in many, even most, circumstances.

7 Competition from low-cost providers in some core service sectors will happen anyway, assuming that international out-sourcing progresses further. Some producers, who might have survived had the internal market created more efficiencies early on, will be driven out of business.

8 Workers who lose their jobs have the right to protection, but such protection has to take the form of flexicurity. We have to

---

[31] Patrick A. Messerlin, 'Liberalising services trade in the EU', *Intereconomics*, May/June 2005.

give especial attention, however, as I shall argue in chapter 3, to those in vulnerable categories, such as those who lack skills, or older workers.

Conclusion

Worries about economic globalization, and more specifically about the Services Directive, especially from those on the left, tend to merge with wider concerns about the power of global capital. Those who think such capital is inherently destructive, however, should ponder the case of Nokia in Finland. Nokia, and other Finnish firms that have to some extent modelled themselves on it, have played a vital part in the success of Finland, including the success of its social model.

The CEO of Nokia, Jorma Ollila, has remarked that 'listing on the New York stock exchange in 1994 was a far more important step than we ever thought. But access to capital was less important than the presence as such.'[32] Presence on global capital markets helps a company gain credibility, and provides a means of developing a clear brand identity. Until the 1990s, foreign capital was tightly controlled in Finland. In 1993 this position was reversed and shares in Finnish companies could be freely bought and sold. The change was in fact made in preparation for EU membership, which took place early in 1995.

Nokia was a key beneficiary. In the early 1990s it was in an acute crisis. The company needed a large injection of cash, which meant going to US capital markets. But American investors were not interested in Nokia as it then was, a firm involved with rubber, cables, paper and TV sets. In order to get listing, the firm developed a new vision – 'focused, global, telecom-oriented and value-added'.[33] It was the beginning of Nokia's rise; the value of its stock grew by 2,300 per cent in five years. Over 90 per cent of Nokia's stock is

---

[32] Quoted in Risto Tainio et al., 'Global investors meet local managers: shareholder value in the Finnish context', in Marie-Laure Djelic and Sigrid Quack (eds.), *Globalization and Institutions*. Cheltenham: Elgar, 2003, p. 7.
[33] Ibid, p. 39.

now owned by foreign investors. The success of Nokia meant that overseas investors brought new capital to other Finnish companies.

There have been tensions and problems. Foreign investors have pressed Finnish managers for higher share value returns and lower costs, creating conflicts in local communities threatened with job loss. On the other hand, a reverse effect occurred too – increased understanding of national and local concerns on the part of investors. Researchers studying these events have shown that there is not a simple one-way flow of power or influence. Rather, there is 'a reciprocal relationship between foreign investors and local actors that is simultaneously pushing for common rules and keeping the world diverse'. They conclude that the idea that exposure to global capital destroys distinctly European qualities in business is a myth, as is the notion that everything has to conform to an 'Anglo-Saxon' framework. 'The responses to common shareholder principles', they say, 'may in the end perpetuate national and local differences or even generate more variation across countries and regions than is observable today.'[34]

[34] Ibid, p. 54.

3

Social Justice and Social Divisions

The Lisbon Agenda quite correctly emphasizes that revolutionary changes have happened in the economy with the shrinking of manufacture. Only a generation ago, close to 40 per cent of the labour force in the developed societies was in manufacturing or related industries. In some states over 10 per cent of the labour force at that point still worked in agriculture. These proportions in the EU15 are now down to an average of 16 per cent and 2–3 per cent respectively. As emphasized earlier, well over 80 per cent of workers have to get their livelihood from knowledge-based or service industries. It is surely right to say we need very different strategies of investment and economic policy from the industrial age.

But there has been no comparable, in-detail examination of connected changes going on in the wider society, or of their implications for inequality and social protection. Consider for example the most recent Commission statement on the 'social agenda'. As part of the Lisbon and sustainable development strategies, the document says, 'The Commission is fully committed to the modernisation and development of the European social model as well as to the promotion of social cohesion'.[1]

But how much *analysis* is offered of changing patterns of class, inequality and social division? In point of fact, in the document in question at least, there is none at all. What concrete *recommendations* are made about how to coordinate the Lisbon strategy with

---

[1] Communication from the Commission, 'The Social Agenda', Brussels, 2005, p. 2.

social justice and welfare reform in the EU countries? Few, if any. The social agenda, it is said, 'aims to modernise the European social model by improving collective capacity to act and to offer new chances to all'. How? All that is offered is the stated intention to promote 'decent work' as 'a global objective at all levels'; increase the adaptability of workers; and 'implement inclusion measures in the labour market'. Of course, there is EU-level legislation concerning work and working conditions, in the shape of the Social Charter and Social Chapter. The Social Charter was adopted at Strasbourg in 1989. The UK initially refused to sign up to it and afterwards vetoed fourteen out of the seventeen draft employment-related Directives. At that point, unanimous approval was required to endorse them. 'Protocol 14', annexed to the 1992 Maastricht Treaty, set up a mechanism whereby Directives could be binding on not all member states. Protocol 14 then became known as the 'Social Chapter'. (After 1997, the UK finally signed up.)

The Social Chapter deals with workers' rights and pay. It sets out provisions for improving standards in areas such as working conditions, social security and trade union rights. EU regulations have also been introduced to cope with most of the cross-border problems that arise with social security. But the Social Chapter has never been integrated with an understanding of how changing socio-economic conditions are reshaping how welfare provisions are best organized. In a way, this fact is not surprising, since the legislation originated at a time when the full force of the changes affecting the economy, and wider society, was in its infancy.

Social protection lies at the heart of the anxieties many citizens feel as they live through the changes associated with the global age. Our societies, and with them people's everyday lives, are changing just as dramatically as the economic order. We have to identify these changes and ponder their implications for policy. It is not enough to make airy statements about reducing social exclusion. Lack of a developed analysis of the changing forms of social justice is one of the main reasons the Lisbon Agenda has proved so hard to implement.

In this chapter I will seek to clarify these issues. I shall look first of all at the changing shape of the stratification system, concentrating especially on the poor and the deprived. Patterns of inequality differ from those of two or three decades ago, a phenomenon that has important policy consequences. There is more erratic fluidity in contemporary societies than was once thought. Life-transitions are less predictable than they were for both good and bad reasons. Policy innovations must respond to these developments.

Differentiated and culturally diverse societies are not likely to have a high degree of equality of outcome. Yet growing economic inequality is not a price that has to be paid to secure good growth rates. On the contrary, a more egalitarian Europe can also be a more competitive Europe. The blocked societies discussed in the foregoing chapter are not sacrificing economic growth in order to preserve equality. Instead, inequalities are growing at the same time as their economies are underperforming. In concluding the chapter I shall look in more detail at child poverty.

New Classes

The class structure and class divisions associated with the knowledge/service economy are quite different from those of the industrial age. The blue-collar working class was the largest class grouping in the old social order. Marx labelled the working class the 'universal class', and of course expected it to be the agent of revolutionary change. Today, the manual working class is very much a minority, and its numbers are set to reduce further as the proportion working in manufacture continues to diminish. The old working-class communities, that used to be the source of much local solidarity, have largely broken up. What used to be the 'middle class' has become much more differentiated, while the land-owning upper class has largely disappeared. Separate agrarian classes have more or less completely evaporated too.

New occupational divisions have come into existence, based upon the social and technological changes associated with the knowledge/service economy. About two-thirds of the jobs generated by the new economy are skilled – they demand a technical knowledge of IT and other skills too. Such jobs are becoming more plentiful in relative terms. Over the period 1995–2004, the

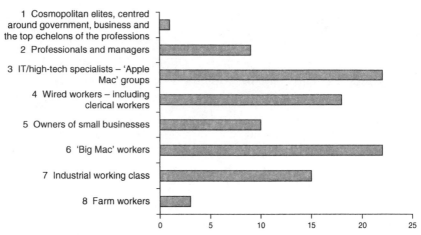

Figure 3.1 Classes in post-industrial society (% of population)

proportion of jobs in the EU15 demanding advanced qualifications in IT – 'Apple Mac' jobs – went up from 20 per cent to 24 per cent. But many people have to work in much more routine 'Big Mac' jobs – serving in cafés, shops, supermarkets or petrol stations. The proportion of such jobs may be declining compared to more skilled occupations, but it remains substantial.

The class structure of a post-industrial society looks as portrayed in figure 3.1. This picture is a generalized one, since different societies vary between themselves to some considerable degree. The percentages given are only rough guides, and refer to individuals, not households. The group at the top is an amorphous one of elites whose power and outlook are as much transnational as national, especially in Europe's 'global cities'. They may include substantial proportions of immigrants. The French banker working in the City of London leaves his office in the early evening. As he departs, a cleaner from the Philippines, who is regularly sending money to her family there, comes in to tidy up after him.

At least 50 per cent of jobs in the knowledge/service economy demand a high level of cognitive and/or personal skills, stretching down into work performed by 'wired workers' – those who use computers much of the day, but are not themselves IT specialists.

All class categories can involve those who work for the state or in state-controlled enterprises. The distinction between those who work for the state and those who don't tends to coincide with divisions in labour markets; but job security is normally highest for those in classes 1, 2 and 3.

One of the distinguishing features of the knowledge/service economy is the high proportion of women in the labour force – although few work in manual occupations. Women are heavily represented in 'Big Mac' jobs and among wired workers. They are also more likely to work part time than men are. Only 7 per cent of men in the EU15 countries work part time, while 30 per cent of women do. Women's wages are on average about 15 per cent lower than those of men doing the same or a comparable job.

These gross figures mask some important trends. The gender gap in pay is tending to become reduced almost everywhere. Moreover, at the bottom end women are actively doing better than men – declining wage levels and job security are much more marked among low-skilled working-class men than among women of comparable skill levels. Crucially, the role of women in providing household income is increasing dramatically. In Denmark, it is reaching parity with men, at 42 per cent, although at the other end of the scale, in Spain and Italy, it is as low as 27 per cent.[2]

Low pay does not necessarily mean that a person lives in hardship if he or she is a supplementary earner in the household. Household inequality is substantially lower than individual inequalities in most EU15 countries. Households most likely to be in poverty are single-earner households and especially households where no one is in work. The proportion of households in the EU15 with no one working ranges from 15 per cent in the UK to 6 per cent in Denmark.

The changing class structure has altered the nature of politics – and much else besides. In the old society, politics was largely shaped around the dividing lines between the manual working class and the rest. There were always 'working-class Tories', and

[2] Gøsta Esping-Andersen, 'Inequality of incomes and opportunities', in Anthony Giddens and Patrick Diamond (eds.), *The New Egalitarianism*. Cambridge: Polity, 2005, pp. 22–4.

social democratic parties needed to appeal to other groups besides the working class. But political activity correlated strongly with class, and voting preferences tended to be quite stable from election to election. Now the major political parties have to appeal to diverse constituencies, while many more voters are 'dealigned' – they do not automatically stick to the same party.

The working class was (and is) very much divided along skill lines. Skilled workers, either craftsmen or those who worked in various areas of industrial technology, normally had quite stable jobs, and often were more affluent than clerical workers and others in the lower reaches of the middle class. Skilled workers in established trades that continue to thrive can still be in much demand – consider again the fabled Polish plumber. However, the position of the unskilled has worsened. Unskilled workers – especially men – have poor work opportunities, above all in areas where manufacturing industries have closed down. Even 'Big Mac' jobs involve face-to-face social skills that those from traditional working-class backgrounds may find it hard to master. Many men from such backgrounds are in any case unwilling to do what they see as 'women's work'. Unskilled men are thus highly vulnerable to spells of poverty or unemployment. This situation often applies with particular force to migrants or those from minority groups.

To refer to the situation of groups at the bottom of the socio-economic scale, the term *social exclusion* has been widely popularized. The point of the concept is to recognize that factors other than poverty alone might prevent individuals or groups from playing a full part in society. The notion is usually traced to the work of the French author René Lenoir. The 'excluded' in his analysis included a variety of groups, making up about 10 per cent of the population – not only the poor, but also the disabled, mentally ill, older people, drug users and so forth. The introduction of the concept was important, because it drew attention to the fact that the existing welfare provisions often did not reach the people in these categories; and because it stressed that it is not only sheer economic deprivation that prevents individuals from realizing their potential.[3]

---

[3]   René Lenoir, *Les exclus: un français sur dix*. Paris: Seuil, 1974.

At one time it became common to speak of the '50/40/10' society in Europe: 50 per cent of the working population are in stable jobs, 40 per cent are in more insecure work, while the remaining 10 per cent consists of the socially excluded, either unemployed or shifting in and out of the labour market (although the percentages varied in different versions). An underclass, in other words, has replaced the traditional working class, or the lower levels of it. A certain percentage of the population is cut adrift from the wider society.

However, this notion has proved to be incorrect.[4] Sociologists are agreed that there is no distinct underclass in this sense in the EU countries – although the notion may have more applicability in the US. Thus the government Strategy Unit in the UK studied four measures of social exclusion – those who are not in employment, education or training; those with a low income (below 60 per cent of median income); those who have few established social ties with others; and those who perceive themselves as living in an area marked by high levels of crime, vandalism or material dilapidation. Only 1 per cent of the UK population is excluded on all four of these measures. Multiple deprivation does exist, but it tends to be concentrated in specific neighbourhoods rather than affecting a 'class' of people.[5] Social exclusion is a concept with some value, but it must not be used loosely and generically. It has essentially the same meaning as 'multiple deprivation', which tends to affect pockets of neighbourhoods and certain groups of individuals in particular (such as the homeless).

New Social Divisions

Class divisions in post-industrial society by and large are no longer behavioural, but are determined by differential life-chances. This change is a very significant one. At one time in most countries people in different class groups could be distinguished from one another quite visibly. Lifestyle variations still exist between those

---

[4] See John Goldthorpe and Abigail McKnight, *The Economic Basis of Social Class*. London: Centre for Analysis of Social Exclusion, London School of Economics, 2004.

[5] Prime Minister's Strategy Unit, *Strategic Audit of the UK*. London, 2003.

in different class groups, but they are often more influenced by taste and custom than by sheer financial constraints. Physical mobility, including foreign travel, is available to virtually everyone. The substantive freedoms most people have, centred around freedom of lifestyle choice, today are greater than for past generations. I shall call this phenomenon *everyday democratization*. Everyday democratization tends to stretch both 'downwards' and 'upwards' in the life-course. In the age of the Internet, childhood can no longer be as sheltered as it once was; and older people feel free to experiment with lifestyles just as much as younger ones do.

Everyday democratization does not necessarily bring greater security, or feelings of security. In fact a series of new insecurities come into being alongside it. Some are directly economic, others more social in nature. Most people want, and expect, more from their lives than previous generations did, leading to aspirations that cannot always be realized.

The degree of experienced security of different class groups tends to produce new ideological rifts in post-industrial societies. Such cleavages are partly based on rational anxieties (for example, fears of job loss) and partly on more free-floating worries. Those who flourish in the new economy tend to be happy with diversity, and embrace cosmopolitan lifestyles. Some may actively court what is seen negatively as insecurity. For instance, they may relish the prospect of moving on from job to job, and neither expect nor want to have a hierarchical career of the traditional sort. The creative industries, high-tech jobs, finance and banking and professional occupations are where such groups tend to be found in highest density.

What Richard Florida calls the 'creative class' now comprises well over 20 per cent of the labour force, with a high concentration in certain metropolitan areas. It is mainly made up of people in classes 2 and 3 in my categories (see figure 3.1). The members of the creative class are diverse in terms of background – it includes people of all ages, from different ethnic groups and of differing sexual orientations.[6]

---

[6] Richard Florida, *The Rise of the Creative Class*. New York: Perseus, 2002. For the author's subsequent reflections, see Richard Florida, *The Flight of the Creative Class*. New York: HarperBusiness, 2005.

To measure the distribution of the creative class in the US, Florida developed a 'creativity index', based on four factors: the percentage of the creative class in the workforce; the percentage working in high-tech industry; innovation, as measured by patents per capita; and diversity, as assessed by the 'Gay Index', the proportion of gays being taken as a proxy of openness. Some cities, such as San Francisco, Austin or San Diego, rank high on all measures. Others are cities bypassed by the creative class, such as Memphis or Pittsburgh.

Those cities near the top of the Florida list head the country in terms of economic prosperity and job creation. The liveliest local economies are characterized by the 'three Ts' – talent, technology and tolerance. They are above all *cosmopolitan*. The members of the creative class are very mobile, and will gravitate towards those cities in areas that offer what they want in terms of lifestyle. They prefer active, participatory recreation and street-level culture – a blend of cafés, restaurants, galleries and theatres. They are into a variety of active sports. They involve a high proportion of qualified migrants. According to one study, almost a third of all businesses set up in Silicon Valley in the 1990s were started by Indian and Chinese-born entrepreneurs.

Some cosmopolitans in Florida's sense may be found in other class groups too, given the available range of possible lifestyles. However, many who feel vulnerable to unwanted change are better characterized as *locals*, who rather want to stick to the existing order of things, or who look back nostalgically to the past – real or imagined. They might look for scapegoats, for example immigrants, upon whom to blame their troubles; and they might be attracted by political populism and economic protectionism. Immigrants themselves are not necessarily cosmopolitans. In their attitudes they may become locals, just as hostile to further immigration as groups in the native population.

Coupled to the other changes, especially in the sphere of the family, the changing class structure alters the distribution of 'at risk' groups, as well as the nature and form of inequalities. The conditions generating 'at risk' groups are structural, but how far they translate into real vulnerabilities depends upon the policy mix of a particular society, as well as specific blockages it might have. The other side of risk is *opportunity*. We must not make the mistake of supposing that risk is always a negative factor. Some of the most important changes are the following:

1   There are on average fewer jobs with secure tenure for people in most work situations, although there are variations, depending upon the strength of insider/outsider divisions in labour markets.

2   Risk (and opportunity) are distributed differently across the life-span from how they were in the past. Risk and opportunity do not just 'happen' to people. More and more people think strategically about their lives in terms of future possibilities – including the decision to have a child/children. Transitions at different phases of life are both less predictable and less mechanical than they used to be. Heightened rates of divorce and separation mean that transition can happen at diverse times.

3   The intensity of technological change, conjoined to a more globalized division of labour, creates new vulnerabilities for some groups. Young men with no qualifications, as mentioned, are likely to fare especially poorly. Older workers in manufacture, whose jobs disappear, risk long spells of unemployment, or the prospect of never working again, unless appropriate policy interventions are made.

4   On average, older people hold a greater share of overall wealth and income than they did in the past, compared to the young. Many, however, are still at risk of poverty on retirement. Older women living on their own are the most vulnerable. However, risks have cascaded down more towards the young rather than the old.[7] Child poverty has become commonplace where child care facilities and opportunities for work for women are under-developed.

5   'Big Mac' jobs tend to offer little chance of a career. This situation may not matter where they are carried out by

---

[7]   Esping-Andersen, 'Inequality of incomes and opportunities'.

groups who have the capability to move into other sectors – such as students who work in coffee-shops during vacations or in gap years. It can matter a great deal for those who have few qualifications to allow them to move on.

6   In the knowledge/service society, credentials – certificates, diplomas, degrees – become of the first importance for career mobility. It is harder for affluent parents to pass on their advantages in a 'direct' way to their children. Hence they concentrate heavily on education. For example, university graduates on average earn significantly more over the course of their careers than those who do not go to university.

7   Ethnic minorities may be significantly at risk where they lack qualifications. Prejudices can be reinforced, and to some extent taken over by the members of the minority themselves. There can be additional problems for women where traditional beliefs confine their role to a domestic one.

8   Not only do many (most) women work, and for much of their lives, but their incomes are quite often crucial for sustaining the standard of living of a family. In an increasing proportion of cases they are the prime earners. This situation is not the cause of Europe's low birth rates. On the contrary, those families with the highest proportion of women in work are also ones with the most elevated birth rates. However, work/life issues become of great importance. Women are still the main carers and their careers are interrupted by having children much more than men's are.

9   There is a great deal of fluidity in contemporary society, but, as mentioned in chapter 1, structural sources of mobility are different from a generation ago. There will not be as clear a 'direction' to mobility between the generations as there used to be when many people from working-class backgrounds moved into white-collar and professional jobs. Structural mobility will depend upon a continuing overall upgrading of knowledge-based jobs at the expense of less-skilled service occupations. There are likely to be many more voluntary and involuntary career transitions, often involving a move

sideways to a different job area, or taking time out from work for education or retraining.

10 Ageing is changing its nature, not just because more people will work longer, but also because there will not be the same discontinuities as before between working and non-working life. The old-age 'retirement ghetto' – a form of social exclusion if ever there was one – is being broken down. The very notions of retirement, and even pensions, might disappear in the future. In their place will come more flexible attitudes towards work and more orthodox sources of social support for those considered to be significant at-risk groups among older people, including especially many older women.

Social Justice in Post-industrial Society

'Social justice' is a notoriously controversial notion. How far does it imply the redistribution of wealth and income, as compared to enhancing equality of opportunity? What can it actually mean in the context of a post-industrial society? The first of these questions can actually be quite easily answered on the level of principle. In a society that depends upon a highly dynamic marketplace for its prosperity, aspiration, ambition and opportunity have to be central. Equalizing opportunities is important because it makes the best use of available talents. However, reducing inequalities of opportunity necessarily involves redistribution, since otherwise those who are successful in one generation could simply hold on to the fruits of their success. In the EU countries, post-tax inequality is significantly lower than pre-tax inequality, a desirable and necessary outcome since it sets a framework for other measures. Further redistribution occurs through the welfare system and through the direct effects of policy measures, depending on the welfare mix a society has. Nevertheless I shall suggest later that the idea of redistribution has its limits.

How social justice should be defined is a difficult issue, about which large philosophical tomes have been written. However, a very useful working definition has been provided by the German political scientist, Wolfgang Merkel. He lists five priorities of social justice in post-industrial social conditions:[8]

1 The fight against poverty – not just because of economic inequality itself, but on the grounds that poverty (above all, enduring poverty) limits the individual's capacity for autonomy and self-esteem.
2 Creating the highest possible standards of education and training, rooted in equal and fair access for all.
3 Ensuring employment for those who are willing and able to work.
4 A welfare system that provides protection and dignity.
5 The limiting of inequalities of income and wealth if they hinder the realization of the first four goals or endanger the cohesion of society.

Obviously, the devil is in the detail, especially in respect of point 5. But the formula provides a down-to-earth scheme that is both simple and clear. It recognizes the role of equality of opportunity in a differentiated society, against the backdrop of current economic imperatives. It quite rightly gives pre-eminence to the struggle to reduce levels of poverty, since poverty limits life-chances and the capacity for self-realization. It follows from the formula that targeting child poverty is of especial significance. The higher the proportion of those who suffer poverty as children, the more likely it is that all five goals will be compromised. In one recent study, cognitive development tests sat by children at the age of 22 months were found to be accurate predictors of educational attainment by the age of 26. Children of equal ability early on fared quite differently over time, depending on the socio-economic status of their families.[9]

[8] Wolfgang Merkel, 'How the welfare state can tackle new inequalities', in Patrick Diamond and Matt Browne (eds.), *Rethinking Social Democracy*. London: Policy Network, 2004. Merkel's standpoint draws upon that of Amartya Sen. Sen argues that policies concerned with furthering equality should centre upon the 'capability set' of an individual – the overall freedom a person has to pursue his or her well-being. Amartya Sen, *Inequality Re-examined*. Oxford: Clarendon Press, 1992.
[9] Leon Feinstein, 'Inequality in the early cognitive development of British children in the 1970 cohort', *Economica*, 70 (2003).

Social justice, social exclusion and social protection all relate to one another and it might be worth indicating how they differ. In my usage, countering social exclusion is only one element in creating more socially just societies. Social justice is a more powerful and encompassing notion. It is concerned with reducing significant inequalities – social and economic – and with equalizing life-chances. Social justice overlaps with social protection, which refers to the apparatus of welfare provision. However, social protection is a broader idea still, since it covers insurance against risk, plus investment in education, health care and other socially desirable goods.

Esping-Andersen has identified the family and the household as being at the centre of concerns with social justice in post-industrial society. 'Women', he suggests, 'emerge as the lynchpin of any new equilibrium between households and the economy.'[10] The knowledge/service economy has the household as its hub. With female employment at an all-time high, families outsource activities that once were carried out mainly by housewives, thereby promoting jobs in service industries. This situation creates a 'double multiplier', since women also by and large work in those same industries.

Gender equality is sometimes thought of as a matter for women, as they strive to improve their position within the family and in the world outside. However, the quality of future welfare hinges on the outcome. 'For good or bad, gender equality becomes therefore a "societal affair", a precondition for making the clockwork of post-industrial societies tick.'[11] Two types of equality are in play – inside and outside the home. The two are obviously connected, but not necessarily in a one-to-one relation. There are still large differences, but it would be true to say that on average women's careers are coming more and more to resemble those of men. However, this situation is cross-cut by the demands of child-bearing and motherhood.

Catherine Hakim points out that the dilemmas faced by women are grouped around three life-course preferences.[12] On the one side

[10] Gøsta Esping-Andersen, 'A new gender contract?' in Esping-Andersen (ed.), *Why We Need a New Welfare State*. Oxford: Oxford University Press, 2002, p. 69.
[11] Ibid.
[12] Catherine Hakim, *Key Issues in Women's Work*. London: Athlone, 1996.

are 'family-centred' women, whose priorities concern marriage and motherhood. If they work, it is out of necessity, and they have no interest in forging a career. In other words, they effectively sustain the structure of the traditional family. While they may widely be represented among older women, they are disappearing, even in countries such as Italy or Greece.

'Career-centred' women are at the other extreme – they have children only if their career is unaffected. In contrast to the first type, this is a growing category – Hakim estimates that a fifth of women under the age of 45 have such an outlook, although the proportion varies in different EU countries. However, by far the greatest number of women have a 'dual-role' orientation. They want a career – and motherhood as well.

When we look across the EU countries, we see the same polarity that we noted in chapter 1. In Denmark, for instance, mothers of two or more children only infrequently interrupt their careers, and mostly remain in full-time jobs. In Germany, Italy and Spain, mothers of families of two or more children are less often in a job.[13]

Does the 'dual role' condemn women to a 'double shift', in which they have to bear most of the domestic burden while still striving for success in the workplace?[14] That question can only be answered if we take a life-span perspective; and if we think of equality in terms of power and decision-making, not just in terms of formal economic parity. It is unlikely (although not impossible) that there could be a large-scale 'feminization' of male careers, where family obligations rank equally with career aspirations. Sweden has so far come closest. Male paternity leave makes up 13 per cent of total child care leave, twice as much as the other Nordic countries. Sweden also boasts the highest level of unpaid domestic work done by husbands or partners – an average of twenty-one hours a week. This is not far short of the level for women, which is about twenty-seven hours a week. There is a small minority of households where the male concentrates on the domestic work while the wife focuses on her career.

<hr />

[13] Esping-Andersen, 'A new gender contract?'.
[14] Arlie Russell Hochschild, *The Second Shift*. London: Penguin, 2003.

Inequality and poverty

Let us now turn to look in detail at patterns of inequality, concentrating upon poverty and deprivation, before considering policy innovations that might follow on. As measured by the Gini coefficient, overall economic inequality is on the increase in most EU countries, although it has recently stabilized in the UK. However, what such increases mean for the distribution of life-chances in the population is unclear where data (as many statistics do) refer to individuals, not to households. Many low-paid people may be supplementary earners in households that have reasonable or good overall incomes. What we can say for sure is that having two earners in a household, regardless of whether or not there are children present, gives almost complete protection against poverty. As mentioned earlier, inequalities between households in most countries are on average significantly lower than those between individuals.

Changing patterns of economic inequality among men have been mainly driven by falling returns to those with low skill levels. Skills, especially those in the forefront of the knowledge/service economy, command a premium. Job precariousness has grown in line with trends mentioned earlier. It is in fact higher relatively speaking in manufacture than in service industries, because of its continuing decline, plus the impact of technological change.

Defined by the standard EU criterion – those earning less than 60 per cent of median national income – as of 2005 there were some 60 million people living in poverty in the EU15 states. This number represents about 16 per cent of the total population. The true proportion may be lower, since we do not have reliable comparative data on households. The new member states cannot be measured off the same baseline, since their statistics are still based upon varying national measurements. The percentage of individuals living below the poverty line as specified in those countries ranges from 8 per cent in Slovenia to 26 per cent in Hungary.[15]

[15] Brigita Schmognerova, *The European Social Model: Reconstruction or Destruction?* Bonn: Ebert Foundation, 2005, p. 70.

The lowest rates of poverty in the EU15 are in the Nordic states, the highest in the Mediterranean ones. Child poverty rates (measured in terms of individuals) show much the same distribution. As of 2004 they were less than 4 per cent in Sweden, Denmark and Finland. They were around 20 per cent in Greece and 22 per cent in Hungary.[16] The risk for lone-parent families of children living in poverty is higher in all societies. Yet a substantial proportion of poor children live in 'standard' families – as high a proportion as 48 per cent in Greece.

Poverty is almost everywhere highly regionalized, in terms of gross comparisons between segments of countries (such as north and south Italy, or the north versus the south-east in England), and in more micro-contexts. In the UK, for instance, half of those on low incomes live in 20 per cent of local areas; and 50 per cent of children of primary school age living in low income households are concentrated in 20 per cent of schools. Much the same proportion applies also to neighbourhoods within cities.

Poverty used to be widely spoken of as though it was (1) a *unitary* condition and (2) an *unchanging* one – once in poverty always in poverty, unless lifted out by active social policy measures. Both assumptions are wrong, and spelling out the reasons why has major implications for policy reform.

The 'poor' are very diverse. As Lutz Leisering and Stephan Leibfried put it, 'the new insight is . . . that poverty has many faces'.[17] For instance, there are many different types of deprived areas and neighbourhoods, driven by differing dynamics. Some poor areas are those where manufacturing, mining or shipbuilding industries have closed down. Some involve a high percentage of ethnic minorities; some do not. Some are in large cities; others are in small towns. Rural poverty often differs from urban, and itself covers a range of different circumstances. Coping strategies may vary widely according to these and other differences.

Even more important, poverty is not a static phenomenon. Until quite recently, there were few or no studies of the experience

---

[16] Figures using a definition of below 50 per cent of median income.

[17] Lutz Leisering and Stephan Leibfried, *Time and Poverty in Western Welfare States*, trans. John Veit-Wilson. Cambridge: Cambridge University Press, 2001, p. 239.

of poverty across time. The arrival of such studies has transformed our understanding of the phenomenon. An emphasis upon time and the life-span is especially significant in the context of post-industrial societies, because movement and flux are more prevalent in them than in earlier periods. Far more people experience spells of poverty than anyone once thought, but most spells of poverty are short-lived. Poverty is more likely to be a one-off experience than it is to be sustained. However, individuals and households quite often suffer repeated spells of poverty – the so-called 'carousel effect'. In the EU15 as a whole, 39 per cent of spells of poverty end within a year. The figure for the Nordic states is over 50 per cent. In the UK it is 36 per cent and in Portugal 24 per cent. In most EU15 countries less than 8 per cent of those who are poor during any five-year period stay poor over that whole period. Long-term or embedded poverty is nevertheless a problem in many or most countries.

Leisering and Leibfried, who have carried out extensive time-series studies in Germany, speak of the following main characteristics of poverty in post-industrial societies (all apply to other groups in the class structure too). One is *temporalization* – the experience of poverty depends upon how long it is experienced, what happens between spells of poverty and at what time of life. The second is *democratization* – the experience of poverty affects large numbers of people and does not necessarily indicate marginality. The third is that much poverty is *biographical* – tied to specific life-events and episodes, such as divorce, illness, leaving the parental home or losing a job.[18]

In the light of such findings, we have to start to look at 'poor communities' with new eyes. Even with substantial numbers of immigrants or ethnic minorities, an area that stays poor over a period of time can have large movements of individuals in and out. Research in Bolton and Bradford in the UK, cities with a high proportion of East Asian minority groups, showed that most immigrants did not stay put. They wanted to get on and move out from the inner city to the suburbs, and many of them did. The immigrant

[18] Ibid, pp. 240–3.

neighbourhoods on the surface seemed to stay the same, but in fact their composition was continually changing.[19]

To draw up effective policies, we have to look at the conditions that cause people to fall into poverty and those that enable them to move on. Many factors influence whether, when there is a labour market transition, for example, individuals or households are able to weather it effectively. A study carried out across the EU15 countries showed that people aged 55–64 weather life crises better than other groups – mainly because they have accumulated assets and their children have normally left home.[20]

Policy implications

In considering the policy implications of the analysis so far, we should bear in mind what has been said in chapter 1 about best practice. I would summarize the discussion as follows:

1   There should be no more empty talk about social exclusion; it needs to be given a precise meaning. We should disentangle inequality and poverty per se from social exclusion, which is in fact a far narrower notion in terms of its application. 'Social exclusion' should only be used to refer to situations in which individuals or households suffer from multiple deprivation; and where such deprivation cuts them off in specifiable ways from wider social and economic participation.

2   To increase levels of social justice, it is above all important to concentrate, as Merkel proposes, on reducing poverty. Since poverty is defined in relation to median income, it is in any case a measure of inequality. In a differentiated society, levelling up is more national than levelling down. However, what matters about poverty is not economic deprivation as

[19]   Yasmin Hussain and Paul Bagguley, 'Citizenship, ethnicity and identity: British Pakistanis after the 2001 riots', Dept. of Sociology, University of Leeds, Working Paper, July 2003.
[20]   Robert Walker, 'Opportunity and life-chances: the dynamics of poverty, inequality and exclusion', in Anthony Giddens and Patrick Diamond (eds.), *The New Egalitarianism*. Cambridge: Polity, 2005, p. 77.

such, but its consequences for individual well-being and capacities.[21]

3 Most social policy is concerned with improving people's lot once they have fallen into poverty, but this traditional approach is inadequate in the context of today's society. Flexicurity is the best way to cope with transitions between jobs, and can certainly help those in poverty, since getting a job is the best route out of poverty, for men and women alike. However, we also need a more preventative approach, which focuses upon the events that precipitate spells of poverty, the factors that bring those spells to an end, and upon the consequences of poverty that shape subsequent outcomes.

4 Investment in children can have a multiple pay-off, not only because of the problem of child poverty, but simply because policies initiated early on can have an impact throughout life. Education has a crucial role in post-industrial society, but it does not automatically act to equalize life-chances. In fact, it can easily become a battleground for the privileged to sustain or enhance their advantages. Active policies have to be instituted to counter these tendencies, since otherwise the new primacy of education can create fresh barriers for the less advantaged to surmount.

5 Policies should not just address the 'poor' or even the 'excluded' as embedded categories – and we must not concentrate only upon those who are poor at any given period of time. Some policy initiatives should be directed at those above the poverty line in the light of known risk factors that might cause them to drop below it, or, having escaped from poverty, might lead to them falling into it again. These policies need to be both structural and personalized. They should not be limited to the human capital side. Together with employers, improving both conditions of work and internal promotion chances are important. Such interventions will help mute the carousel effect.

6 We must take an interest not just in pathways the unemployed may use to get into work, but also in the dynamics

[21] Sen, *Inequality Re-examined.*

of low-paid jobs. The British Household Panel Survey has interviewed the members of more than 5,000 households each year since 1991, including in their interviews questions about people's experiences before the research started. The panel provides a rich and detailed source of information about the low paid. As one would expect, those on the lowest pay grades are most likely to experience spells of unemployment. Over the period 1991–4, 30 per cent of men in the bottom quarter of earners spent some time out of work, compared to 12 per cent among those in the top quarter.[22] The study confirms the importance of job tenure – low-paid men who have held a job continuously for more than five years are 80 per cent more likely to move out of low pay than those who have held their current job for less than two years. Skill level is an important influence. Over 40 per cent of men who begin their careers in low-paid jobs lack formal qualifications. They are the least likely to move to higher earnings at any subsequent point.

7   Generalized policies promoting skills, and aimed at reducing educational under-achievement, are obviously essential to improving the life-chances of these groups. However, more targeted and personalized interventions could clearly make a major impact. Programmes should be directed to trying to ensure that those who start work unqualified stay in jobs for lengthy periods and are able to progress in them. Training opportunities at work could be part of the policy package, and would be particularly important for women. Unions could and should play an important role here.

8   For those who are genuinely excluded, quite different sorts of policies are appropriate, although a passage into work remains a major aim. Addictive behaviour, often producing a deteriorating cycle in the ability to cope, is a significant influence. Material help, even the offer of concrete job opportunities, will make little impact on their own. Targeted policies at a micro-social level are needed. They should

---

[22] BPHS data quoted in John Rigg and Tom Sefton, *Income Dynamics and the Life-Cycle*. Centre for the Analysis of Social Exclusion, LSE, 2004.

include the specific provision of counselling services, neighbourhood support groups and means of helping those
affected by domestic or other forms of violence.

9 Targeted policies are also required to deal with externally
generated shocks, especially where large numbers of workers
are made redundant in the short term. They should involve
close collaboration of the social partners and other agencies.
Just like 'poverty', however, 'redundancy' is not a singular
experience, and the range of coping strategies both before
and after the event may be quite wide. They always have to
be understood in terms of wider life-situations and life-
projects.

10 Flexicurity is highly important in such situations, but on its
own it is not enough. A number of approaches have been
suggested in the US that might have relevance in Europe too.
Pre-emptive re-employment schemes are one idea – workers
in threatened industries could apply early on for retraining
as an insurance policy; or encouragement could be given for
early job search. The most effective way, Gene Sperling suggests, would be to expand local college training courses over
the Internet, allowing currently employed workers to start
training at home. Internet services providing job search facilities have proved to be one of the most effective options. The
state could contribute, since there should in fact be net
savings from such schemes if periods of unemployment are
cut.[23] A high proportion of workers, including increasing
numbers of women, would like to start their own businesses.
There are some encouraging results from pilot schemes. Two
such schemes were set up in Washington, DC and in the state
of Massachusetts in the US. Those who took part in the programme were twice as likely as others to start a business in
a period of eighteen months after training. Their earnings
increased by US\$7,500. Other programmes have been set up
to provide opportunities for those who might want to
combine starting a business with a part-time job.

---

[23] Gene Sperling, *The Pro-Growth Progressive: An Economic Strategy for Shared Prosperity*. New York: Simon & Schuster, 2005, pp. 77–82.

Flexible education accounts could help workers cross skill barriers within enterprises as well as help with pre-emptive training. The Clinton administration introduced lifetime learning credits, under which workers could get a 20 per cent credit for costs of up to US$10,000 a year for learning and retraining while in work. The percentage would probably have to be substantially higher for such a scheme to be really effective. But what others have called a 'learning bank', in which investments could be made against future transitions, should give those who choose this option more long-term control over their lives.

It should be possible to bring high-speed Internet access, and training facilities, to the low-cost areas of the EU. Labour costs are falling in the production of some kinds of products – for example, the cost of labour in producing a computer is only about 2 per cent of the total production cost. Poorer areas of Europe should be able to compete effectively with low-cost areas abroad if the necessary skills are there. The social dumping argument can be turned on its head, because job and production facilities would be kept within Europe; and convergence would be facilitated.

The support of companies should be enlisted to exercise responsibility in lay-offs. Such an approach is by no means naive or unworkable. There are almost always some areas of managerial discretion, even in a company facing severe problems of profitability. Thus in 2001 Southwest Airlines in the US faced declining revenues as many people refused to fly in the wake of 9/11. The company deployed various cost-saving techniques – including cuts in executive salaries – and weathered the crisis without a high lay-off. A year later the airline went back into profit.[24]

Is there a role for protectionism where workers are threatened with redundancy? The answer to the question surely has to be 'no', if the term refers to the propping up of firms that have become outmoded technologically, uneconomic or uncompetitive. There are a few examples of companies that have managed to weather an economic storm and subsequently return to profitability. But they are very much the exception rather than the norm; there are far more cases where companies have been artificially rescued only to

---

[24] Ibid, p. 88.

collapse a little later, often with worse consequences for the workers involved than if the 'rescue' had not happened. Any form of protection offered by the state to a company should be temporary, and should be geared to retraining and assistance in finding new job opportunities.

Reform of public services so as to increase responsiveness to client needs should be the backdrop to most of the other points made above. The aim should be to empower welfare recipients to make responsible choices rather than respond to need in a bureaucratic way. Personalized service plus choice open to the welfare client where possible should be central to the options that are made available. In education and health care, choice of alternative options should not just be open to the affluent, much less only to those who 'go private'. However, it is important to offer enough incentives to persuade affluent groups to make use of public services, so that they retain a commitment to them.

When we talk about economic inequality, we should not forget about what is happening at the top, even if the proportion of people involved is tiny compared to those in most countries living in poverty. The proportion of income taken by the top 1 per cent of earners has increased in most, although not all, EU countries over the past thirty years – reversing a trend established for several decades previously. (We know little, however, about distribution by households.) The distribution of wealth is everywhere more unequal than of income, although there are wide variations across the EU countries, as well as differences with the US. The top 1 per cent of the population possesses about 25 per cent of total wealth in France and Denmark, although only 15 per cent in Sweden. In the US the proportion is 35 per cent.

Should we be worried about the disproportionate amounts of income and wealth going to the top 1 per cent? In terms of helping the more deprived, what happens to the incomes of high earners makes little difference. Whatever redistribution were to take place from the very affluent to the poor would have only a small impact, since the numbers of those who experience poverty are far too large. Most countries have reduced their top rates of income tax for high earners, which in some countries at one time reached over 90 per cent. However, evidence shows that either in spite of or because of this change, the proportion of income paid by the highest earners in tax has actually increased rather than dropped compared to that period.

It is in terms more of solidarity and power that the position of the top 1 per cent should cause more concern. Are those running the large corporations living up to their citizenship responsibilities? Are their earnings in line with their achievements? There is reason to have concern on both these points. For instance, tax evasion and pushing tax avoidance to its very limits are more the norm today than used to be the case. Quite often – even characteristically – there seems little relationship between the earnings of corporate directors and actual performance of companies.

What should, and can, be done? Given the mobile nature of capital, incentives are likely to work better than punitive regulations – except where the latter can actually be applied at transnational level, as in the case of anti-monopoly legislation. Tax breaks for philanthropy are one policy. In some EU states – such as the UK – the rich give a smaller percentage of their income away to charitable or public causes than do the poor; in the US the reverse is true. The earnings of the best-paid American executives seem shockingly high by European standards (and are regarded as such by many among the American public). Yet some high earners follow the maxim of Andrew Carnegie, and give away most of their fortune in their lifetime. Bill Gates has given more to anti-AIDS programmes in Africa than has any single country (including his own).

Inequalities of wealth are higher than those of income, and here it makes sense to think of taking action. Wealth can be transferred from generation to generation, unlike income unless it is derived from wealth. The obvious mechanism for egalitarian policies is inheritance tax. Some OECD countries have moved to abolish inheritance tax, but a far better case in terms of social justice can be made for rendering it more progressive. The way to do so is to close down tax exemptions, such as those that make it possible to pass on gifts *inter vivos* without tax having to be paid. It is both possible and desirable to have progressive banding for inheritance tax – and to make it steeper where it exists.

Such an innovation has been suggested, for example, for the UK. At present, tax is charged at 40 per cent for every £1 of inheritance over £263,000. This system is progressive, since it means that an estate worth £300,000 is taxed at only 5 per cent; one of £1 million is taxed at 29 per cent. Overall, however, in spite of rising wealth inequality, only 6 per cent of the value of estates every year is taken in tax. Introducing more steeply progressive bands would both increase overall revenue, and produce a fairer overall outcome. The authors of the proposal argue that the extra money generated could be spent on a trust fund for children, or for long-term care for the frail elderly.[25]

Transitional Labour Markets

Whatever happens to the rich, it is certain that the vast majority of people's lives will be affected most directly by their own work prospects. The relationship between work and non-work has grown more complex. Being able to profit from transitions, rather than being brought low by them – whether it be unemployment, a spell of poverty, divorce or becoming disabled – comes to the forefront. In social policy terms, these considerations suggest quite fundamental changes in how we should look at labour markets.

In the typical labour contract in the past, employment was defined as simply the state of having a job at a given time. But we might start seeing employment in a very different way – as a temporary state or *current expression* of long-term *employability*. The point of labour market policy should be to enhance positive market transitions, based on enhancing employability and minimizing downward spirals into precarious employment.[26]

In social policy terms, we have to learn to concentrate on the life-course, and upon the transitions people experience and have to cope with. Transitions have become more 'open' and less predictable than they used to be. The notion of full employment as formulated by Beveridge in the 1940s is plainly outmoded. Creating

[25] Dominic Maxwell, *Fair Dues*. London: IPPR, 2004.
[26] Bernard Gazier and Günther Schmid, 'The dynamics of full employment', in Schmid and Gazier (eds.), *The Dynamics of Full Employment: Social Integration Through Transitional Labour Markets*. Cheltenham: Edward Elgar Publishing, 2002, p. 6.

jobs for all on the model of the male head of household (at that time) working for a fixed period each week for most of his life would make no sense today. Not only must part-time work have a significant role, but the boundaries between paid work and activities directed to other life-goals often need to be quite fluid.

Gender relations are particularly important here. In the past, most men followed a standardized work pattern with fixed hours of employment, in jobs stretching over a long time period. Women's employment patterns were almost completely the opposite – they worked as occasional secondary earners or carers, and their jobs were not standardized at all. The fact that this opposition has now broken down – although by no means completely – is a progressive development, but means we must have new ways of thinking about policy. It is significant that France, Germany and Italy still approximate more to the traditional gender distribution of work than do the UK, the Netherlands or the Nordic countries. No country has yet come close to what one might take as a guiding ideal, both of gender equality and lifetime flexibility – a situation in which, as measured over the life-span, both men's and women's jobs would converge around, say, a thirty-hour week (with periods of longer and shorter working hours for both).[27]

Because of the stress now put upon globalization, analyses of the changing nature of labour markets tend to emphasize external shocks as the source of discontinuous life-situations. In line with the earlier emphases of this study, however, one must point out that many (most?) transitions are endogenously generated, although once more very few are completely uninfluenced by globalization. These may include changing patterns of taste that undermine a product or market, poor management on the side of the employer, and so forth, but also many factors (negative and positive) on the side of the worker. Examples are health problems, relationship changes or time off for retraining. Those in demanding jobs may suffer from burn-out, or change occupations after a break.

[27] Günther Schmid, 'Towards a new employment contract', in Schmid and Gazier (eds.), *The Dynamics of Full Employment: Social Integration Through Transitional Labour Markets*. Cheltenham: Edward Elgar Publishing, 2002.

Positive factors are also many. A person (man or woman) may decide to take a less – or a more – demanding job at a certain time of life. Many of those who commit themselves to 'burn-out jobs' plan to move on quite early in their lives. For example, a high proportion of workers in financial services jobs plan a career change at around the age of 40 – and many go on to make it, jumping rather than being pushed. Other positive influences include the birth of a child, a decision to enter or re-enter higher education, a return to health after illness, or the discovery by someone who is disabled that he or she can work in a rewarding job after all. The birth of a child is quite a different phenomenon from the classical period of the welfare state. It is now far more of a conscious decision, one that may be weighed and reweighed before being taken.

'Internally' produced spells of unemployment, or a move to part-time work, differ from traditional sources of unemployment produced by cyclical movement of the economy or by technological change. Even where they are produced by negative shocks, they may spark positive life-transitions, producing higher salaries or more fulfilling jobs. But they can mark the beginning of a downward spiral. For example, if older men lose their jobs, they might find themselves out of work for the rest of their lives. To cope with these issues, we need a politics of *second chances* – the provision of opportunities to start again after set-backs, whether in work, the family or other areas.

A fundamental problem is how to create positive transitions for those in 'Big Mac' jobs. In the EU15 states half of these jobs are occupied by young people (under 25) and older people (over 60). There is no reason why a still higher proportion of older people should not work in these jobs – there are more who would like to do so than can find such work. The reason is wholly social – resistance from those who manage and frequent businesses such as coffee shops. Such prejudices hopefully in the future can in large part be overcome, as the population itself ages further, and as ageist prejudices decline.

A certain proportion of young people in 'Big Mac' jobs are already in transitional labour markets – they are working casually prior to entering further or higher education, or are taking time off to travel before resuming a new career path. A high number of young people working in hotels, restaurants and cafés in London, for example, are there in a transitional situation – to learn English, experience London, or perhaps get some professional training in the service industries.

A further proportion consists of those – predominantly women – who are secondary earners in households with others in work. Their chances of promotion are low, though they do not necessarily live in poor households. Examples are those who work as check-out clerks at supermarkets, as industrial or domestic cleaners or as shop assistants. Should we worry about them, given that many may want part-time and relatively undemanding work? Yes, because if the opportunities for advancement were there, they might certainly be interested in taking them up. Moreover, those most likely to be impoverished are (predominantly) women who are either heads of households in which no one else works or whose partner is also in a low-paid occupation. Statistics show that the proportion who make a direct transition from 'Big Mac' jobs to more stable and worthwhile employment is worryingly small.

Making transitions

What kind of policies might be implemented to deal with the possibilities and problems of post-industrial labour markets – especially ones that are preventative rather than of the safety-net variety? Günther Schmid suggests a number of approaches. We should aim for policies that:

- maintain or enhance income *capacity* during transitions between education or training – or re-education and retraining;
- provide income *security* during significant transitions between employment relationships, particularly between part-time and full-time work and between contractual employment and self-employment (or vice versa);
- offer income *support* during phases in the life-course where income capacity declines because of social obligations, such as caring for children or other caring tasks that consume much of the time of the individual;

- provide income *maintenance* during transitions between employment and unemployment;
- supply *income replacement* where income is reduced or undermined by disablement or other causes that make paid work impossible. To secure a higher proportion of older workers in the labour force, retirement as a qualification for income replacement has to be limited as far as possible, by a mixture of incentives and sanctions.[28]

To these we should add:

- the introduction of training schemes that can be used by those in low-level service jobs who wish to move to more skilled occupations. Employers should be offered incentives to construct career ladders from 'Big Mac' jobs to other job possibilities.

To facilitate these policy proposals, we might start to think in terms of *employment insurance* or wage insurance rather than the unemployment insurance systems that exist at the moment.[29] Such an approach is consistent with a stress upon full employment as a lifetime concept. Unemployment benefits, even in active labour market conditions, only come into play once an individual loses his or her job. Employment insurance is oriented not only to these circumstances, but is aimed also at the more positive side of transitional labour markets. A prime function of employment insurance would be to encourage people to take risks that could have positive outcomes – such as taking time out to enhance employability through arrangements for lifelong learning, or to make transitions that would defer retirement.

The conditions that would balance autonomy, increased social justice and economic dynamism in the knowledge/service economy would be a far cry from deregulated labour markets. They would ideally involve close collaborations between the social partners –

---

[28] Ibid, pp. 394–8.
[29] Erik de Gier and Axel van den Berg, *Making Transitions Pay!* Amsterdam School for Social Science Research, June 2005.

employers and unions – and government. Available policies are of several different types; some are already in operation to some degree in certain countries. Possibilities include the use of vouchers for in-work training as part of a package involving the acceptance of lower initial wages; and 'employment companies' to develop local networks that would come into play when large numbers of workers are laid off and also help the long-term unemployed. Experiments with such ideas are under way in the Netherlands, Belgium and Austria, among other countries. In the Netherlands, for instance, a not-for-profit agency, START, temporarily employs people unable to get into the labour market by orthodox means, loaning them to private employers to gain work experience or offering them training if employers will not take them.

The work foundations that have been set up in Austria offer interesting possibilities of further generalization. Their objective is to provide a network of resources for redundant workers so that they do not have to deal with the transition to a new job in isolation. The work foundations are an excellent example of social partnership. Where a company makes mass redundancies, those workers who stay in their jobs pay 0.25 per cent of their wages as a contribution to the foundation – a gesture of solidarity to their former workmates. The company itself makes a larger capital contribution. A further payment is made by the redundant workers themselves, who give over 50 per cent of their redundancy payments to the foundation. Finally, the state guarantees the payment of unemployment benefit for a maximum of four years, covering most of the costs. The experiment seems to have worked. A comparison between those who participated and others who did not showed a much higher proportion of the former group had found employment over a relatively short period.[30]

A move towards an employment insurance system as detailed above would not necessarily be more expensive than the more fragmentary programmes that currently exist in most states. Experiments such as that just mentioned meet their own costs –

[30] Schmid, 'Towards a new employment contract', pp. 417–18.

more than meet them if the overall net benefit to the economy is included in the calculation.

Active labour market policy has been successful – indeed it has been a crucial element in the policy used in countries that have lowered unemployment and achieved high employment. However, in line with the above emphases, there should be a shift towards *activating* labour market policy, a broader concept. Most active labour market schemes at the moment become operational only when a person has already been unemployed for a certain period. As has been observed: 'This is rather like throwing the unemployed in at the deep end of the swimming pool and waiting to see whether they manage to get out unaided, instead of asking them beforehand whether and how well they can swim.'[31] It would be better to make an immediate assessment of the risk of medium or long-term unemployment. Active labour market policies normally provide the costs of whatever retraining options are offered. But such a system has no built-in incentives to make sure the placement office is efficient; it is preferable to have co-financing, as in the work foundations just described.

In the traditional labour contract, the roles of the social partners mainly concerned negotiating wages and working conditions. In activating labour market policy, bargaining would centre just as much on working-time arrangements, including periods when work can be combined with family commitments or periods of training. Extra costs should fall upon employees as well as employers. Firms should also develop human resource programmes in order to enhance their flexibility and competitiveness, in line with employee needs as far as possible. In traditional schemes of unemployment benefits, the state picks up virtually all of the cost of human capital investment. But it would make sense to provide incentives for companies themselves to assume part of this role, especially since in the knowledge/service economy it can conform closely to their economic interests. Some new labour market programmes of this sort have been introduced in Finland, although at the moment they remain rather marginal. Instances include job rotation schemes and counselling schemes in the event of substantial restructuring of the firm or business.

[31] Ibid, p. 427.

Box 3.1 The new egalitarianism

1 Concerned not just with social justice but with economic dynamism. We know that the two can be closely reconciled, although there are trade-offs.
2 Traditional redistributive mechanisms stay in place, although in modified form. For instance, progressive taxation is still highly important, but is altered where known to compromise economic needs and job creation.
3 Some policy orientations have to be towards the long-term poor and the genuinely excluded; but we have to be especially concerned with transitions, most notably with transitional labour markets.
4 Policies that benefit more affluent groups are important if they have the effect of consolidating commitment to the welfare system.
5 Gender-sensitive policies are crucial, not only to continue to improve the economic position of women, but also to help men in vulnerable categories.
6 Emphasis upon activating labour market strategies.
7 High standards of social and economic citizenship demanded of the top earners.
8 Reducing child poverty has a particularly central place.

Like active labour market policy, activating labour market policy involves obligations as well as rights for all involved. The obligations of the unemployed at the current time involve primarily the requirement to enter training programmes at a certain point, and to accept job offers made. But the responsibilities of benefit recipients could be extended. For instance, they could be obliged to contribute to wage investment funds.

Children, Childhood, Child Poverty

Finally in this chapter let me return again to the issue of children. Economic issues here overlap with more general social ones. In post-industrial societies we live in an era of the 'prized child'. The decision to have a child is almost wholly an emotional one, but also very special and distinctive. A child only rarely any longer just 'comes along'. Parenthood has thus changed dramatically, while childhood itself is still evolving. Childhood might not have 'disappeared', as some have argued, but children are arguably exposed to an adult world much earlier than they were a generation ago, because of the ubiquity of the media.[32]

Child poverty is perhaps the most pernicious form of poverty there is, and the one with the most ubiquitous consequences. But now it extends into more subtle and difficult forms of under-privilege too. We don't know what effects there are from the fact that some children grow up with everyday access to the Internet and a diversity of media, whereas others do not. It is possible that the 'adulting' of childhood affects children from poorer backgrounds in more negative ways than the children of the better-off. For instance, there is evidence that street gangs, even quite violent ones, develop among children at an early age, in which role models are taken directly from TV. These differences are fraught with implications for education and educational experience.

In the era of the 'prized child', parents and prospective parents recognize (or should do) that responsibilities for children stretch for twenty years or more, with corresponding implications for income security. Flexibility of working conditions when children are young does not solve that problem and, if further career opportunities are not provided later for women, could actually compound it. Policies for transitional labour markets, with a life-span perspective, should play a fundamental role here. For many families in Europe, two incomes are now required to stay above the poverty line, not only early on but in the long term, too. Access to adequate housing is a very important factor, especially given the elevated prices of property in many parts of Europe.

Policies for investment in children need to be tied in a thoroughgoing way to concerns about gender equality – and therefore have to involve men as well as women. In spite of difficulties noted earlier, policies that emphasize greater equality in the distribution of

[32] Neil Postman, *The Disappearance of Childhood*. London: Vintage, 1994.

domestic work can have some effect. For instance, as a result of such initiatives in the Netherlands, the ratio of men in part-time work has risen to 23 per cent, as against an EU15 average of only 7 per cent.

Many of the EU countries at present are far from meeting the Barcelona targets for child care spaces. Lack of affordable places is a major issue, but so also, as Jane Jensen points out, is design.[33] Thus the Barcelona targets are sometimes met by setting up nursery school places. Since these are part time, parents have to find other sources of child care for the remainder of the day and week. While mothers might be freed for paid jobs, these cannot be for more than a few hours and produce only marginal income.

Some ways forward have become clear in recent years. Reducing child poverty means not focusing upon children themselves, but upon households. It is households that are at risk rather than children as such. Households with no one in work are most prone to child poverty – followed by those with only one earner. Income supplements designed both to help the earnings of households and get more people in them into work have been proven effective. An important example has been the use of tax credits in the UK – some 750,000 children have been lifted out of poverty over the period from 1997 to 2004.

Providing help to lone parent families is important in reducing child poverty, but it is by no means decisive – the attention concentrated on lone parent families in recent years in policy terms seems to be misplaced. A study showed this to be so by calculating what would happen if all advanced countries had the same proportion of single parent families. The results showed that the ranking of countries would not change if in every country one in ten families was a single parent family – reinforcing the conclusion that it is households that matter.[34]

The Nordic countries are again in the lead in their low levels of child poverty and of 'social inheritance' – equality of life-chances. There is much other countries can learn. In Sweden, child poverty stands at only 2.6 per cent: before taxes and transfers the level is

[33] Jane Jenson, 'The European social model. Gender and generational equality', in Anthony Giddens, Patrick Diamond and Roger Liddle (eds.), *Global Europe, Social Europe*. Cambridge: Polity, 2006.
[34] Ibid, p. 165.

23 per cent. The difference comes almost wholly from policy rather than from direct redistribution of income. Most such policies can be replicated by countries with lower overall tax rates, through the deployment of tax incentives, private-sector involvements and other mechanisms. Universal and effective child care appears to be the single most important factor that ties together low rates of child poverty and low rates of social inheritance – although, as we have seen, the implications for women are to some extent problematic.

Deficiencies in skills and in literacy in some EU countries affect some 20–30 per cent of youth population – a dire situation in a world where the prospects of semi- or unskilled manual work are all but drying up. Traditional ways of improving this situation have concentrated upon in-school reforms – such as avoiding early streaming by ability, introducing comprehensive schools, literacy classes and other strategies. However, there might be more to be gained by concentrating on the family milieu. Evidence indicates that more important than sheer poverty in influencing the cognitive development of children are the cultural resources of the home. 'Culture' and 'money' are not closely related, as a study of international data on school achievement showed.

Research compared the effects of parents' education, income and cultural level with the cognitive performance of their children aged 15.[35] Household income does not come out as an important explanatory factor in the differences noted, but culture does, as measured by available information sources in the home, frequency of discussion of cultural issues and attending concerts or the theatre. Children with few cognitive resources start with a handicap that becomes magnified later – sometimes actually as a result of the school environment. When one controls for parents' income, education and even immigrant status, those who score highly in pre-school years or cognitive tests have two to three times as much chance of making the transition into upper secondary education as others.

If lowering child poverty rates has to be a main objective in (most) EU countries, so also does elevating the birth rate. Falling birth rates are not confined to the EU – the birth rate in Singapore, at 1.1, is the lowest in the world. Chile, the most economically

[35] Esping-Andersen, 'Inequality of incomes and opportunities', p. 33.

advanced society in Latin America, has a birth rate of 1.7. The EU countries, however, have a very much larger combined population, and the issue has become an acutely important one.

It is generally acknowledged that there is a gap between how many children people say they want and how many on average they actually have. Lack of state support for child care is clearly one factor. Those countries that have the lowest birth rates in the EU, such as Spain and Italy, offer the least support in these areas. Countries with higher birth rates, such as Denmark or France, offer vastly better child care services. But this explanation is only part of the story. Part of what is happening is a result of a fall in the numbers of those who had *more* children than they wanted – the capacity to avoid excess child-bearing is greater than the past.[36]

Child care facilities and flexible working time are important. But surveys also show that fear of unemployment – for oneself or one's partner – ranks very high up on the list of people's stated reasons why they have fewer children than they would like. In the era of the 'prized child', having a child and providing for him or her appropriately is an expensive business. Prospective parents worry about bringing a child into the world when their own economic future looks less than rosy. This conclusion is highly important, because it suggests how far coping with Europe's demographic problems is tied in to reform of the social model more generally.

The future of the European social model is bound up with successful investment in children – for economic reasons and reasons of social justice. However, it will not do to concentrate on children to the neglect of the implications of policy for gender relations. There are some possible trade-offs to be faced. For instance, flexible working hours for women allow for a balance of family and work responsibilities, but may leave many stuck later on in poorly paid jobs with little chance of moving to full-time work. Women employed by more affluent mothers for domestic child care risk a similar fate. There is a major overlap here with issues of migration, since many such women are from ethnic minorities. I shall discuss some of these issues further in the next chapter, which concerns the reform of welfare.

[36] Jenson, 'The European social model', p. 159.

4

From Negative to Positive Welfare

In discussing welfare reform, we might begin by disentangling the two elements, 'welfare' and 'state'. In post-industrial societies the role of the state can no longer be just to 'provide' welfare. It has to assume a wider, but looser, regulatory role. The task of the state is to help create an effective public sphere and worthwhile public goods. It is far from being the only agent involved. For example, the effective distribution of food products to shops, supermarkets, etc., is a public good, but it is not the place of the state to do more than provide an overall regulatory framework for it.

The notion of 'public services' has to be treated with care. The 'state' and the 'public sphere' or 'public goods' are not the same. State-provided services may or may not create optimal conditions for the delivery of public goods. The state may be inefficient, overly bureaucratic, dominated by producer interests or over-centralized – all of those and other traits have hampered the provision of welfare in the 'welfare state' in the past.

'Welfare' is also an ambiguous term. The *Oxford English Dictionary* gives two prime meanings. One is 'economic assistance to people in need'. The other is more general, and refers to a 'state of being happy and healthy', as in 'well-being'. The welfare state was conceived by its founders mainly as a system of insurance or risk management, hence using the narrower definition of welfare. William Beveridge, for example, saw the welfare state as a way of attacking the 'five giants' – Want, Disease, Ignorance, Squalor and Idleness. But his approach to welfare is as outdated as the industrial order within which it was developed. The post-industrial society is characterized by higher levels of individualism, and by much greater lifestyle diversity than was true before. In such a society, it makes less sense to think of the state as a mere insurance mechanism, or to see welfare as defined only in terms of economic risk.

We should start to understand 'welfare', I shall argue, more as well-being, or as the positive pursuit of life-goals. We could term this a move from protective risk-management towards *positive welfare*. Each of Beveridge's negatives could be replaced with a positive. In place of Want, personal autonomy or freedom; not avoidance of Disease, but active health; instead of Ignorance, education, as a continuing part of life; rather than Squalor, prosperity; and in place of Idleness, initiative. Turned into positives, the five make up a core of positive life-goals, to which social policy should be oriented. Americans, as many surveys show, on average tend to be more optimistic than Europeans. Could this be something to do with the fact that positive life-goals were already structured into their constitution: life, liberty and the pursuit of happiness?

The traditional welfare system sought to *transfer risk* from the individual to the state (see box 4.1). Security was defined as the reduction of risk, and was presumed to be the main goal of the welfare state, alongside the search for increasing social justice. But this view is again quite negative, especially in a world where many people are bent on exploring new lifestyle opportunities. Rather than 'the welfare state', we should speak of a *society of positive welfare*, in which the state plays a central, but not a dominating, role. The state is primarily a *social investment* and *regulatory* agency. Many over recent years have talked of the state as an enabling force, but it is better to speak of the *ensuring state* in the positive welfare society. An enabling state uses social investment whenever possible to help people to help themselves. But this notion suggests that, once provided with resources, people are left alone to sink or swim. The ensuring state, by contrast, seeks to influence outcomes in the public interest, or even sometimes to guarantee them. The ensuring principle applies in such areas as minimum wages or income guarantees, child benefits, or a floor for pensions commitments.

Box 4.1 The traditional welfare state

1 Policies are 'after the event' – picking up the pieces after things have gone wrong. The welfare state is essentially a collective insurance system, based upon the idea of a safety-net.

2 Apart from the fields of education and, to a lesser extent health, the welfare state is not seen as a generative agency. This orientation is partly because lifestyle is not seen as problematic – behaviour and many structures (such as gender roles) are dictated by custom.

3 The welfare state is designed to increase cohesion, but above all through the reconciliation of classes. 'The' social problem is the problem of class conflict, centring upon the division between the manual working class and other major class groups in society.

4 The welfare state develops primarily through the extension of rights. T. H. Marshall quite correctly distinguished three successive 'layers' of rights: legal rights (such as freedom of speech), political rights (universal franchise) and economic rights (unemployment insurance and so forth) (see below).

5 Producer interests tend to dominate over those of clients, who by and large have to 'take what they are offered'. 'Doctor knows best' mentality predominates in most spheres. Citizens assumed to be largely passive as recipients of services.

6 Policies oriented to here-and-now problems as they occur in people's lives, but overall life-span presumed to be stable and predictable. Pensions are built around these assumptions, but so are most other policies.

7 Education has a central place, but is understood primarily in terms of primary and secondary education, and in terms of its extension to groups whose access was restricted.

The old welfare state defined benefits primarily, in some contexts exclusively, in terms of rights – the right to a job, unemployment benefits or free education. However, in a society of more open lifestyles, rights normally also involve *obligations* – obligations that have to be spelled out, or sanctioned in law. In the sphere of labour markets, for instance, unemployment benefits are tied both to incentives and sanctions, designed to ensure active job search and job placement.

Welfare should be redefined in terms of personal *autonomy* and *self-esteem*. These values become important in a society that is aspirational, but also one where lifestyle issues are close to the surface, since they imply active behaviour change. Self-esteem, or rather lack of it, has been shown to be involved with a range of social problems, including poverty, crime and health among other areas. Low self-esteem limits autonomy, and the capability to better one's life; but it can actually produce self-damage or aggression towards others. A whole range of behaviour that centres around addiction, including eating disorders, alcoholism and even aspects of sexual violence, relates to self-esteem and lack of a stable sense of self.[1]

To speak of self-esteem might seem vague or unrealistic, compared to narrow economic notions of welfare. In fact, in the knowledge/service economy, self-esteem actually connects closely to some very mundane, on the ground issues. Consider, for example, transitional labour markets. In the employment conditions that come to prevail in the new economy, the network labour market has flexible entries and exits, depending upon opportunities, work–life balances and paths of accumulating work experience. Such labour markets seen from a positive angle 'foresee the end of purely dependent labour, the individual's release from the bonds of the firm and the beginning of a new form of self-employment'.[2] For these possibilities to be realized, the individual should have sufficient self-reliance to be able to cope with change, or even engineer it if necessary.[3]

In this chapter I shall try to connect these ideas to a broadranging assessment of the welfare state and its future. The classical

[1] Anthony Giddens, *Modernity and Self-Identity*. Cambridge: Polity Press, 1991.
[2] Bernard Gazier and Günther Schmid, 'The dynamics of full employment', in Schmid and Gazier (eds.), *The Dynamics of Full Employment: Social Integration Through Transitional Labour Markets*. Cheltenham: Edward Elgar Publishing, 2002, p. 6.
[3] Ibid.

welfare state, I shall argue, has become largely obsolete, or at least in need of a thoroughgoing rethink. Some of the reasons why were discussed in the last chapter, since social justice is an abiding concern of any welfare system. However, there are many other concerns to be tackled, especially those to do with social solidarity. Most important among them is what I call *the* social problem of today – how our societies should react to their new-found cultural and ethnic diversity. The questions involved are so crucial that I devote all of the second half of the chapter to them.

Interventionism and Activism

A positive welfare approach should be *interventionist* or pre-emptive rather than only *remedial*. Interventionism means wherever possible seeking to tackle problems at source, rather than following the format of the classical welfare state – covering risks and picking up the pieces later. The image of the safety-net is a misleading one for current times. There is a clear coming together here between economic dynamism and social justice. Investment in human capital, ensuring as much equality as possible in life-chances in the early years of life, upping the educational qualifications of those who at present fare poorly – these are all policy orientations that can act to promote economic competitiveness as well as greater equality.

Interventionism goes along with *activism*. Activism has two senses. One is that whenever possible welfare services should be designed to help people to help themselves. We have to take seriously the fact that the welfare state has sometimes, or in some contexts, been counter-productive for the very citizens it was designed to help. Benefits can create passivity. The welfare dependency that critics started lambasting the welfare state for in the 1990s is real, even if it was greatly exaggerated by some people at the time.[4] Again, the social justice element can be very plain, at least if

---

[4] See Charles Murray's various writings on the 'underclass' and the welfare system – for example, Institute of Economic Affairs, *Charles Murray and the Underclass*. London: IEA, 1996.

policies are properly designed. Consider disability. The very definition of 'disability' can create passivity or dependency in those to whom it is applied. This fact is indeed the reason why the terminology has changed – 'handicapped' was an even worse term.

There are many disabled people who want to work, or otherwise lead more fulfilling lives than they do. For those who are seriously disabled, technology obviously can help, with, for example, artificial limbs, speaking or hearing devices. The recent increase in the category of those classified as unable to work, however, also includes large numbers whose incapacities are less clear-cut – and shades over into those suffering from depression or mental disorder. The wider availability of therapeutic services is one way of helping people to stand on their own two feet again. 'Disablement' – if it means a form of social exclusion, being unable to play a full part in society – is to some large degree dependent on the attitudes of the sufferer, given that resources are available to help. Think of what the actor Christopher Reeve achieved when reduced to circumstances in which he could not move his body, or even speak. We see again the importance of self-esteem in such a context. Overcoming disablement is never a matter of technology or resources alone – although these can help generate the self-esteem that in turn makes greater autonomy of action possible.

The labour market reforms of the 1990s in Denmark involve the use of an 'individual action plan' (IAP). The client engages in a dialogue with a social worker, to build up a profile of his or her life and ambitions. The stated ideal of the IAP is to balance the needs of the individual with those of the labour market.[5] The IAP is a contract. The individual agrees to act in the manner specified so far as retraining and job search goes; the resources have to be made available to make it possible to fulfil these objectives. Where employment is unlikely to be found, the aim of the IAP is to stabilize the life-situation of the individual, and prevent a process of alienation and loss of self-esteem.

Although the system has its critics, the overall results seem encouraging. 'An IAP', it has been said, 'makes it possible for the

[5] Asmund W. Born and Per H. Jensen, 'Individualising citizenship', in J. G. Andersen et al., *The Changing Face of Welfare*. Bristol: Policy Press, 2005.

unemployed person to function as a responsible and reflexive citizen, as it activates unemployed individuals in the solution of their own problem.'[6] An important consequence is that individuals are encouraged to think about their likely job future in an active and also a long-term way.

The other meaning of 'activism' is social activism. We know from the failure of endless anti-poverty programmes, for example, that passive transfers of income have their limitations, especially when poverty goes along with other forms of deprivation. Local activism and involvement are crucial. Civil society organizations have to be central to the delivery, and the shaping, of welfare programmes. This proposition applies with even more force to the resolution of welfare issues that presume lifestyle change.

However, we cannot legitimate civil society organizations en bloc. Effectiveness and legitimacy are as necessary here as anywhere else. Old-style charitable organizations can at best have a limited role. Third-sector groups and non-governmental organizations (NGOs), no matter how local or more all-encompassing they may be, have to meet measures of public responsibility, since they are neither elected nor subject to the pressures of the marketplace in the same way a business firm is. These should include publicly published accounts, effective and open internal governance, and a preparedness to work directly with a variety of groups in government, the non-profit sector and business. The entrepreneurial spirit can often play a vital role – there is no reason to suppose it should be confined to business firms. Social entrepreneurs should be as alert and alive to new opportunities to pursue social goals as business leaders are in respect of economic ones.

Social policy can no longer cover just those areas to which it conventionally applies at the moment. As far as problems of cultural integration are concerned, for instance, it has to connect with debates about civil liberties and cultural relativism (see below). Tolerance and freedom of speech have mostly been kept in a separate policy box from welfare, but this division has broken down. In his classical formulation of the development of citizenship rights – which was also an account of the evolution of the welfare state –

---

[6] Ibid, p. 152.

Box 4.2 The post-industrial welfare society

1 Policies are based on preventive welfare and investment in human capital. Safety-net approach remains in place, but integrated with more generative policies. Policies are oriented towards positive life values.

2 Lifestyle change becomes a core concern of the welfare system. Incentives and sanctions are deployed to help secure positive outcomes. These have to be shaped through orthodox democratic mechanisms and should be geared to substantive freedoms.

3 The welfare system is designed to increase solidarity, but above all through helping to reconcile cultural and lifestyle diversity with overall social cohesion. 'The' social problem is that of creating this balance, and ensuring the full participation of minority groups.

4 Rights go along with obligations or responsibilities in virtually all areas of the welfare system. However, once established, rights cannot be just taken for granted. They might need to be reformed, and also can come directly under threat (such as freedom of speech).

5 The clients of the welfare system are empowered through a series of mechanisms, such as availability of information, personalization of services and choice.

6 Policies are oriented towards transitional problems in people's lives, many of which are unpredictable, but which also are often actively taken decisions. Policy aims to invest in people's capabilities and where possible has a long-term perspective.

7 Further and higher education become of great economic and social importance, as does learning across the life-span.

T. H. Marshall analysed three sets of rights, the legal, political and economic.[7] As he described them, such rights developed in sequence, each providing a foundation for the next one. Legal rights, including especially a range of personal freedoms, developed first. They were largely a creation of the eighteenth century. Once those had been achieved, the path was open for the acquisition of political rights, which got under way in the nineteenth century. Political rights in turn allowed the more deprived members of society to push for economic rights – the benefits that became built into the welfare state. The welfare state has been largely a twentieth-century creation.

Neither legal nor political rights were as firmly founded as Marshall thought. Each generation has to defend them afresh. Threats to civil liberties and freedom of speech have in fact been ever-present. One has only to recall the rise of Fascism, and then Communism, in Europe to see that this is so. Today, new tensions have arisen, coming from cultural contexts in which freedom of speech and individual liberties can clash with strongly held sacred values.

Consumer-Citizens and Citizen-Consumers

It will not do to suppose that the state automatically acts in the public interest; or, *per contra*, that market initiatives necessarily run against it. We must find a way beyond such crude characterizations, which have dogged debates about the future of the welfare state. Part of the problem is the ambiguity of the term 'public services', which refers in fact to state-based services. State-based institutions, or groups working within them, can be as sectional or self-interested as anyone in the 'private' sector. Privatization can sometimes serve the public interest very well, as the deregulation of telecoms shows.

A good society can be defined as one in which there is an effective balance between a competitive marketplace, a robust third

---

[7] T. H. Marshall, *Citizenship and Social Class*. Cambridge: Cambridge University Press, 1950.

sector or civil society and the democratic state. The boundaries between these are often contested, but that there are boundaries is obvious. In areas where markets have full rein, the individual functions as what might be termed a *consumer-citizen*. Standards in the marketplace are guaranteed primarily and directly through competition. A TV set that is inferior to others at the same price will be forced out of the market. The state and other public authorities play a role, but this role is limited to overseeing the general framework of the market, preventing monopolies and providing the means of guaranteeing contracts.

In non-market domains – the state and civil society – there may, and should, be significant consumer choice, but these areas are not organized primarily through market principles. For instance, in the state sector there may be choice between medical practitioners, schools or social services. However, standards cannot be guaranteed through competition as they can in the marketplace; they have to be supervised in a more direct way by professionals and public authorities. In these areas, one might say, the individual is a *citizen-consumer* – he or she has a right to expect standards to be applied vigorously by external authority.

The state is not the embodiment of the public domain. The state often needs reform precisely in order to pursue public goals and purposes. One of the difficulties with the Lisbon Agenda is that it concentrates almost wholly on markets and market efficiency, without a concomitant emphasis upon reform of the state.

The limitations of a society where the state is too dominant are well known. Yet it would be a mistake to suppose that such societies are alien to recent European experience. They are not. Several West European countries (Spain, Portugal and Greece) were state-based dictatorships only some three decades ago, while most of the new member states in the EU are ex-Communist societies, where the state was the prime actor.

Some such countries, perhaps understandably, have swung the other way, towards radical free-market philosophies. Such a stance can be regarded as at best provisional and temporary. A radical free-market approach does not create a fair or just society, nor does it create the conditions for longer-term economic growth. The experience of the UK under Mrs Thatcher's governments in the

1980s and after make these conclusions plain. The economic situation of Britain improved, but income and wealth inequalities increased sharply, public services and the transport infrastructure decayed. Productivity stagnated because of the lack of investment in the longer-term conditions of growth.

A society – local, national or transnational – that allows too much invasion from markets suffers consequences for welfare too. Market incentives might be important for welfare goals, ranging from health to the environment. But they normally have to be deployed within a broader framework of regulation. It is important to recognize that a society that gives too unrestricted a role for markets will suffer a decline in the civic order – inequalities become too large, commercial motives dominate other goals and crime and vandalism multiply.

Welfare Delivery

The post-war welfare state developed at a time when collectivism was still respectable, or at least acceptable. Attitudes of stoicism and self-sacrifice – coupled to feelings of solidarity with fellow countrymen and women – were commonplace for some time after the war. But the result was a system geared to the suppliers of services rather than recipients. Queuing, waiting, being at the disposal of the purveyors of services rather than having the chance to influence them, were characteristic features.

Some suggest that it is the advance of consumer capitalism which has made people dissatisfied with what they were once prepared to accept. For in markets the consumer has to be treated as a customer. No doubt there is some truth in this argument, but changing attitudes are probably more the result of everyday democratization. Individuals are empowered not just as consumers, but because of the progress of everyday freedoms, including access to a much wider range of information than previously. The welfare system often still lags painfully behind. In a study carried out in Germany, for example, researchers sat in social security offices to see what actually happened when unemployed people registered or came to enquire about job opportunities.

They found that the officials took no interest in the lives of applicants, or what had led them to apply for benefits. They asked them only for bureaucratic details – their date of birth, address, age and so forth.[8] (Agenda 2010 has introduced a more person-centred system.)

Welfare services, including the two basic areas of education and health, need to be personalized and their 'users' empowered. Such developments do not threaten authority or solidarity; they are the condition of them. Personalization is not at all necessarily the same as privatization. Zuboff and Maxmin have argued persuasively that most corporations in the private sector do not address the individual needs of their customers. Not just state-based institutions but many business organizations too still reflect the era of mass production, in which needs were assumed to be standardized. In spite of the fact that we are all consumers now, many experiences of the consumption process are in fact rather adversarial – call-lines where a computer answers rather than a person, long waits in line at the airports, insurance companies that devise all sorts of escape clauses to limit liability, data mining that treats individuals as statistical units, and so forth.

'People have changed more', Zuboff and Maxmin say, 'than the commercial organizations on which they depend.'[9] They don't want any longer to be treated like pawns in market games of segmentation and manipulation. They want to make their voices heard, and the customer services provided to them need to be tailored more effectively to the specific demands of their lives. As Zuboff and Maxmin put it, people (from all backgrounds) 'experience themselves first as individuals and share a common longing for psychological self-determination'.[10] As they quite rightly stress, although many associate this phenomenon with the decline of community and the spread of narcissism, it actually has quite different implications – an active search for connection and for involvement with others.

[8] Lutz Leisering, Stephan Leibfried and John Veit-Wilson, *Time and Poverty in Western Welfare States*. Cambridge: Cambridge University Press, 2001, p. 8.
[9] Soshana Zuboff and James Maxmin, *The Support Economy*. New York: Viking, 2002, p. 8.
[10] Ibid, p. 25.

Choice and competition are crucial within the sphere of public services – this question goes back to the debate about the Services Directive. Whether in health, education or social services, it cannot be acceptable any longer to suppose that those using public services have to make do with whatever the state cares to offer. Providing greater information, and means of more direct participation (such as government through local trusts) can help. But diversity of provision and effective incentives are vital.

In the early years of the post-war welfare state, up to the late 1970s, it was assumed by most policy-makers that those who worked for the welfare state were driven mainly by altruistic goals. In other words, corresponding to the designation of state-based services as 'public services', there was a public service ethos. Civil servants and professionals in state agencies were supposed to be motivated mainly by an ethic of serving the greater good. Those who used welfare services – the general public – 'were considered to be essentially passive'. They were to wait patiently in queues at general practitioners' surgeries or at out-patient clinics; if they needed further treatment they had to be prepared to wait their turn on hospital waiting lists. In much the same way, 'the parents of children in state schools were expected to trust the professionals and to accept that teachers knew what was best for their children'.[11]

In the 1980s and after, these assumptions came under fire. Academic studies showed that the welfare state supported the middle classes as much, or more, than it did the poor. 'New management theory' proposed that the behaviour of civil servants, bureaucrats and professionals was more self-interested than altruistic. Clients of the welfare state began to expect a higher quality of service. The neo-liberal right looked at the public services, and saw monopoly, which breeds inefficiency and indifference towards users, who have nowhere else to go. Partial privatization and quasi-markets became the order of the day in many countries.

Research does disclose overall differences of outlook between workers in the public sector and those outside. One study in the UK, for instance, interviewed samples of managers from state, non-profit

---

[11] Citations from Julian Le Grand, *Motivation, Agency, and Public Policy.* Oxford: Oxford University Press, 2003, p. 6.

and commercial sectors. Of sixteen possible goals, the one placed first by public-sector managers was providing a service for the community. This aim did not appear at all in the top ten goals for managers in the commercial sector. The contrast was just as great among younger as among older workers. Another survey of doctors found that only 2 per cent agreed that medicine was 'a job like any other and that doctors have the right to work normal hours and forget about work when they get home'. Much the same findings appear when non-profit groups are compared with commercial organizations.[12] However, there are important caveats. Those who accept the public service ethos tend to support the idea that 'the professional knows best'. Customer service, by contrast, ranks as the highest value among those in business, followed by efficiency. (In neither case, of course, are motivations necessarily the same as outcomes.)

Choice and Empowerment

I have argued that client empowerment in the public services is not the same as consumerism, but is driven by everyday democratization (plus changing notions of welfare) – as in fact are attitudes towards the marketplace. Choice in the context of public services cannot, and should not, mirror that in situations of straightforward commercial competition. However, even if it is limited, choice – or the possibility of choice – is still the key basis of empowerment. 'Trust me', says the doctor. A patient may decide to vest more or less complete trust in a physician, but it is important that such trust is (in principle) 'decisionable' – not only a decision made by the patient, but one that concerns this particular doctor at this particular time.

'Doctor knows best'. Well, yes, since he or she has access to a body of knowledge and expertise that the patient does not. This situation is particularly true of specialists, as compared to GPs, who must have knowledge of hundreds of ailments. However, in current social circumstances, patients can easily get detailed information and 'expert assessment' from the Internet or other sources.

[12] Ibid, pp. 32–3.

A doctor sees a patient for perhaps a short period in rapid succession from others. Patients have to make decisions only for themselves. Moreover, although doctors may indeed be motivated by an ethic of service, or care, there are bound to be circumstances in which their interests diverge from those of the patients – for example, the doctor may be under pressure and take decisions too rapidly, or give some types of patient preference over others.

Choice, and more generally client empowerment, helps to drive up efficiency and cost-consciousness. But what other techniques might help? If appropriately set, targets can work, especially in the early phases of reform of state institutions. But targets are of limited use. They do not encourage continuous improvement. Once a target has been attained there is no incentive to go further. Staff may actively rebel: 'What is the point of setting the target when, as soon as we achieve it, you ask us to go further?' Moreover, there is the disadvantage that targeting skews priorities – in those areas where there are no targets, nothing is done. In addition to all this, there is pressure to manipulate results where targets are in danger of not being reached.[13]

Public services need to have incentives built into them. How to do so if it is recognized that they cannot mimic markets? Innovations pioneered in the Nordic countries, at state or city level in the US, and more recently in the UK, point the way. User choice has to go along with user voice. The key elements have been well analysed by Julian Le Grand. Choice is empowering for users and provides greater incentives for providers, as long as money follows it. Choice is only effective if it has consequences – if rewards follow being chosen, and unfavourable consequences follow for those who are not chosen. But there must also be real choice between providers; empty choice is worse than none at all. New kinds of provider must be introduced to develop such choice – such as the independent schools introduced in Sweden, the voucher system in use in some cities in the US, foundation trust hospitals such as introduced in Spain and the UK.[14]

---

[13] Julian Le Grand, 'The Blair legacy? Choice and competition in public services', public lecture, LSE, 21 February 2006.
[14] Ibid.

The main objections to such innovations come again from those who are worried about the implications for social justice. They offer two types of argument: that with increasing diversity, those who are more affluent will profit at the expense of the poor; and that choice and competition undermine public-sector values, perhaps even the values of the welfare state itself.

What does comparative research show? It reveals first of all that people do want choice – and that poorer people are more adamant on this point than the better-off. Surveys in the UK, for example, show that over 70 per cent of people consider that having more choice over which schools their children attend is 'very important' or 'fairly important'. Of those earning less than £10,000 a year, 70 per cent wanted more choice of hospitals, compared to only 59 per cent of those earning more than £50,000 per annum. Very similar results were found when questions were posed about having more choice in local government services. The same sorts of pattern have been found in other EU countries and in the US.[15]

In most public services, lack of choice is concentrated more among poorer groups – it itself is a stratifying factor. More affluent people have more choices partly because they have more money, but also because they are typically better at manipulating the system to their advantage. The question is whether introducing a greater range of providers will simply consolidate those advantages. Schemes already in place in several countries or regions demonstrate how the right policies can reverse these tendencies. The less well-off can be helped, for example, with transport costs, plus advice on contemplating decisions – in the field of health care, for example, by the allocation of patient care advisers.

Policies can adjust costs so that inequalities of income can be counterbalanced. For example, in education the funding a school receives could be connected to an area deprivation index; students from poorer areas would carry more 'weight' (money) than those from more affluent ones. If the weighting were sufficiently substantial, it would in fact give schools clear incentives to specialize in such children's education. We should remember that with competition there is greater motivation for improvement among

---

[15] Ibid.

schools that lag behind. Evidence both from Sweden and the US shows that competition improves performance by state schools at the bottom end rather than opening out larger divisions within the system.[16]

What about the charge that choice and diversity corrode the public sector, undermining the altruistic values that distinguish it from market enterprises? We should first of all remember the point about the ambiguity of the term 'public' in 'public services'. We are talking of state-provided services, and the state by no means automatically acts in the public interest. When asked what they think of various types of state-provided services, citizens' opinions do not at all necessarily confirm the idea that beneficiaries are treated well by those in state-based institutions. A study by the opinion survey organization MORI in the UK, for instance, asked people to rank adjectives applying to public services. The highest ranked included 'bureaucratic', 'infuriating', 'unresponsive' and 'unaccountable'. Only one positive term – 'hard-working' – appeared in the top five. At the bottom were 'friendly', 'efficient', 'honest' and 'open'.[17]

Social Solidarity

One of the defining features of the traditional welfare state is a concern with promoting solidarity or social cohesion. But solidarity of what? What social entity or entities does the notion apply to, especially in a cosmopolitan world? What are the mechanisms that produce it? Considering how widely the terms 'solidarity' and 'cohesion' are used, it is amazing how little attention has been devoted to giving them some measure of precision (I shall treat them as having the same meaning).

Solidarity, I suggest, can be understood in terms of three dimensions – the psychological, the behavioural and the structural. *Psychologically*, a solidary society is one where there is a generalized attitude of care towards others, including towards others less

---

[16] Caroline Hoxby, 'Satisfaction with public services: a discussion paper', available online at <http://www.strategy.gov.uk/downloads/files/satisfaction.pdf>.
[17] Le Grand, 'The Blair legacy?', p. 15.

fortunate than oneself. One might call this the attitudinal dimension of citizenship. Care might take the form of generosity, but can mean simply accepting the duty to pay one's taxes, or other duties that enhance the greater good. Care does not stop at the local community and it does not stop at national boundaries either – as the donations widely given to global causes of one kind or another show.

Can government – local, national or transnational – help create a caring society? Yes, it can and should. We can define 'care' in quite a mundane way as the acceptance of obligations that go along with rights, even if at its edge it shades over into altruism. Altruism itself can to some degree be institutionalized – as in the case, for example, of philanthropy. Philanthropy expresses an attitude of care, but can also be bolstered by directly material incentives such as tax breaks. Where the underlying motivation is less altruistic, of course, incentives may be balanced by sanctions.

The *behavioural* aspect of solidarity could be understood as *civility*. Civility is a disputed notion.[18] As I use it here, it refers simply to responsible behaviour in public places, both towards others and to the built environment. Civility is the everyday expression of cosmopolitanism, implying as it does respect for others and the acceptance of difference. Civility is above all about interactions between strangers, rather than relatives and intimates, since in these cases there are deeper bonds that form the basis of the association. Where a society is divided or fragmented, civility is the first casualty, for it is the very medium of everyday interaction. We can trace out processes that create downward spirals in public behaviour in neighbourhoods where social divisions come to triumph over mutuality, or where fear takes over from ease in relations with others.

The *structural* dimension of solidarity refers to the level of integration of the community, nation or other form of social

---

[18] See, for example, James Schmidt, 'Civility, enlightenment and society: conceptual confusions and Kantian remedies', *American Political Science Review*, 92/2 (1998); Tom Rice and Jan L. Feldman, 'Civic culture and democracy from Europe to America', *Journal of Politics*, 59/4 (1997); Anna Bryson, *From Courtesy to Civility: Changing Codes of Conduct in Early Modern England*. New York: Oxford University Press, 1998.

association. It concerns how far a community sustains close contacts between groups, or how far, alternatively, divisions or schisms exist. In general, where integration is at a low level, care and civility will suffer too. Just as some look back to the 'golden age' of the welfare state, so there is also for many a period when solidarity and consensus were more marked than today and when local communities were more intact. Yet images of a golden past are as misleading in this area as they are for the welfare state.

It is certainly true that local communities, or some of them, thirty years ago were more integrated than in current times. Society as a whole was more local than it is now. Yet in practice not many people would want to go back to the communities that existed in an earlier age, even supposing that was possible. Many offered only a life of manual labour – industrial or mining towns, for example, where few other work opportunities were to be found and where local pollution was high. There were infrequent job openings for women in such communities, mostly in poorly paid work with no career opportunities. Moreover, small communities of the traditional type tended to be socially backward. There were strong local norms that governed local behaviour. You can have too much cohesion!

When we speak of solidarity in present-day society, this term cannot refer to an us/them identity, or simply an inclusiveness that builds from the we-feeling of the community to the nation. Solidarity or social cohesion now has to refer to networks, sometimes centred in localities, but often more diffuse, and quite often also crossing the boundaries of nations – for instance, kinship relations sustained over large distances through modern communications and transportation technology. Such networks are likely to overlap and confer multiple identities or feelings of obligation and belonging (or, sometimes, antagonism or isolation). (See box 4.3.)

We can define social solidarity as the integration of a network society, having porous boundaries, where positive citizenship creates an effective set of social obligations and a discernible civic culture of respect for others – stretching from encounters in everyday life up to abstract dealings with remote cultures.

'We-feeling' can no longer be taken for granted – it has to be actively created and re-created as a more or less continuous process.

Box 4.3 Social solidarity in post-industrial societies

Dimensions

- attitudes of care towards others within a social, national or transnational community;
- civility towards others in the public settings of everyday life;
- integration of groups, communities and societies at different levels.

Mechanisms

- active trust: trust in which there is two-way negotiation and regular monitoring, operating in the context of
- everyday democratization: the range of substantive freedoms of day-to-day life.

Social groups

- the nation-state;
- local and regional communities;
- social networks: local, regional and transnational.

Traditional communities, and the classic nation-state, were largely based upon *passive trust* – an acceptance of 'established ways of doing things' and of established systems of power and deference. Passive trust has been for the most part suspended, and for good reasons rather than bad. With the progress of everyday democratization, not just deference to those in authority, but tradition and custom more generically play less part in people's lives than they used to do. Hence far more areas of life are open to decisions than once was the case; and there is much more information available to sift through than there was. Most of us have been 'forced' into freedom – although many new pressures and tensions come along with this change.

Although I shall not develop the point, one might say that the increasing democratization of everyday life is one of the prime reasons for widespread disaffection with orthodox democratic institutions. They appear remote from the flux of everyday life, and periodic elections happening every four or five years neglect the long period in between, when citizens want more and more to monitor and question the activities of their political leaders.

In almost all spheres of life we have moved from passive to *active* trust as the main bond of social cohesion. Active trust is trust that has to be won from the other and others; where there is two-way negotiation rather than dependence; and where that trust has to be consistently renewed in a deliberate way. The prevalence of active trust has direct implications for inequality and poverty. It presumes an open form of life, being able to deploy new information and a certain public confidence. But these are exactly some of the qualities that people in poorer neighbourhoods tend to lack.

The move to a society of active trust does not signal a breakdown of social cohesion – far from it. Nor does it inevitably mean, as so many have suggested, the emergence of a 'me first' society. Many new forms of cooperation develop, both within the family (see below) and in larger groups and organizations. Flattened organizations, and networks, are much more based on active trust than the hierarchical firms characteristic of industrial society. Yet they are probably more durable than the old type, exactly because they are more flexible and adaptable to change.

The work of Robert Putnam, which analyses declining social capital in contemporary societies, has quite rightly received a great deal of attention.[19] Although his earlier books were about Italy, most of his work has concentrated upon the US and almost certainly has its greatest purchase there. But one could reinterpret the data Putnam provides to suggest that what he is discussing is the transfer from passive to active trust relationships. This is a situation of decline, to be sure, in traditional patterns of community and mutual reliance; but it is also marked by the rise of new forms of solidarity, sometimes more intensive locally than the old ones, but

[19] Robert Putnam, *Bowling Alone: The Collapse and Revival of American Community*. New York: Simon & Schuster, 2001.

stretching across much larger spatial arenas. Solidarity is easier to define in a society of passive trust than in one of active trust; and in a world where 'society' fits closely with the bounds of nation, rather than over-spilling them as now. Solidarity originally meant bonds of common dependence, visible in stable local communities and a sense of being part of a 'community of fate', the nation. It is no doubt significant that the welfare state in most countries was shaped through war. In wartime one's antagonists are clear and a sense of one's own collective identity becomes intensified; war also breeds a sense of self-sacrifice in the face of the common good.

The question, 'solidarity of what?' is more difficult to answer today than it was thirty or forty years ago. Given the continuing importance of the nation, solidarity – along its three dimensions – at the national level remains of great importance. But there are many complexities. Regional solidarities might become so strong that they actively threaten the continuing integration of the nation. 'Nations without a state', such as the Basques, might feel little in common with the overall national community or communities to which they belong.[20] Where regional divisions overlap with linguistic or cultural ones, integration at the national level may again compromise national identity, as is the case in Belgium. Moreover, as nations become more culturally diverse, problems of integration – and therefore of care and civility – also become more acute.

Diversity and Welfare

With the exception of some of the smaller states, the EU countries have long been ethnically and culturally diverse. What we now accept as culturally relatively unified nation-states were built in some large part through the suppression of minorities and of minority languages. But the recent arrival of millions of immigrants, sometimes from very different cultures, has put things on a different plane. The European countries have been used to sending emigrants elsewhere; they are much less used to receiving them in such

[20] Montserrat Guibernau, *Nations Without States: Political Communities in a Global Age*. Cambridge: Polity, 1998.

117

large numbers – and in a quite short period of time. The implications for the welfare system, solidarity and citizenship are large.[21]

The classical welfare state has always contained an important element of redistribution towards the less fortunate. Several possible grounds exist for supposing that cultural diversity might affect willingness to redistribute in this way, where the underprivileged include substantial proportions of minorities.[22] Cultural difference might undermine the readiness of the better-off to support those poorer than themselves because the latter group is no longer defined as part of the same social community. The more the beliefs and practices of minority groups are alien to the majority, it might be supposed, the greater this effect. Another possibility is that cultural diversity makes it more difficult for poorer groups to express their interests and fight for them, because of linguistic handicaps and other barriers. Studies across a number of countries seem to show an inverse relationship between cultural diversity and strength of union organization and representation.

A third possibility is that the welfare state itself tends to promote segregation. Van Parijs gives the following illustration from his home country, Belgium.[23] In Brussels the rate of employment among Belgian citizens is 64 per cent. But it only averages 33 per cent in local immigrant communities. This outcome owes something, he argues, to the generosity of the Belgian welfare system, which gives high levels of overall benefits, unemployment support without a time limit, and so on. Such a situation shelters immigrants from the labour market. Since their separation is reinforced by low skills or poor knowledge of the language, it tends to become self-perpetuating, provoking hostile attitudes from the native population. In particular, and most dangerously, the minority becomes seen as sponging off the welfare state. Generalized to a larger group, Van Parijs argues this is essentially what happened to Afro-Americans in the US.

---

[21] Will Kymlicka, 'Immigration, citizenship, multiculturalism', *Political Quarterly*, 74 (2003).

[22] Philippe Van Parijs, 'Cultural diversity against economic solidarity?', in Van Parijs, *Cultural Solidarity versus Economic Solidarity*. Brussels: Bibliothèque Francqui, 2004.

[23] Ibid.

How plausible are these arguments? A number of studies have been published looking at the relationship between cultural diversity and economic solidarity.[24] They seek to show how far the presence of new minorities is associated with changes in the nature or level of social spending. There seems in fact to be very little relationship, and what there is suggests the reverse of the hypotheses mentioned above. Looking at the OECD countries as a whole, rather than just the EU, Australia and Canada, which both have large new minority populations, have done best in terms of trends in economic solidarity. Of course this research result may be influenced by the fact that their welfare systems differ from some of the European ones, as do their systems of labour market regulation. However, these findings are encouraging.

If European assertions about solidarity are to mean anything, we must avoid the situation that has developed in the US, where 'welfare' for most people, including recipients, has become a pejorative term. When Bill Clinton spoke of the need for welfare to be a 'hand-up rather than a hand-out', he touched a real nerve in the American psyche.

Overcoming divided labour markets where they exist is one way forward. Such labour markets all too easily lock out those from minority or immigrant communities. Another is to place an emphasis upon the contributory principle. One of the most frequently heard complaints about immigrants is that they are getting something for nothing – receiving benefits that others have paid for. A hand-up rather than a hand-out applies in European welfare states too. Of course, the more job vacancies there are around, the more easily immigrants – or workers coming from new member states – become direct taxpayers. The Polish plumber is a feared figure in countries with high levels of unemployed, but a welcome one in those where unemployment is low.

Migration and Citizenship

'Immigration' is not all of one piece, but a highly complex and differentiated affair; and the same is true of the situation of more

---

[24] Ibid, pp. 20–1.

established cultural minorities. There is no doubt that immigrants are more readily assimilated, and usually more ready to adapt freely to the host culture, when they are ethnically and culturally similar to it. In the US, waves of migrants have been assimilated – without necessarily dropping all the traits of their culture of origin – but Afro-Americans remain anchored at the bottom. Racism and fear of the alien outsider play their part. Whites who migrated from Spain to France during Franco's regime were readily accepted and integrated, as were those from Algeria. The same has not happened for other ethnic groups.

If the appropriate instruments of citizenship are in place, it is clear that second-generation immigrants can have a substantially different – although sometimes ambivalent and tangled – identity from first-generation migrants. In the 1990s and early 2000s there were riots in Oldham, Leeds and other towns in the north of England. Those involved were Pakistani groups and indigenous whites. In the aftermath of the riots, serious worries were expressed about the level of segregation between Asian and white communities. It was widely suggested in the press that social policies involved with multiculturalism were to blame.

The reality on the ground in the communities was different, as in-depth surveys of local attitudes have since shown. The British Pakistanis involved were second-generation immigrants. In the conflicts, they were not rejecting the wider society, but the fact that it does not deliver on its promises. They sought to assert their rights as British citizens.[25] First-generation immigrants' sense of identity amounts to being what the researchers call a 'denizen' rather than a citizen. They have a right to be in the country, but do not feel they fully belong to it, and experience their situation as precarious. For the second generation, on the other hand, feelings of being British citizens are central to their view of themselves and the wider world. They understand the threat presented by local white vigilante groups affiliated to the far right. But they feel these antagonisms more as an attack upon their rights as British-born citizens than on their identity as Pakistanis.

[25] Yasmin Hussain and Paul Bagguley, 'Citizenship, ethnicity and identity: British Pakistanis after the 2001 riots', Dept. of Sociology, University of Leeds, Working Paper, July 2003, p. 12.

'Britishness', with its suggested multiculturalism, is a popular identity with minority groups in the country as a whole. In the UK, 59 per cent of ethnic minorities in surveys refer to themselves as 'British', while only 45 per cent of whites do so. Only 11 per cent of ethnic minorities refer to themselves as 'English', compared to 54 per cent of whites. Pakistanis are Muslims, but the Muslim aspect of their identities barely surfaced in the clashes at that time. They are distinguishing their own Britishness from that of the far right, with its claims to ethnic purity.

The difference between the generations comes out clearly in the words of the interviewees: 'The general outlook in the older people is "don't do that or they'll deport you". Whereas in the younger people it is: if we don't stand up for what we believe in, you know we will have no future here. And they can't deport us – we are British citizens . . . It is the only way you can change things, if you stand up and fight.'[26]

There are some significant lessons here, as the researchers point out. Accounts of citizenship – and policies that are put forward – often emphasize communality and uniformity. Yet citizenship for minorities – and perhaps to some degree for everyone – is an open and fluid enterprise. Citizenship has to be experienced as real and meaningful, however. Here there seems a difference between the rioters in British towns and those in French cities and towns in 2005, most of whom felt their citizenship to be something of a sham.

Bradford at first sight seems an ethnically polarized city. In the wake of the 2001 riots, a number of official reports diagnosed ethnic segregation as a source of long-term social disorder. As one author put it: 'Separate educational arrangements, community and voluntary bodies, employment, places of worship, language, social and cultural networks means that many communities operate on the basis of parallel lives.'[27]

However, subsequent research has shown that these conclusions are mistaken. One of the main reasons why earlier studies

[26] Ibid, pp. 12–13.
[27] T. Cantle, *Community Cohesion*. London: Home Office, 2001, p. 9. As the major critical source, Ludi Simpson, 'Statistics of racial segregation', *Urban Studies*, 41 (2004).

were deficient was their lack of a dynamic perspective – the same flaw as we have seen in conventional studies of poverty. When researchers looked at neighbourhoods in Bradford over time, they found a more or less continuous movement in and out of them. Many South Asians have in fact moved out of the inner-city wards to middle-class neighbourhoods or rural areas. Because new immigrants have moved in, it looks as if there is continuing segregation when in fact there is not. Contrary to the idea that South Asians wanted to keep to themselves, survey data also showed 'evidence of the desire for more mixing on the part of all ethnic/religious groups . . . [most wanted] a more independent lifestyle, away from the sanctions and gossip of the ethnic cluster'.[28]

It is possible that for third-generation immigrants there is a further change, although the research in Bradford did not cover this issue. Research suggests that, for some such groups, there can be a move back towards elements of the migrants'. 'original' culture. Third-generation immigrants may feel that their parents' generation mimicked the host culture too much, betraying their own cultural roots. Hence they create new hybrid cultural forms. The possibilities here are much greater than in the past, because of the ease and immediacy of electronic communication. Individuals or groups can be radicalized, for example, through identifying with movements elsewhere or on the basis of events happening thousands of miles away in the world.[29]

Multiculturalism

These findings are germane to the debate about multiculturalism, which is today going on at two levels. On the one hand, there is a popular – and populist – rejection of the idea, as a perspective that tends to exacerbate conflicts rather than help resolve them. On the other, there is a much more complex and detailed debate in the

[28] D. Phillips, *Movement to Opportunity?* ESRC Report, School of Geography, University of Leeds, 2002, p. 10.
[29] I owe this point to Montserrat Guibernau, who made extremely helpful comments on the multiculturalism sections of this work.

academic literature about multiculturalism, much of it emanating from North America rather than from Europe.[30]

If one looks at the academic literature, it is evident that in much of the popular debate multiculturalism is widely misunderstood. Among its more sophisticated proponents, it has never meant a policy that looks to keep cultural groups separate, each free to develop its own identity as it wishes. The 'home' of multiculturalism is Canada, both in terms of policy practice and intellectually, since some of the leading scholars in the field are from that country. In Canada, it has long been accepted that language tests, citizenship ceremonies and oaths are axiomatic for immigrants. As Will Kymlicka points out, the ceremonies are welcomed by immigrants as a sign of acceptance and mutual commitment.[31] They are wholly uncontroversial, among the host population as well as immigrants. Becoming Canadian does not demand renunciation of one's previous identity. Hence few migrants see becoming Canadian as a betrayal of their country or culture of origin.

According to Kymlicka, the use of public money is a core test of whether the rules of citizenship function as a basis of inclusion or not. Taxpayers do not mind paying for programmes that demonstrate the active involvement of immigrants in the society to which they have come. Canadian policy may stress citizenship and national identification, but it is openly multicultural. Pre-existing ethnically biased policies that prevented non-whites from feeling Canadian have been publicly repudiated – a highly important step. In other words, an effort has been made publicly to repudiate past episodes of racism and maltreatment of minorities.

In most EU countries, citizenship is seen as a reward that depends upon a lengthy period of probation. In some states, such as Germany until recently, it has not even been on offer for those of non-Germanic background. Immigrants in Canada, by contrast, can apply for citizenship after only three years if they have

---

[30] See especially the complex debate surrounding the work of Charles Taylor. Charles Taylor, *Multiculturalism*. Princeton: Princeton University Press, 1994.

[31] Kymlicka, 'Immigration, citizenship, multiculturalism'.

resided in the country for most of that time. Moreover, citizenship is not seen as an end-process, but as a halfway stage – as part of the way towards becoming a more effective member of Canadian society.

All is not rosy in Canada. There is hostility to immigrants in some quarters, and public disquiet about fraudulent asylum claims. High-profile cases alleging discrimination have been brought by indigenous peoples; the tensions surrounding Quebec continue. However, unlike Europe or the US, Canada does not share any borders with developing countries. Moreover, the country has never been a colonizing power, and immigrants do not face the feelings of hostility that may linger, or which they may harbour, when they move to a former imperial state.

'Multiculturalism', to repeat, is not a description of a society in which there are diverse cultural groups. It is best to reserve the term 'cultural pluralism' for that. Multiculturalism is a policy or a set of policies. It refers to policy programmes that recognize the authenticity of different ways of life within a social community, and seek to promote fruitful and positive transactions between them – but within an overall, and singular, system of citizenship rights and obligations. The European countries have a lot to learn from Canadian multiculturalism. British citizenship policy, in fact, including the introduction of citizenship tests and ceremonies, has self-consciously borrowed from Canadian practice. In most EU countries, however, as Kymlicka points out, there is little visible public policy commitment to multiculturalism, or attempt to promote a sophisticated understanding of it. In a sense, the British Pakistanis in Bradford, although in a situation of conflict and intimidation, are pioneering on the ground what should be a more open component of public policy across Europe.

What has happened in Canada has not yet happened in Europe – but it is high time it did. This is the development of policies aimed at changing the attitudes of the *host* population, specifically in order to disown historic forms of racism and prejudice. When a report on multiculturalism was published in the UK in 2000 (the Parekh Report), suggesting that British citizens rethink some of their attitudes towards minority groups, it was attacked from all sides of the political spectrum.[32] It says something about the distance to be travelled in Europe that the UK is probably the country that so far has done the best job of absorbing immigrants and containing far right parties of any country in the EU.

Kymlicka has identified three conditions that facilitate the successful adoption of multiculturalism. First, it is difficult to gain public support if the main beneficiaries are illegal immigrants. In most countries such migrants are seen as flouting the rule of law and 'jumping the queue'. There is a continuum here. At one end is Canada, which has the lowest level of illegal immigration among advanced countries and the highest public support for multiculturalism. At the other is Italy, which has the highest level of illegal immigration in Europe, and where multicultural policies barely exist – storing up big problems for the future, because of the marginal position of cultural minorities.

A second influence is what kind of cultures figure in multiculturalism. Public support is very hard to get if the cultures in question are perceived as illiberal – a situation that primarily today concerns Muslims. In much of Western Europe, the largest minorities are Muslims – some 80–90 per cent of minority groups in France, Spain, Italy and Germany. 'The numerical predominance of Muslims, combined with racism and Islamophobia, generates a general perception of immigrants as illiberal, and hence of multiculturalism as morally risky.'[33]

The third factor is the perceived economic impact of immigrants. Where those who would benefit from multicultural policies are seen as taking more from the welfare state than they contribute to it, public support again tends to lapse. In Canada, immigrants are largely seen as net contributors – reflecting the reality that they have mostly been chosen for their skills or education levels. In many European countries, by contrast, a high proportion of migrants are ex-colonial groups or illegal migrants with few or no qualifications.

The future of multiculturalism, Kymlicka suggests, may depend upon whether governments can persuade citizens that the benefits

[32] Bikkhu Parekh et al., *The Parekh Report: The Report of the Commission on the Future of Multiethnic Britain*. Available online at <http://www.runnymedetrust.org/projects/meb/report.html>.
[33] Kymlicka, 'Immigration, citizenship, multiculturalism', p. 32.

of multicultural policies are worth the risks. Will this be difficult? Possibly – but consider the alternative. It is the very failure to implement multicultural policies that leads to polarization and mutual suspicion between minority communities and the host population. Multiculturalism has so far barely been tried in Europe. The main exception is the UK, which, in spite of many difficulties, has proved so far to be the most successful country in coping with cultural pluralism and turning it to positive effect.

Managing Migration

I shall not trace out the arguments for and against immigration in any detail – they are well known, even if some issues remain highly controversial. There can be no going back on pluralism, and immigrants will keep coming, legally or illegally – although in most EU countries there is a good deal of outflow too. At the moment, the proportion of people born abroad varies significantly between different countries, especially if we look at the OECD countries rather than only the EU. The proportions in 2002 ranged from 5.3 per cent in Spain, 8.3 per cent in Britain, 10 per cent in France and the Netherlands, through to 12.4 per cent for the US, 19.3 per cent for Canada and 23 per cent for Australia.

Not just cultural acceptance, but economic integration is crucial. During the first phase of large-scale migration into Europe, in the 1960s and 1970s, labour force participation was very high – at that point immigration was actively encouraged in Western Europe because of high levels of job vacancies. In Germany, for example, 75–80 per cent of migrants from Turkey, Yugoslavia and Portugal were economically active.[34] Most found jobs in manufacturing or building industries. By the early 1990s, however, these proportions had declined. In 1995 the employment rate of Turkish men in Germany was only 61 per cent, and their rate of unemployment was high. The unemployment rate of men and women born abroad is over 20 per cent today in France, Belgium and Germany. There

[34] Susan Martin, 'Economic integration of migrants', Discussion Paper, Transatlantic Learning Community, 12 August 1991.

are clear differences here with countries such as the UK and Sweden, where employment rates of immigrants, on average, are higher and unemployment rates much lower than elsewhere.

Although disputed by some, it is widely accepted that immigration tends to have overall net economic benefits for the host society. In the US, the National Research Council's panel on immigration, in an exhaustive study, specified the reasons. Immigrants increase the supply of labour, and most are highly motivated to work. They help to produce new goods and services. As they are paid less than the total value of these new goods and services, domestic workers gain. Immigration also makes it possible for domestic workers to be used in a more productive way, by specializing in the production of goods and services at which they are more efficient.

Such gains only occur, however, if the employment levels of immigrants are reasonably high. Where there is substantial immigrant unemployment, as is true in some countries in Europe and regions within them, the theorem no longer applies. The point at which a society loses out is lower in the EU countries than in the US, because benefit levels are higher. Nor is immigration necessarily beneficial to local native workers. The overall national economy has a net gain, but workers in specific localities might find their jobs threatened. Since this situation is especially true of unskilled native male workers, locally there can be those who lose out.

Circumstances are different of course with skilled workers, especially in the high-tech and knowledge-based industries. Most EU states, even those with high levels of unemployment, have labour shortages in these categories of job. In countries with low unemployment, there are also shortages in other trades. Thus, in the UK construction companies report shortages of skilled workers of three times the national average in other categories. There are also shortages in some types of unskilled or semi-skilled work. For instance, many farms depend upon migrant seasonal labour.

Most countries (rightly) want to limit the number of unskilled workers coming in, and at the same time increase the number of skilled ones in the relevant sectors. Quotas have been widely introduced. Those for unskilled workers, however, are always exceeded – legally or illegally – while those for skilled workers are rarely if ever achieved. The annual quota for unskilled or unqualified workers in the US is 10,000; 50,000 visas are also granted by a worldwide lottery, and many of those selected by this method lack qualifications. Each year, 11 million enter the lottery, but illegal immigration vastly exceeds the numbers who get in by this method. On the other hand, countries that have tried to increase their numbers of well-qualified workers, in Europe at least, have not succeeded even when they have made the offers attractive. The green card system introduced in Germany, for example, fell well short of expectations in terms of numbers recruited.

Quotas seem to have a rebound effect – increasing, in fact, illegal immigration of the unskilled. The countries in Europe that have sought to regulate immigration through quotas have been obliged to have recourse later to regularizing the flood of illegal migrants who come. Spain and Italy are two such countries. In Italy, 800,000 such applications were made in 2004 under such a scheme, and about the same number in Spain in 2005. These very large numbers have only been exceeded once before anywhere in the world – in the process of legalization that took place in the US in 1986.

There is no single or simple policy framework for dealing with the questions all this raises. But several avenues for moving towards a more effective economic balance can be explored. Most countries are tightening rules on family reunification. When family reunification is interpreted liberally, it has the effect of bringing in large numbers of unskilled individuals, or women who stay outside the labour force. Some are parents, who choose not to join the workforce even when they could. If such new entrants are supported economically by the original immigrant or immigrants, no overall cost to the host society accrues. Often, however, they do not receive such support, and for the more elderly significant medical costs might be incurred.

It is surely appropriate policy to follow the examples of the US, Canada and Australia, where family reunification has been limited to nuclear family members, priority being given to spouses and children under 18. Parents of those who have become citizens can be admitted, but only if those who petition for them to come can show that they can provide full financial support. There is to be an end to chain migration created by the free admission of siblings.

It will not be possible to stop all illegal immigration, but there is hope that it can be contained. Border management is one way, although the stricter it is the more likely it is to produce tragic situations in which those trying to enter illegally suffer hardship or loss of life. Interior management can include penalties for employers who hire illegal migrants, and deportation; and the effective sorting out of genuine asylum-seekers from others. Country-of-origin policies certainly have to play a part. What happens in North Africa and the Middle East, as well as in countries such as the Ukraine, Moldova and Belarus, will certainly have a medium and longer-term impact on pressures for immigration into the EU.

A further possibility is to create the right of 'recirculation' to skilled and professionally qualified workers. Many qualified workers who come to the EU states do not return to their countries of origin for fear of being denied access to the host country when they want to return. Such a situation is unfortunate for the individuals involved and denies the countries from which migrants come the possibility of making use of their skills. Given the ease of transportation and communication now possible across the world, it makes sense to think of allowing them free entry back into the host country even when they are not full citizens. 'Return tickets', making possible easy movement back and forth, could be established, with specific prescriptions for different categories of workers – for instance, for professionals, skilled manual workers or seasonal workers.[35]

Free Speech

Immigration has changed its nature in a world of instantaneous communication. 'Internal globalization' – the internal make-up of societies – mirrors globalization on a world scale. There were always diasporas, but they take on a more direct and continuous form. Migrants and cultural minorities can interpret their local experience in terms of events happening elsewhere in the world. Nowhere is this situation clearer than in the case of Muslim minorities.

[35] Patrick Weil, 'A flexible framework for a plural Europe', in Anthony Giddens, Patrick Diamond and Roger Liddle (eds.), *Global Europe, Social Europe*. Cambridge: Polity, 2006.

'Islam and the West' is the key motif of the moment, and with good reason. Quite apart from global events outside Europe, there have been many conflicts, clashes and incidents. The war in ex-Yugoslavia 'rediscovered' Muslim culture as an object of derision and hate. The line between Muslims and others was not a salient feature of Tito's Yugoslavia. Most of those of Muslim background were not especially conscious of the fact, certainly not as a divisive feature of everyday life. It became such as the conflicts began and escalating antagonisms gave new force to old stereotypes.

The last few years have seen terrorist attacks by Islamic radicals in Madrid and London; the murder of Theo van Gogh in the Netherlands; and marches and demonstrations in many countries across the world in protest about the publication in a Danish newspaper of satirical cartoons about the Prophet Muhammad.

The cartoons appeared in *Jyllands-Posten*, a paper with a circulation of 150,000. The editor took the decision after a conversation with Frank Hvam, a comedian. Hvam commented that he did not dare make fun of the Koran. Kåre Bluitgen, a writer of children's books, added that in the book he had just written about the Prophet Muhammad, the artists he had approached to do illustrations for the book had only been prepared to work anonymously. When the cartoons were first published, the only response was limited to some angry letters. When two of the cartoonists received death threats, this fact was widely reported, and the debate spread more widely. After the cartoons were republished, and appeared in newspapers in several countries, the row became truly global. The cartoons sparked violent confrontations in several countries across the world, and more than thirty people lost their lives as a result.

The problems of the world are no longer just 'out there' at a remote distance, but tend to be brought into the centre of everyone's lives. Global problems confront us personally, no matter how much we would like to switch off from them. The decision of a young Muslim woman in London about whether to wear a headscarf in the streets, at school or college can no longer be an innocent one. It is fraught with meanings and potential meanings. Some wear the headscarf as a religious symbol, a mark of orthodoxy; others do so for feminist reasons, a rejection of the sexual gaze of men. But all realize, and in some sense react to, the wider world significance of their style of dress.

There are difficult issues of how societies that have become fundamentally secular confront religiosity and a reaffirmation of the sacred. Battles that seemed to lie in the past now reassert themselves in the present. One could argue that the very principle of an open society is the acceptance that 'nothing is sacred' – all beliefs, of no matter what kind, are open to critical scrutiny. In the US, although not to any significant degree yet in Europe, fundamentalist religious groups are attacking science – rejecting evolution and seeking to prevent certain types of research (such as stem-cell research).

Inherent tensions exist when sacred symbols are invoked in relation to social attitudes and practices in everyday life – and where these conflict with those of the majority, or even the foundational principles of a democratic society. The issue of freedom of speech, which once seemed more or less wholly resolved in contemporary societies, comes to the fore again in a dramatic fashion. There are two reasons: one is the return of the sacred, and the other is the threat or actual use of violence where beliefs or symbols are in some sense said to be defiled.

In the aftermath of 11 September 2001, the French newspaper *Le Monde* published an article declaring 'We are all Americans now'. Following the episode of the Danish cartoons, several European newspapers carried headlines saying 'We are all Danes now'. Well, are we? And if so, what can that statement really mean in practice? Are we all Danes now? Yes, in the sense that freedom of speech, action and enquiry, including the results of democratic decisions, must not succumb to violence or to the threat of violence. It is not only religiously motivated groups that are a matter of concern here. The same principle applies to animal rights activists who threaten or attack scientific establishments.

Are we all Danes now? Yes, if that statement also means standing up to dogmatism and intolerance. In the context of religion, the issue is that of confronting fundamentalism – of not allowing a small minority of believers to speak for the majority within a religious denomination. A big responsibility hangs on the shoulders of the moderate leaders in all religions, since fundamentalism is not confined to Islam. We must not make the mistake of reducing fundamentalist beliefs to economic causes. They are extreme and stylized versions of religious doctrines, and have a fervour all of their own.

Nonetheless, their appeal is greatest to those who feel themselves oppressed or without hope. Fundamentalist groups such as those associated with radical Islam provide unambiguous answers to questions about those who are the cause of their misery. So it isn't surprising that, when Communism as a utopian belief system has all but disappeared, fundamentalist religion is ready to step into its place. The importance of social and economic deprivation in this context is obvious. In the Arab world, for example, of the 90 million young people aged between 18 and 30, 14 million are unemployed, as are many of their counterparts living in Europe.

Are we all Danes now? The question is much harder to answer if it means whether the cartoons should have been published in the first place. Freedom of speech is one of the conditions of a free society, but by no means the only one; it is not, and cannot be, an absolute principle. In all democratic societies free speech is hedged around with qualifications, and there are always disputes around where the proper boundaries lie. There are laws governing libel, slander, obscenity, the protection of minors, blasphemy and, these days, hate speech. In some European countries, there are laws forbidding Holocaust denial and anti-Semitic statements. Those who contravene such laws face prison sentences.

In the debate about the rights and wrongs of the Danish cartoons – which was truly a global debate, involving uncountable thousands over the Internet – there were many comments from Muslims drawing attention to this fact. Why should people not be free to make jokes about and even ridicule the Holocaust, they asked? What is the difference between that and caricaturing some of the most sacred symbols in Islam? The difference is a narrow one, and directs our attention to the always complex relation between rights and responsibilities. It is surely correct to recognize that some beliefs have an especially sensitive character, and to acknowledge that such sensitivities have a particular resonance when those beliefs are held by underprivileged groups in a society. The decision to print, and reprint, the cartoons in Danish newspapers was complicated by the fact that some portions of Danish society have turned xenophobic, with marked and growing hostility directed towards Muslims.

The cartoons were bound to further inflame an already tense situation (although to a greater degree than anyone can have realized), and for this reason I do not think it was either wise or principled to publish and republish them. But there are no general rules that can be set up to regulate such decisions, and they are bound to be largely contextual – a matter of balancing principles and consequences. We can venture some observations. First, rights and responsibilities are always linked – because one has the right to say or do something, it does not follow that it is a responsible act to assert it in a particular context. Second, we have an obligation to develop a sensitive understanding of systems of belief and practice that are different from those of the majority. And this sensitivity should extend to an understanding of the specific qualities of sacred beliefs.

Some policy recommendations can be summarized in conclusion:

1 Multiculturalism should be reaffirmed, not abandoned (whatever that would mean). It is entirely compatible with a stress upon the importance of learning the national language, acceptance of overall national identity and recognition of the obligations of citizenship. The problem with the European countries is not that they have been too multiculturalist, but that they have not been multiculturalist enough.
2 Progress will depend in a fundamental way upon wider social and economic reforms, especially in those countries that have high unemployment, divided labour markets, and have allowed neighbourhood ghettos to develop, or all three. However, we cannot reduce the problem of reconciling pluralism and solidarity solely to socio-economic considerations.
3 Specific policies have to be put in place to counter racism. However, the best 'policy' against racism is to help those from ethnic minorities achieve success. Several decades ago, levels of prejudice against Chinese and Japanese minorities were higher than those against Afro-Americans. These perceptions

changed as groups became more successful in American society (and also as Japan and China became increasingly so on the world scene). The same is now happening with Indians, both in the US and Europe.

4 All the points made about welfare reform are relevant to issues of cultural pluralism and migration. Policies directed at creating a solidary society have to be interventionist – in respect of language learning, for example, and much else. The goals of positive welfare are especially relevant to underprivileged minority groups, perhaps struggling to gain acceptance in the wider society. Multiculturalism itself presumes these involvements.

5 Europe cannot cope with floods of unskilled migrants, and needs to find policies that will limit illegal migration. Skilled migrants are needed, and positive inducements should be in place to attract them.

6 Topics once thought separate from questions of welfare have moved to the centre of the agenda. They include those of freedom of speech, enquiry and action. Policy initiatives can help mute clashes that might occur around these, but there are problems whose solutions will always be partial and contextual.

5

Lifestyle Change

The classical welfare state developed in a society where scarcity was the main social problem, especially in the context of the immediate post-war period. But in many circumstances in post-industrial societies we are dealing not with problems of scarcity of resources, but with issues of lifestyle. Consider the example of obesity. In 2004, about 23 per cent of adults in the US were rated as obese. There are only two states in America, Massachusetts and Oregon, where the prevalence of obesity is under 20 per cent. According to the World Health Organization, the proportion in the EU15 is not far behind, the average level standing at 16 per cent – and the gap with the US is closing. Obesity comes from following an unhealthy diet, and from lack of exercise, not from scarcity of food. It comes from eating too much, rather than having too little to eat.

Most ecological issues, including global climate change, are not to do with scarcity of resources, but with the profligate use of them. Traffic congestion and pollution are good examples. Los Angeles once upon a time looked like the city of the future, maximizing the effective use of space in relation to individual mobility. But with the multiplication of car ownership it has become a social and ecological dead end. The main freeways are choked with cars for much of the day, and are often almost at a standstill. In spite of rigorous control measures, levels of air pollution are high. European cities, which were not designed for car travel, are in many cases just as clogged up with traffic and polluted.

The solutions to such problems nearly all depend upon lifestyle change on the part of individuals, change that cannot easily be imposed from the top. The role of government and other concerned agencies is to find a mixture of incentives and sanctions that will have real purchase on behaviour. Research on obesity, for instance, shows that government programmes favouring healthy eating can have an effect, especially where they are backed with sanctions (more on this issue below). Evidence from seat-belts to smoking and AIDS suggests that the citizens are responsive to public campaigns. Change in attitudes can occur even when there are very powerful groups lined up in opposition. For example, the giant tobacco companies vociferously opposed the curtailment of smoking in public places, but in some countries a total ban has been successfully instituted.

It is important to notice that lifestyle issues overlap heavily with social divisions. Some of the biggest dilemmas for social policy lie here. Obesity, habitual smoking, alcoholism, mental illness and other destructive life-habits are more prevalent among lower-class groups than among the more affluent. In the UK, average life expectancy for unskilled male manual workers is seven years less than for men from professional backgrounds. The difference is six years in the case of women. The relation between ill-health and class is the reverse of what used to be the case until some point into the early twentieth century. A century ago, obesity, diabetes and heart disease were most prominent among the wealthy. For most of history, and in most cultures, being fat was a sign of affluence; but now, the more affluent are mostly thinner than the poor.

One of the problems is that those who most need to be reached by public health messages are least likely to be influenced by them. Somewhat perversely, health campaigns sometimes have the effect of shoring up rather than reducing social divisions, since more educated and literate groups tend to be the most responsive to publicly and privately disseminated health information. Following Richard Wilkinson's analysis, the psychological factors that link unhealthy or self-destructive lifestyles to social exclusion need to be dealt with at source.[1] Traditional notions of health care were based on

---

[1] R. G. Wilkinson, *Unhealthy Societies: The Afflictions of Inequality*. London: Routledge, 1996; and subsequent publications of the author.

treating illness once it is experienced or discovered. Of course, much medical care still falls into this category. But we need to shift more to positive ideals of health, especially in a society in which so many major illnesses are lifestyle-related.

Freud wrote extensively of obsession-compulsion at the turn of the twentieth century. As he discussed it, compulsive behaviour applied to only relatively minor traits – such as endlessly remaking the bed or washing one's hands. In post-industrial societies, however, compulsive behaviour becomes much more widely diffused and intersects directly with health hazards. The reasons are bound up with the erosion of custom and tradition that are the other side of a society of expanding lifestyle choice. Choice is part and parcel of everyday democratization. It promotes freedom and autonomy and is in this sense a liberating force. On the other hand, new pathologies arise. These are easily seen in relation to food, eating and diet. Rising rates of obesity are only one example of eating habits that have a compulsive quality. Anorexia, at the other end of the scale, has the same character. Everyone in modern societies is 'on a diet' since the advent of supermarket culture and global food production. That is to say, everyone has to 'decide what to eat' in relation to how to be – how to live their lives. But habits, once established, can turn into compulsions, and create a downward spiral which the individual finds it difficult or impossible to control.[2]

Addictive behaviour correlates closely with lack of self-esteem, even among those who are nominally highly successful. Mental problems, and associated depressive states, emerge as core mental disorders in an age that privileges individualism. According to Richard Layard, it is not the poor who are most unhappy in post-industrial society, it is the mentally ill. In the UK, measured unhappiness is three times as frequent among the mentally ill as among the poor (although these categories overlap to some degree). The cost to the economy is estimated at around 2 per cent of GDP. Out of a total population of some sixty million in the UK, five million at any one time are suffering from depression or clinical anxiety

---

[2] See Susie Orbach, *Hunger Strike: Starving Amidst Plenty*. New York: Other Press, 2001.

states, many of whom are unable to take up regular work. 'Mental illness', Layard says, 'is now our biggest social problem – bigger than poverty.'[3]

The very notion of positive welfare implies lifestyle change, whether or not such change comes primarily from the efforts of the individual, or is primarily the result of intervention from outside agencies. 'Lifestyle' shouldn't be understood in terms just of consumption – the sort of ideas that crop up in glossy magazines. It refers rather to the habits and orientations people follow in their everyday life – and how these relate to their sense of self, goals and aspirations. Lifestyle becomes important in post-industrial societies because of everyday democratization. Most of what we do today is in some sense 'decisionable': we take decisions each and every day, not against a relatively stable background of engrained tradition or custom, but one of shifting information. The decision 'what to eat', for example, may for many operate against a backdrop of scarcity (what a budget can afford), but is no longer driven by scarcity.

Lifestyle issues cover work as well as consumption. They have a dominant position in decisions surrounding transitional labour markets. For example, now there is no longer a clear division of labour between gender roles, decisions have to be taken by partners about paid work, domestic labour, when life transitions will occur and why. Of course, they are not always deliberative decisions, often just a particular course of action adopted among options, or within a tight framework of constraint.

Ageing is not normally thought of as a lifestyle issue, since it seems to refer only to the ravages that time can wreak upon the human body. It could be seen as a quintessential problem of scarcity, since time is a scarce resource for us all. I shall argue, however, that we cannot understand the issue of the 'ageing society' except in lifestyle terms; nor can we develop appropriate social policy except in such terms. In this chapter I shall discuss ageing alongside health and the environment. What ties these policy areas together is that evolving lifestyle patterns, persuading

---

[3] Richard Layard, 'Mental illness is now our biggest problem', *Guardian*, 14 September 2005.

people to make different lifestyle choices, or both, are at the core of them.

Ageing and 'Youthing'

In post-industrial society the relationship between the generations shifts. The 'ageing society' is not the best way to describe these issues. We could just as well speak of the 'youthing society' (and I shall do so, even if the phrase sounds somewhat odd). The old are getting younger. One of the distinctive features of our society is that increasing diversity of lifestyles goes along with a 'flattening' of the life-course. Take sexual behaviour, for instance. Typically, young people become sexually active at a younger age than before, quite often at the age of 14 or even younger. Yet sexuality and the formation and re-formation of relationships now also continue almost to the end of life for an increasing number of people. Lifestyle drugs are not solely the prerogative of the young. After all, what else is Viagra?

It is not, therefore, just that the society is ageing, but that the whole nature of ageing is changing, and will doubtless do so more and more. Ageing poses many problems for the wider society, to be sure. But in its altered forms it also contributes to the solutions. Why should older people be considered unfit to work just by virtue of having reached a certain age? Recent research into brain function suggests that – if one standardizes for diet and lifestyle – there is very little decline in mental capacities between the ages of 20 and 70. The long-held belief that brain cells die out with ageing has proved to be false as new methods of measurement have been developed. Functional magnetic resource imaging shows that the brains of healthy people in their eighties are virtually as active on a metabolic level as those in their forties.[4]

In the US, over a third of those aged over 65 now stay on in their jobs, or go on to new careers. Surveys show that 50 per cent of Americans expect to work into their seventies, either by choice or

---

[4] Dennis Selkoe, 'The ageing mind: deciphering Alzheimer's disease and its antecedents', *Daedalus*, Winter 2006.

because they need to earn money. In Japan, 78 per cent of those aged between 55 and 59 say they plan to work beyond the age of 60, the official age of retirement. In France, by contrast, the average worker still retires at the age of 59, in spite of the fact that the average life expectancy is 83. Other European countries have done more to change things around. In the early 1990s, among Finns aged 60–64, only 20 per cent were in the paid labour force. The country subsequently set up 'bonus pensions' for those who agreed to work to the age of 68 or beyond. Employers are legally obligated to have health programmes in place to prevent minor work injuries such as repetitive stress syndrome. The idea is to extend work life for several years for those who might otherwise give up or register as disabled. In just over ten years the rate of employment among those aged 60–64 has doubled. The result is a virtuous circle. Pensions costs are lowered, tax revenue is increased and economic growth furthered.[5]

Older people eventually become the elderly, many of them frail elderly, in need of care. Yet there are on average twenty years or more between conventional retirement ages and that time. For much of that period many are fit and active. We need therefore to detach pensions from the concept – and most of all from the legal requirements – of retirement. If the future of the European social model depends upon investing in the young, it depends also upon mobilizing the human and social capital of the old. At one time, it was considered enlightened to reduce the age of retirement to the lowest possible age. That policy has rebounded disastrously. If the retirement age is fixed at 60, the result is that firms start to treat workers as on the scrapheap ten years earlier. Ageism becomes heavily entrenched – the exact opposite of what a post-industrial welfare society needs.

Nations should therefore move towards abolishing a formal age of retirement altogether – as has been done on a federal level in the United States. There is only one real way of solving the 'pensions crisis' in most EU countries, and that is to have far more older people in jobs. Once more, we see how closely specific policies are tied to general structural reforms of the social model. Those

---

[5]   Stefan Theil, 'The new old', *Newsweek*, 30 January 2006.

countries with the highest levels of unemployment also have the lowest proportion of older people in work. If there is no fixed age of retirement, the term 'pensioner', with its pejorative connotations, will cease to exist. Pension funds should be available at a diversity of ages and also able to be used for a diversity of ends. They should be far more integrated with transitional labour markets than they are anywhere at present. For example, incentives could be put in place to use certain pension funds to finance re-education, or career breaks.

Ageism and age-discrimination are the most important barriers facing attempts to create more productive opportunities for older people – and to make more productive use of their talents. The basic difficulties are attitudinal and cultural. Ageist stereotypes are not just a problem when they come from those in younger generations. They can be taken over by older people themselves, reducing self-esteem and perhaps even affecting physical and mental capabilities.

Ageism, one could say, is the sexism of our time – and of course older women suffer from both. Legal action to counter discrimination on the basis of age can help, since it can provide a lever for changing more general attitudes. The EU directive on equal treatment in employment obliges all member states to introduce legislation prohibiting direct and indirect discrimination at work on the grounds of age. The issues are not as simple as they may look, since younger workers rightfully expect to have preference where their abilities or skills outstrip those of older competitors; and age is now rarely, as it used to be, a basis for securing durable skills.

The youthing of society will itself in some part help to counteract ageism, both external and internal. Most of the remarks made earlier about positive welfare also apply. The adoption of a healthy lifestyle, for instance, has been shown to inhibit the development of some illnesses once thought to be largely an inevitable part of ageing. There is evidence that it may also help combat some of the main disorders and disabilities of the frail elderly. We don't know at the moment how far the boundaries can be pushed here, or whether social and medical advances may actually increase the numbers of the frail elderly, by further prolonging life. There are some remarkable stories, though. One is that of Fauja Singh, who lives in the UK. He took up running in his eighties and in his mid-nineties was still competing in marathons.[6]

Along with dropping the formal age of retirement is the right of people to be in work at any age, subject only to the normal constraints of competence and diligence. But the opportunities have to be there. Governments need to collaborate with employers to identify and promote job opportunities for older people – in conjunction with fighting ageist attitudes within the workplace. There is no reason why older people shouldn't be encouraged to start small businesses, on their own or in collaboration with others. 'You can't teach an old dog new tricks' – the assertion is a false one, as recent research is making clear. The young, it is said, are the IT generation, while many older people can't even operate a video-recorder. There is no doubt a good deal of truth in the observation, but much of the reason may simply be habit. Studies show that older people are as quick at mastering IT as the young, if put in a situation where there is both motivation and opportunity.

What is missing in most countries so far, for obvious reasons, are widely available opportunities for retraining and re-education for older people. Most of the opportunities that exist are essentially recreational, such as the University of the Third Age. Lifelong learning in most countries is very far from meaning what it says. One reason may be that the current generation of over-65s experienced work environments of a more traditional form, where retraining opportunities were few. The spread of re-education in earlier transitions or periods of life could very well create more appetite for extending them to later years. The involvement of women is again a central factor here, and an issue that has in some part to be solved by providing job opportunities, and networks of help and information, at a time when they might otherwise become caught up in part-time jobs with no prospects.

Finally, we should mention local involvement. The needs of older people should be integrated within urban and community planning, including for employment opportunities, social services, housing and transport. Advances made in creating job chances for the disabled should not be limited to younger people. Moreover,

---

[6]   Richard Askwith, 'Contender', *Observer Sport Monthly*, 6 April 2003.

there are many third-sector occupations, with and without salaries, in which older people could play a large role.

Retirement, of course, will continue to be a very widespread practice, and many people quite rightly look forward to it. However, it will lose its sharply defined, all-or-nothing character as transitional labour markets become more fully established for younger age groups. Even those who are 'finally retired' might still be offered opportunities to come back into the labour force or take part in socially useful endeavours. The frail elderly are a different proposition, since the costs of care are often very high.

A substantial proportion of the frail elderly are women, since women on average outlive men. But many carers are also women, paid and unpaid. There are major tensions here that have to be addressed by future policy. In the classical welfare state it was assumed, and is still largely taken for granted today, that younger women in the family would take most of the responsibility for care of the elderly. However, this assumption is in conflict with the fact that the work and family responsibilities of younger women do not allow time for such caring tasks. Should they take them on, and as a consequence give up paid work, there is a threat to their own incomes when they in turn become elderly. Hence, it happens more and more often that older people (normally women), and even the elderly (say, those over 80), have to provide care for others, a task for which they have no training and where they may sometimes have to take charge of complex regimes of medication.[7]

Over 40 per cent of the population, men and women, will experience a lengthy period of frailty and endemic illness towards the end of their lives. Alzheimer's disease alone affects more than 6 million people in the EU countries, and this number is expected to grow threefold by mid-century.

The state, third sector and commercial organizations will all need to play significant roles. Household service provision will often be organized via partnerships – where, for instance, the state provides some financing, as well as direct medical care, with the

---

[7] Jane Jensen, 'The European social model. Gender and generational equality', in Anthony Giddens, Patrick Diamond and Roger Liddle (eds.), *Global Europe, Social Europe*. Cambridge: Polity, 2006.

private and civil society sectors providing a mix of paid and unpaid work. Again, there are significant possible conflicts with gender issues. Care and domestic provision for older people are provided overwhelmingly by women – in every EU country the proportion of women workers in these tasks is over 90 per cent. Pay rates and job security are very low. Policy initiatives concerning the frail elderly must at a minimum be integrated with programmes to ensure that there are more positive gender outcomes.

Concerns about ageing and health are intimately linked. While we know that many diseases and disabilities of old age are lifestyle-related, we don't know as yet how far these inevitably induce frailty near the end of life. A joke in circulation among the medical profession observes: 'You fitness freaks are going to look foolish one day, lying in hospital dying of nothing!' Like most jokes, this one has a serious point to make. You have to die of something. Yet it is not clear how far frailty itself is inevitable, or whether earlier lifestyle changes could reduce its incapacitating impact.

Health and Lifestyle

Changing lifestyles in a positive direction can be done. It isn't a matter of the state imposing regulations upon its citizens against their will. The point is to lead individuals – and organizations – to different patterns of behaviour by helping to create a new consensus. The wearing of seat-belts provides an instructive example – both for what can be achieved and what remains to be achieved. Originally there was much resistance in Western countries to the wearing of seat-belts in cars, partly on civil liberties grounds and partly on the grounds of inconvenience. Today in the EU15 over 70 per cent of the population wears a seat-belt in the car all or most of the time, even on short journeys. In some countries, such as the UK, the average is over 85 per cent.

Yet in all the developed countries, including the US, a high proportion of young drivers, especially young men, do not wear seat-belts. There is a more or less direct correlation between level of GDP per head and the wearing of seat-belts. The incidence of seat-belt wearing is lowest – and the level of death and injury on the roads highest – in Portugal and Greece. The difference is not just a matter of poverty, as virtually all cars in those countries are fitted with seat-belts. Since car accidents cluster highly among younger male drivers, the statistic probably reflects the persistence of machismo attitudes.

In the US, about 80 per cent of drivers wear seat-belts, although it took long and concerted campaigns to reach that figure. The fatality rate of male drivers under 21 is twice as high as for older groups. Recent research shows that more than half under 21-year-olds who die in crashes are not wearing their belts. Fatalities in car accidents are the leading cause of death for adults under about 30. In a typical year, some 32,000 people die in traffic accidents in the US. It has been said that 'we have a vaccine for the leading cause of death for Americans aged 2–33: safety-belts'. In the US, as in Europe, the next stage in the battle to influence opinion and actions is that of enforcing the wearing of safety-belts in the rear of motor vehicles.

Safety and security – they apply just as much to death and injury on the roads as to other areas usually treated as within the penumbra of the welfare state. Diet and health supply another key area. In the US, the incidence of diabetes is rapidly increasing, in tandem with obesity, since diabetes is closely related to that condition. Of those over the age of 20 in the US, 9.6 per cent – more than 20 million people – have diabetes. The proportion amongst those over the age of 60 is 21 per cent. The total annual economic cost of diabetes in 1992 was estimated at $132 billion.[8] Treatment for diabetes represents 11 per cent of total US health care expenditure. Of the complications of diabetes, cardiovascular disease is the most common. Much of this toll of illness is, in theory, avoidable.

Whether a person is designated overweight or obese is measured by the 'body mass index' – a ratio of height to weight. Someone with a BMI of between 25 and 30 is considered overweight; a person with a BMI of over 30 is categorized as obese. The dubious distinction of having the highest proportion of obese people in the

---

[8] There are counter-voices. See Paul Campos, *The Obesity Myth: Why America's Obsession with Weight is Hazardous to Your Health*. New York: Gotham, 2004.

EU is held by the UK (22 per cent), followed by Malta (20 per cent).[9] However, high proportions of people in some countries are overweight – for instance, 45 per cent of men in Greece and Slovakia. In some EU countries, more than half the adult population is overweight (BMI >25), and in a few regions in Europe the combination of men who are overweight or obese exceeds the 64 per cent prevalence found in the most recent US survey.[10] The cost to the population as a result of unhealthy diets and inactivity is extraordinarily high: a small increase in BMI, e.g. from 28 to 29, will increase the risk of morbidity by around 10 per cent.

The number of EU children who are overweight or obese – one in four – is estimated to be rising by more than 400,000 a year, adding to the 160 million of the EU population who are overweight. In Spain, Portugal and the UK, more than 30 per cent of children between the ages of 7 and 11 are overweight or obese. The rates of the increase vary, with Britain and Poland showing the steepest growth.

The rise in obesity is not confined to the US or Europe: the rate for Japan has now reached 16 per cent for men and is climbing, threatening that country's status as the leading country in the world in terms of longevity. The traditional Japanese diet is high in protein and low in saturated fat, but consumption patterns have altered. The younger generation in particular has shifted towards Western-style diets.

In December 2005 the European Commission published a Green Paper on 'promoting healthy diets and physical activity', marking an important intervention in the area. The paper speaks of 'the rising prevalence of obesity across Europe' as 'a major public health concern'.[11] Among a range of other proposals, the Commission has suggested creating EU-wide rules to ensure that foods high in salt, fat and sugar cannot proclaim health or nutrition benefits.

Examples from some member states show how lifestyle change can be achieved. One of the best known is that of Finland. In the

[9] European Commission, *Health in Europe*. Eurostat, 2005.
[10] American Obesity Association: AOA Fact Sheets, at <http://www.obesity.org/subs/fastfacts/obesity_US.shtml>.
[11] European Commission, Green Paper, Brussels, 8 December 2005.

1960s Finland had the highest rate in the industrialized world of deaths among men from heart disease. The most elevated levels were in an area in the eastern part of the country, North Karelia. Farming, especially dairy farming, was the dominant industry in the region. Consumption of high-fat dairy products, such as whole milk and cheese, was commonplace. Smoking was more widespread than in other regions.[12] A concerted attempt to produce lifestyle change in North Karelia provided programmes that were later instituted in other parts of the country. Schemes were set up in workplaces to persuade people to eat more fruit and vegetables, lose weight and give up smoking. TV series were created in which experts would help people to make health-promoting changes in their lifestyles. Local debates were organized about health-related issues, leading to pressures being placed on local stores to increase the variety of fruits and vegetables they offered for sale. The anti-smoking legislation that came into effect in the 1970s was rigorous and well ahead of anything similar in other countries at that time. Smoking was prohibited in most public buildings; all tobacco advertising was banned; taxes on tobacco were devoted to anti-smoking propaganda. Those running the project worked closely with food producers and retailers to develop low-fat foods and reduce the salt levels in manufactured food.

The changes that occurred in everyday habits were dramatic, and have since been generalized to the rest of the country. The average diet in Finland moved from being one of the highest in saturated fat in Europe to among the lowest. Average cholesterol levels dropped sharply over a period of some ten years. A high proportion of people in North Karelia were suffering from high blood pressure. Most were not aware of it, and it went largely untreated. As a result of dietary change and more frequent regular measurement, average levels of hypertension were greatly reduced. The reduction in heart disease in North Karelia, and then in Finland as a whole, has been remarkable. By the early 1990s, the incidence of heart attacks had been reduced by 75 per cent as compared to

---

[12] Sirpa Seppanen, 'Finland: a case study in healthy eating', available online at <editor@medmedia.ie>.

twenty years before. Importantly, these changes were spread across the whole population, including those from poorer groups.

Many lessons were learned that could be generalized to other areas of lifestyle change. Awareness of the lethal consequences of not wearing seat-belts is not enough alone to persuade people to use them, and the same is true of abandoning harmful dietary habits. Incentives and sanctions have to be put in place, together with campaigns that press home the importance of behaviour change. As with smoking, there is also a proportion of people who embrace destructive habits in an attitude of deliberate provocation or defiance of fate.

Positive behaviour change usually takes place in a relational context, not as a set of decisions taken by the isolated individual. A separate Finnish programme to reduce diabetes had great success. It emphasized the interaction of several lifestyle changes, drawing upon local groups of 'initiators' in order to do so, and also providing counselling for those finding a change of habits difficult. The One Small Decision a Day project, which lasted from 2000 to 2003, is an example of such an endeavour.[13] Participants received peer group support in adopting step-by-step changes in their lifestyles, via self-help groups. The results were again striking.

A health care group in the UK developed a programme along the same lines as those in Finland. The aim was to reduce obesity, and with it levels of heart disease and diabetes. The group calculated that for every kilogram of weight lost for people with diabetes, there is an increase in life expectancy of 3–4 months. For each kilogram of weight increase, the chance of developing diabetes increases by 4.5 per cent. The programme involved group counselling, held once a week, exploring people's habits, motivations and levels of self-confidence. Out of 915 people reviewed after twelve weeks, 76 per cent had lost weight in spite of repeated and unsuccessful attempts to do so before the programme started. Almost all had further loss of weight after six months. 90 per cent increased their fruit and vegetable consumption, and 100 per cent

---

[13] Programme for the Prevention of Type 2 Diabetes in Finland 2003–2010, at <www.diabetes.fi/English/prevention/programme/chapter12_3.html>.

had become more physically active. The cost of the programme per patient was only £113 for twelve months.[14]

As in the case of the wearing of seat-belts, it would be a mistake to think of these programmes and approaches as somehow limiting individual freedoms. Freedom is to be found in increased autonomy of action, in having the opportunity to take lifestyle decisions in an effective way. Studies of obesity and diseases connected with it confirm how closely they are linked to addictive behaviour, where the individual in fact loses control of major parts of his or her life. Changes in lifestyle patterns are almost always accompanied by a recovery of self-esteem. These factors are even more important among those from deprived backgrounds than among the more affluent.

Perhaps adding years to life simply stores up a problem for society. After all, won't it cost more in medical terms if those who foreshorten their lives now live to become frail and in need of care? The answer is 'no', so long as most continue to live active lives up to that point – and some work beyond what is now retirement age. It has been estimated that the welfare gain from increased longevity between 1970 and 2000 was equivalent to total economic growth between those dates.[15] Reductions in the incidence of heart attacks yielded benefits worth several times the cost of medical care involved later.

National and transnational campaigns in relation to the large food corporations have already shown that they can have considerable effect. There have been major shifts in the ways in which companies both produce and distribute food products – shifts of consciousness that can in principle proceed hand in hand with public education and changes in taste. Perhaps these policies should be more draconian than they are at present. One way of making this move might be through the insurance principle. Foods that contain large amounts of salt and sugar, for example, have known outcomes in terms of harmful effects on health; companies that refuse to alter their products could be brought within a

[14] Diabetes UK, 'Sharing practice in diabetes care', available online at <www. diabetes.org.uk/sharedpractice/spexample.asp.id=1258>.
[15] Henry J. Aaron, 'Longer life-spans: boon or burden?', *Daedalus*, Winter 2006, p. 16.

framework of liability laws. The environmental principle, 'the polluter pays', is still very far from being implemented in any society. But it could be the basis of policy reform well beyond the environmental field narrowly defined. Food products that don't observe basic principles of nutrition – that would have to be specified in law – could be subject to insurance claims, as happened with smoking.

Concentrations of cholesterol are directly affected by diet, and these concentrations in turn influence the prevalence of ischaemic heart disease.[16] The incidence of ischaemic heart disease can be predicted from average levels of cholesterol concentration. An increase of 0.6 mmol/1 generates a 38 per cent rise in heart disease mortality; the same applies in reverse when cholesterol levels are lowered.

The heart specialist Tom Marshall has argued that taxation could be used to prompt changes both from manufacturers and consumers. Quite small changes in the relative prices of substitutes can produce substantial changes in behaviour. Thus, introducing a 10 per cent difference between the prices of leaded and unleaded petrol in the UK resulted in a major shift towards the use of unleaded fuel and helped encourage manufacturers to produce cars using the environmentally less damaging fuel. There is no VAT at the moment on most foods. A simple way to alter the existing framework would be to extend VAT to foodstuffs having a high content of saturated fat. The consequence in the UK could be a fall in mortality from heart disease of up to 2,500 deaths a year.[17]

The principle of preventative intervention applies with even more force in terms of health than it does elsewhere. Of course, medical experts have always in some sense promoted active health. Keep-fit exercises, physical training lessons and participation in sports were often on the agenda – although especially stressed in times of war. Fifty years ago, however, the health horizon looked very different from how it does today. The proportion of illnesses

[16] Tom Marshall, 'Exploring fiscal food policy', *British Medical Journal*; available online at <http://bmj.bmjjournals.com/cgi/content/full/320/7230/301>.
[17] However, Marshall's proposals have been criticized. See Eileen Kennedy and Susan Offutt, 'Attentive intuition outcomes using a fiscal food policy', at the same site.

known to be related to lifestyle was less and the same applies for those associated with ageing. Health care systems concerned with the aftercare of illness evolved faster than those to do with preventative medicine, a perspective that needs substantially to be reversed.

It is quite often said that a large part of the reason why poorer people have more unhealthy lifestyles than the more affluent is simply that they cannot afford to eat healthily. But this is not the case. A study carried out in the US found that in 1965 the poorest groups in America ate far better than the well-off. Grains, beans and whole rice figured strongly in their diets. At that time, they could not afford foods such as red meat and butter.[18] The differences in diet between the poor and the affluent in current times is also quite often exaggerated. There is an increasing tendency among all groups to eat away from home, where there is difficulty in controlling intake of fat, salt and sugar. The differences between class groups in terms of health and mortality is explained partly by eating habits, but also reflects higher average levels of exercise and lower levels of smoking.

How free should we be to abuse our own bodies when no one else is involved? The answer is self-evident: we must be free to do so. But that freedom must be substantive or real rather than just formal. And here the issues are far from straightforward. Why is heroin consumption banned in most countries? It is not (necessarily) because of an inherent authoritarianism; it is because of the inference that the addicted person is less free, because less autonomous, than someone who stays away from any such habit.

A second reason is that the drug-user potentially creates costs for others. Drug-users may turn to crime to support their need, may become violent, might be incapable of forming stable social relationships and build up medical costs. There are in fact very few sorts of bodily abuse that do not impose penalties on other people. Hence the idea that those who engage in heavy alcohol

---

[18] Daniel Haney, 'Better US diets mean that everyone eats more like the poor', available online at <http://archive.tri-cityherald.com/HEALTH/nutrition/nutris.html>.

consumption should be encouraged to break the habit receives very general public support. Not only public programmes but also self-help groups play a substantial part in seeking to limit the phenomenon. Alcoholics Anonymous, in fact, was one of the first worldwide self-help organizations, and has proved highly successful in changing behaviour.

Significantly, self-help groups work by helping to reshape a person's sense of identity and, as a result, their self-esteem. In group meetings, individuals recount their life histories in an open way, engaging in a mutual process of psychological reconstruction. Addiction is not only to alcohol as such, but reflects other problems and uncertainties in an individual's life. It isn't as yet generally accepted, but why shouldn't similar approaches be extended to harmful habits in other segments of people's lives, including harmful eating habits?

These ideas and proposals do not imply a sort of new Puritanism, a society run by fitness instructors and dieticians. There is surely a lot more to the good life than that. The nineteenth-century French writer, Jean Brillat-Savarin, proposed that the way to good health was to dispense with carbohydrates. He knew what response his admonitions might bring. People would say: 'But what a wretch the Professor is . . . he forbids us everything we most love, those little white rolls from Limet, and Achard's cakes and those cookies and a hundred things made with flour and butter, with flour and sugar, with flour and sugar and eggs!'[19]

A 'hundred things' to make life just that little bit better – but this observation is a long way from habits that threaten the very capacity of the health services of a society to cope. In some parts of Europe, established diets are known to be healthy, including the famous 'Mediterranean diet'. They are not exactly lacking in the tastes and sensations that can make eating so pleasurable. We should seek to generalize these rather than watch them drain away. People talk a lot about European values. Shouldn't a healthy diet, integrated with the pleasure and rituals of eating, be among these values?

---

[19] Gina Kolata, 'Roasting the notion of low-fat diets', *Herald Tribune*, 16 February 2006.

The Environment

There are intimate connections between health and the environment. It is well known that environmental pollution can have toxic effects. Air pollution, for example, affects those with asthma or other respiratory problems. How deeply environmental factors might affect health is a matter of fierce controversy. A few years ago, Theo Coulborn and co-authors wrote a book called *Our Stolen Future*.[20] The book carried a preface by then US Vice-President Al Gore. The writers argued that man-made chemicals are disrupting human hormonal processes, causing, among other things, a long-term decline in male fertility, plus increases in various forms of cancer. Their thesis was attacked on grounds of inadequate evidence and faulty reasoning. Yet the suspicion that pesticides and other chemicals could adversely affect normal human functioning continues to be widely held within the scientific community.

The environment is not just 'out there' – because of our interactions with it, in the course of our individual lives as well as collectively, it enters into many aspects both of who we are and what we do. This statement is true, for instance, of the food we eat, which even when grown organically is no longer 'natural'. At a deeper level, it is true of all the scientific advances that what once appeared to be 'outside' the human sphere becomes more on the 'inside', with genetic engineering being only one example of such a phenomenon.

These innovations have become part of our lives and there is no going back on them. It is a great mistake to treat science and technology as the enemies of the environment. We would not even know about some of our major ecological difficulties without them, and we certainly would have no hope of resolving them. The world owes a great deal to the green movement, which helped force environmental issues onto the political agenda. However, one must enter some reservations about its impact. Too often it has presented itself as anti-science, anti-markets, as well as (especially in the earlier days) anti-growth.

[20] Theo Colburn et al., *Our Stolen Future*. New York: Dutton, 1996.

The idea of a 'return to nature', upon which the very term 'green' is based, is a non-starter, since the boundary between what is 'natural' and what is 'human' is now constantly shifting and will continue to do so. For instance, it will not do to be against genetically modified (GM) crops simply on the basis that they 'distort' what should be left to 'nature' to deal with. The balance of risk and opportunity has to be dispassionately assessed. The greater 'intrusion' into nature represented by GM crops might reduce the dependence upon pesticides and insecticides that possibly have harmful environmental consequences.

Those in the green movement often despair of the passivity of citizens in the face of environmental threats. As one of them puts it: 'Let the age-old assumption that information alone can save the world be laid to rest. For a long time the green movement has pumped out information, assuming it leads to awareness of threats and problems, concern and finally action.' However, the writer continues, 'most of the lifestyle decisions of "ordinary" people are not determined mainly by rational consideration of the facts'.[21] Yet 'ordinary people' are not as foolish as the writer thinks. For a long while many of the assertions made about environmental dangers were more controversial than they have become as the scientific evidence has hardened. The fact that the original Club of Rome projections on the limits to growth turned out to be erroneous didn't help. Reputable scientists raised critical objections to claims made by environmentalists in the 1970s and 1980s, and there are still a few – a dwindling minority – who argue that threats from climate change are exaggerated.[22] Only relatively recently has the consensus become overwhelming – as well as danger signs becoming more visible to the public.

The motivation for behaviour change is almost certainly growing in the face of these developments. But behaviour change towards what? Here we need to think more radically than has mostly been the case at the moment. We might begin by placing in question the notion, and the whole set of terminologies,

---

[21] 'Focus on public participation: the green-engage project and painting the town green', available online at <www.transport2000.org.uk>, p. 2.

[22] See especially the debate around Bjørn Lomborg, *The Skeptical Environmentalist*. Cambridge: Cambridge University Press, 2001.

associated with 'being' or 'becoming green'. The imagery and connotations are almost wholly wrong, suggesting as they do rural rather than urban imagery and implying a recovery of 'nature'. Why are so many in the green movement against nuclear power? There are, of course, cogent reasons why the spread of nuclear power might be opposed, but part of the hostility comes from an intuitive unease about science and technology – even though they have to be central to the resolution of environmental problems.

On these grounds I would drop most of the associated concepts of 'greenness' – such as the 'ecological footprint' and even 'sustainability' (because of its inherent vagueness). We should be looking for a different environmental consciousness, that can be integrated more easily both within a wider framework of welfare politics and citizenship and in such a way as to connect directly with everyday life decisions that people make. The environment, in brief, needs to be brought much more centrally into the mix of rights and obligations that define other areas of welfare and social responsibility – and with a similar conjunction of self-interest and altruism.

How to achieve these aims? First, there must be a clear and generalized awareness of risk, not as a remote potential future, but in the here and now. The danger coming from climate change and from geopolitical threats to energy supplies come together at this point. The management of risk is an extremely difficult issue for governments, since endless scaremongering is counterproductive. But there is no doubt that, as in other areas, public informational campaigns, particularly if based on engagement with local groups, can be effective in consciousness-raising.

A far wider range of tax incentives and sanctions impinging on everyday behaviour must be introduced than exists in any country at present. The environment can no longer be available as a free good, at least as far as the damaging aspects of everyday human actions are concerned. Tax incentives should be geared above all to market forces, since shifts in customer demand help drive technological innovation and product change from manufacturers. Some countries, of course, have introduced carbon taxes, and the EU has set up 'carbon markets', where units of consumption can be bought and sold so as to reduce pollution. Such arrangements anticipate the mechanisms to be set up on a more global level through the Kyoto agreements.

Alterations in everyday habits can make an enormous difference, in respect both of energy demands and pollution. Full insulation of a house can cut down heating costs, and consumption of energy sources, by up to 50 per cent. Low energy light bulbs last ten times longer than ordinary ones and reduce energy consumption by up to 80 per cent. They should be supported by tax breaks, but backed up by explicit obligations of good citizenship.

We should look as far as possible for policy innovations where environmental objectives and other life goals coincide. There are many. Congestion charging in cities, and other modes of limiting traffic, positively improve the everyday environment for other users and have significant health benefits. Taking exercise has positive health benefits for everyone; walking rather than taking mechanical transport is an individual as well as a social advantage. Reducing crime and improving the safety of neighbourhoods has overlapping consequences too – for example, allowing parents and children to walk or travel by public transport to get to school rather than being ferried by car.

Climate Change Shock, Energy Shock

Change in environmental practice is likely to require a shock to get off the ground. The shock or shocks are already happening, and they might be enough to stimulate a step-change in everyday attitudes. No one knows whether hurricane Katrina was influenced by global warming, but that it was seems likely, especially as the annual number of hurricanes in the Caribbean area seems to be growing – a happening in line with predictions from climate change. Hurricane Katrina made a big impact in Europe, no matter that it was far away in terms of geographical distance. It showed that a major coastline city, in the richest country in the world, could be devastated by flooding in a few short hours. And it demonstrated how much more destructive such an event could be for the poor than for the better-off.

Unusual flooding incidents have occurred in several areas in Europe, such as in Boscastle and Carlisle in the UK. Citizens in the Netherlands are alarmed, as they should be, since so much of the country already lies below sea level. Was the exceptionally hot summer in Europe in 2003 the result of climate change? We don't know, but all the signs are that it was, since over the past twenty years the proportion of exceptionally hot summers in Europe has risen steeply. What is sure is that some 75,000 people lost their lives in the EU countries as a direct result of the episode, and health services were ill-prepared to cope.

Local climate patterns appear to be changing, also in line with global warming computer predictions. London in the average year is now drier than Barcelona. Providing more water supplies has become a matter of some urgency, unless people can be persuaded to alter their consumption habits. When one thinks of an environmentalist, the first thing that comes to mind is not a water engineer. But more water engineers is precisely what is required, because, in spite of the proliferation of degrees in environmental studies, engineers and water scientists are in short supply. One of the main challenges is to ensure that scientists concerned with terrestrial, marine and freshwater ecosystems work closely together, because of the intimate connections between these.[23]

Environmental shock is converging with fuel supply shock – the two are obviously closely related, but the change here is partly geopolitical. The Iraq war was initiated by the Bush administration for several reasons, one of which was certainly to help make world oil supplies from the Middle East more secure. That result has not happened – rather the opposite – and one outcome is anxiety about oil supplies from the region, especially given, in addition, the tensions surrounding Iran. President Putin possibly did Europe a service by reminding Europeans of their large-scale dependency on Russian gas. Gazprom is essentially a nationalized industry and hence can lend itself to geopolitical deployment. Moreover, the pipelines that bring oil and gas into Europe come through countries that are unstable and subject to domestic conflicts.

[23] James Kingsland, 'Eco soundings', *New Scientist*, 24 July 2004.

Surveys seem to indicate a decisive change in public attitudes towards environmental responsibility. A poll taken in south-east England in August 2004, for example, showed that 95 per cent of respondents said they were willing to recycle more and 84 per cent were prepared to take specified steps to reduce water use. Four in five were in favour of other proposed moves to lifestyle change, and 82 per cent were willing to act on prescriptions to cut pollution. Only 5 per cent of those interviewed said it was not their responsibility to take notice of environmental problems.[24] In Eurobarometer surveys, 73 per cent of Europeans now think that the state of the environment is having a harmful effect on their quality of life.

In spite of the fact that the EU15 countries have made significant progress with environmental objectives, at least compared to other developed societies, major problems remain. In 2004, 1.3 billion tonnes of waste was generated in the EU countries; about 40 million tonnes of it was classified as hazardous. From 1995 to 2004 the amount of waste actually grew by 10 per cent. Recycling options have increased overall during that period and as a result the amount disposed of in landfill has gone down. However, landfill remains by far the most prevalent practice in spite of the secondary pollution it can cause. Municipal waste in 2002 in the EU states was disposed of in 56 per cent of cases by landfills, 17 per cent by being incinerated, 7 per cent in other ways and only 20 per cent by recycling.

The three main environmental challenges facing Europe – high oil prices, security of supply and adapting to climate change – will require major new investment, as well as lifestyle adaptation, and this investment will have to be made in such a way, as far as possible, to enhance European competitiveness rather than reduce it.[25] Higher oil prices could be a blessing in disguise (if inflation can be avoided) because not only might they motivate change in energy practices, they also make non-oil-based alternatives more competitive. Such a

[24] 'People willing to change lifestyle to help the environment', WWF-UK, 27 August 2004; available online at <www.wwf.org.uk/news/n>.
[25] Dieter Helm, 'European energy policy: securing supplies and meeting the challenge of climate change', paper prepared for the UK Presidency of the EU, 2005.

change in market conditions could be very consequential, because many electricity producers in Europe are dependent upon fossil fuels; most plant is ageing and is due for replacement over the coming decade. This situation includes nuclear power, since current generation nuclear power stations are coming to the end of their lives. It is not clear what the consequences of such large-scale investment will be for economic competitiveness, although this question surely has to be an integral part of forward planning.

A certain amount of work has been done on the impact of existing environmental policies on competitiveness, although the results are not fully conclusive. The issue has a great deal of importance for ecological modernization. There are two ways of expressing it. The weaker proposition is that those states or regions leading the way in environmental terms have not suffered in terms of levels of economic growth. The stronger thesis is that such countries or regions have actually improved their relative competitiveness. One of the leading students of the issue concludes that the weak thesis is consistent with research findings, and that those findings do not disprove the strong thesis.[26] The countries that have pursued the most assertive environmental policies – most obviously again the Nordic countries – have been most economically successful.

Profit is a short-term affair. What incentives are there to invest in the long term? If there aren't any, then such investments would have to be undertaken by governments, with major consequences for other expenditures involved in the European social model. One of the ways of making progress with this issue might be to enlist the help of directors and investors in pension funds. After all, these are funds that by definition have long-term objectives. Pension funds are in fact mostly managed in the short term, to seek to take advantage of day-to-day changes in the market. But pension fund beneficiaries should care about the world they will inherit, especially since without action much of the inheritance, even on a financial level, will be squandered. A world that is not only battered by climate change, but where welfare expenditure has been

[26] Mans Lonnroth, 'The environment in the European social model', in Anthony Giddens, Patrick Diamond and Roger Liddle (eds.), *Global Europe, Social Europe*. Cambridge: Polity, 2006.

undermined by the costs of coping with it, is not going to be an attractive one to live in thirty years down the line.

Civil society groups and NGOs should also play a significant part in tackling most or all of these problems, whether such groups are linked to the green movement or not. They can influence public attitudes, but they can also affect the decisions of governments and, in particular, help monitor the activities of corporations. This is a world where everything is visible to those who wish to make it become so. Firms that might seek to escape environmental regulations in one part of the world by transferring some of their operations elsewhere can be subject to scrutiny. This is already happening where companies are using sweat-shop labour, or are otherwise contravening generally held norms of labour regulation, even where they are not enshrined in international law. Some companies have been forced to modify their actions very substantially as a result of such global pressure. The worldwide NGOs actually have a big advantage over the large companies – they have a far better brand image, and they are trusted more by the public.

There is no doubt that pressure put on governments and corporations will help lay people to develop a greater sense of environmental citizenship. For without such a sense it is hard to see serious progress being made. Of course, such a development should cover the workplace as well as the domestic milieu. Many options are worth exploring. For example, the further replacement of products by services might help. Here, the added value doesn't attach to the product itself, but to the function it has. Renting or leasing, for instance, can create basic changes in patterns of consumption. Thus rental via the Internet can be substituted for the purchase of video tapes or DVDs. New markets for services that have an ecological pay-off may develop. Large-scale washing and pressing of clothes uses 52 per cent less primary energy, 73 per cent less water and 85 per cent less detergent than home laundering. Perhaps we might see a time when the domestic washing machine, having conquered all, goes into retreat again.

'Functional systems' – where services are leased rather than bought – might help reconcile the divergent interests that frequently exist between producer and consumer. The producer's interest is in keeping the life-span of products short, so that new ones have to be purchased. The consumer's interest is normally in products that are durable, reliable and long-lasting. However, this division of interest is much reduced where use is based on function. Producers are concerned with the use and after-use of the product, with efficient delivery to the customer – but also with its preservation for the longest possible period of time. The outcome is a reduction in the consumption of energy and material resources.

The 'dematerializing' of solid matter used in production and domestic services provides a significant point of connection between IT and environmental goals. We've heard a great deal about the paperless office in the past, but the volume of paper passing through most offices grew rather than lessened – until recently. The advent of email has certainly changed the situation. For everyone in the business world, and many in domestic life, the proportion of electronic communications now far outweighs those that arrive through the traditional post.

Hard copies are kept of some of it, but the apparatus of transportation and delivery is not needed – the main reason postal services all over the world are in trouble financially or are moving on to new tasks. Obviously, it is very hard to trace out the net balance of such changes in a society as a whole. Thus the Internet makes possible the direct delivery of all sorts of products and services directly to the customer's door. Does this innovation increase net energy consumption, because of these new delivery services, or decrease it since there may be fewer trips to the shops by car or public transport? No one really knows the answer.

It does seem as though local initiatives can be successful. The Danish city, Kolding, has set up an integrated plan to reduce paper use. Virtually all material sent out is distributed electronically, but in a proactive fashion. Signals are sent to citizens either by email or on their mobile phones about new local developments and how they can access information about them and interact in a direct way if they want with those involved. The Brussels region has also instituted a wide-ranging plan for 'dematerialization', involving offices, schools and homes. It is aimed at rationalizing the use of IT, calculating and responding to the levels of waste generated by it, and replacing products with services. Those who have initiated the project anticipate that local administration can become more efficient and responsive to client needs. At the same time, paper consumption can be reduced by over 30 per cent and energy consumption by about the same amount.[27]

Such initiatives may be capable of far greater generalization – they would have to be so to have any major effect. For widespread lifestyle change to happen, there has to be not just a sense of urgency among the public, but also the introduction of incentives and sanctions – which should be geared to reflecting the true cost of use in relation to environmental damage or investment. I don't think we should any longer call these 'green taxes', as if they have some special quality that sets them apart from other fiscal measures. They should form a core and transparent part of citizenship obligations, since they concern everyone in the social community. They should involve tax breaks as well as tax rises. The benign scenario of ecological modernization may not be fully realizable, but as far as possible lifestyle change should connect with the values of positive welfare, not be simply a programme of self-denial.

Car drivers and manufacturers have strong lobbies in all countries. Drivers often claim they are already over-taxed, but such is nowhere the case. The environmental cost of the car and truck is huge, and of course spills over into geopolitical concerns (and costs) too. In cities the car has become counter-productive because of congestion, often reducing traffic almost to a standstill. Pollution and associated health problems are a more diffuse but very real public cost. Congestion charging in cities – with the revenue used to fund public transport – has to be widely introduced. Rising fuel costs may help move consumers away from large-engined vehicles, but steeper incentive systems need to be put in place. And if Brazil can run a significant number of its cars on bio-fuel, why can't similar patterns be followed in Europe?

How could one bind the various issues involved in environmental policies together? Could we see clear links between them and the Lisbon Agenda? How can such policies also have an output for

---

[27] Municipality of Kolding, 'Dematerialization: a special feature of the Third Waste Management Plan for the Brussels-Capital Region', Kolding, Denmark; available online at <www.kolding.dk>.

social justice? The most obvious way is to tie them closely to key concerns of the social model, most particularly security and welfare – defined as positive welfare – in the context of citizenship. The risks from environmental change are no longer abstract or only long term. They have an immediate character and mesh with risk that the welfare state has more traditionally been equipped to cover (such as health risks, risks to property and so forth). They connect closely to economic concerns too – to productivity and competitiveness. Some of the main growth and job-creating possibilities will be in sectors closely related to, or directly involved with, environmental concerns.

Environmental and energy problems demand transnational collaboration. They make up a prime area where EU-level involvement is crucial. I shall discuss what form such involvement should take in the following chapter.

6

At the Level of the EU

When I speak of 'the EU' in the title of this chapter, I have in mind the European Union governing institutions. I don't mean to separate off these institutions too much from the member states. All the preceding chapters have been about 'the EU' and 'Europe' in the broader sense of member states acting together to resolve common problems. However, in this chapter I shall concentrate upon how the EU agencies can contribute in a direct way to the reshaping of the social model.

I shall first of all offer an assessment of where the Lisbon Agenda stands now. I will then look at the question of social and economic inequalities at the European level, moving on from there to higher education and innovation. Finally, I shall consider in some detail what needs to be done at EU level about the environment and energy.

Assessing the Lisbon Agenda

There are many ways in which EU-level decisions have an immediate impact upon national welfare systems. The 'minimalist' interpretation of social policy, which holds that the member states retain almost complete control over welfare, can be put in question.[1] Legal decisions taken by the EU can directly affect welfare provisions in

---

[1] Stephan Leibfried and Paul Pierson, 'Semi-sovereign welfare states', in Leibfried and Pierson (eds.), *European Social Policy*. Washington: Brookings Institution, 1995.

member states. For example, the European Court of Justice ruling that there must be equal retirement ages for both sexes directly impinged on national policy. If the ruling had been applied retroactively it could have had immense financial implications for some countries, but a fierce lobbying campaign from those nations blocked that outcome. The Court has in all delivered more than 300 judgements on social policy coordination. Indeed, some observers have argued that there should be a specialized EU Welfare Court because of the volume of such legislation. EU legislation has been most important in the fields of employment rights, anti-discrimination measures and the transferability of social security rights.

Yet it is plain enough that, for better or for worse, there is a structural imbalance at the heart of EU decision-making so far as the social model is concerned. The Single Market and the Single Currency are creating large changes in national economies. In the Eurozone, key monetary powers have been transferred to the Central Bank. Yet member states jealously guard their autonomy in fiscal and social policy.

It was this imbalance that the open method of coordination in the Lisbon Agenda was invented to correct. The OMC is described in the Kok Report as a process whereby 'member states agree voluntarily to cooperate in areas of national competence and to make use of best practice from other Member States, which could be customized to suit their particular national circumstances'. 'Peer pressure' is supposed to act as a stimulus to recalcitrant member states. Many member states, it accepts, have not taken the whole exercise seriously enough. The report touches on the social model and speaks of 'eradicating poverty'. It also mentions 'environmental sustainability', speaking of the need for 'spreading eco-innovations and building leadership in eco-industry'.[2] However, few of its recommendations bear directly on these. The emphasis is firmly on growth and employment. One could speak of the report as 'Lisbon minus', in the sense that it proposes to concentrate especially on these two concerns, an emphasis subsequently accepted by the Commission. The proposal of the Kok Report, however – that

[2] Wim Kok, *Facing the Challenge*. Report of the High Level Group, November 2004, pp. 9 and 6.

there should be more 'naming, shaming and faming'[3] – was not. In its conclusion, the report is candid about the problems that remain. There is no ducking the fact, it concludes, that in the end most progress with the Lisbon Agenda will depend upon what happens in national contexts.

In accepting the overall thrust of the Kok Report (and proposals from the Sapir Report too), the Commission unveiled its fresh Lisbon strategy in February 2005. A focus upon economic growth and employment would be accompanied by a 'Partnership for Growth and Jobs', with an action plan at the EU level and national action plans for the member states. Lisbon should 'become part of a national political debate', including within that debate citizens as well as political, business and union leaders. The announcement of the new perspective produced some hostile responses. The social and environmental aspects of the Lisbon Agenda seemed to some critics to have been put on the back burner. Commission President José Manuel Barroso replied to his detractors by saying: 'If one of my children is ill, I focus on that one, but that does not mean I love the others less.' It's a nice metaphor, but not an accurate one. In the case of the EU, the health of all three 'children' – the economic, social and ecological – is at stake.

Early in 2006 a further report – the Aho Report – appeared, which concentrated upon research and innovation, this time as a result of the Hampton Court summit meeting in October of that year. It was produced by a group chaired by the former Finnish prime minister, Esko Aho. Their report proposed a 'pact for research and innovation'. The Kok proposals and the Commission's response to them, it argues, are not going to work. Resources for R&D are not increasing. Nor will their proposals help preserve the social model, which will be eroded because of decreasing resources. A pact should focus more specifically on certain areas of innovation, and should recognize that difficult decisions need to be taken about where these should be, rather than supposing that progress can be made by upping the lowest common denominator.

The proportion of EU structural funds dedicated to research and innovation, the Aho Report argues, should be elevated from the

---

[3] Ibid, p. 43.

current 6 per cent to 20 per cent. So far as the new member states are concerned, for example, such investment might allow them to jump certain phases in economic and technological development. A number of areas should be prioritized, especially e-health, energy, the environment, transport and logistics and security.[4]

What should one make of the continuing debate about the Lisbon Agenda? At the risk of adding to the paper mountain which the agenda has generated, I would offer the following observations and proposals.

First, on an intellectual level – some ten years since the original academic work informing it was done – the Lisbon Agenda has stood the test of time pretty well. As I sought to show earlier in the book, much of what was proposed in Lisbon in 2000 corresponds to demonstrable best practice today. Nonetheless, the criteria deployed to improve competitiveness should be reviewed in a continuous way, since well-informed projections or intuitions from even a few years back can turn out to be wrong or misleading. To give a concrete example: in the late 1990s most business analysts believed that travel agents would be the fastest-growing service industry. In fact, jobs in this area have contracted significantly, since many people now book online – a possibility that didn't even exist a few years ago.

Second, the problems with the open method of coordination derive in some part from the fact that originally it was not contextualized. This failing has been recognized in the latest shift on the part of EU practice, involving the submission of country profiles from each of the member states. It is not clear, however, that the rethinking has been far-reaching enough. Benchmarking is less effective than might appear at first sight. Politicians and voters can compare and contrast the overall economic performance of the EU countries, such as their rates of growth or their unemployment rates. However, it is much less easy to compare policies and reforms, as the impact of any specific reform processes depends upon a multiplicity of factors, many of them particular to the

---

[4] Esko Aho, *Creating an Innovative Europe: Report of the Independent Expert Group on R&D and Innovation Appointed Following the Hampton Court Summit*; available online at <http://europa.eu.int/invest-in-research/>.

country in question. Also, in order to appreciate trade-offs – for instance, between high employment and the existence of 'Big Mac' jobs – more information is needed than just the publication of economic indicators.

Third, the Lisbon Agenda is an EU-wide initiative, but its success or otherwise will not come from the open method of coordination, even if this approach becomes more successful than it is at the moment. It will depend not only on national policy-making, but even more so on national political will. Reform of the state, rather than only economic influences, may be needed. Watching and hoping has to be part of the 'strategy', but perhaps there are some useful interventions to be made. The open method of coordination is essentially a top-down process. Member states (and regions) could be encouraged to compare experiences and learn from each other in a more directly 'horizontal' way – not just in terms of policies but also in terms of surmounting political barriers. Joint initiatives could be encouraged and could draw upon the resources of the Commission as well as being organized locally.

Fourth, as the French economist Jean Pisani-Ferry proposes, some reforms should be concentrated on the Eurozone, since the countries within it have some specific common needs.[5] Where there is a monetary union, a country that, for example, reforms its labour markets and lowers its unemployment rate exerts a medium-term externality on another country that does not. As a consequence of reforms in country A, the aggregate structural employment rate goes down and aggregate productivity goes up – in both cases lowering inflation. The central bank can as a consequence lower interest rates, boosting domestic demand in country A as well as in B, which has not reformed. For country A, the interest rate reduction is lower than it would be if each had control over its interest rates; for country B, the reverse holds. Suppose now that other governments besides B hesitate to undertake reforms, in a situation where reforms impose short-term costs for longer-term gains – as they quite often do. Here, macroeconomic policy might be utilized. What such policy can do is to alter the distribution of

[5] Jean Pisani-Ferry, 'What's wrong with Lisbon?'; available online at <www.bruegel.org/doc_pdf_47>.

costs and benefits through facilitating convergence to a new equilibrium. Hence it can render reforms less costly in the short term and make it easier for national politicians to take reform-minded decisions. Monetary policy inside a currency union can only support the reform endeavours of a particular government to the degree to which it makes a contribution to aggregate performance. For any government acting on its own, especially where there are constraints like high indebtedness, the incentive to reform is reduced. Without coordinated efforts at reform, this situation produces a deadlock in which no government makes needed reforms.

Fifth, at the moment the Lisbon Agenda has a catch-up feel to it – after all, it was designed to help the EU emulate some of the achievements of the US economy. It may be ambitious, but there is a sense in which it plays to Europe's weaknesses rather than to its strengths. Its social model and its environmental record are (in principle) two such strengths, although crucially only in the context of a strong economy. If reforms can be made in the right countries, and in the right directions, the EU should look to progress beyond the attainments of its leading competitors. In many respects the EU countries are ahead of most of the rest of the world in terms of environmental policy. Far more concrete targets have been developed in relation to environmental issues than in relation to social justice, partly because of the leading part the EU has played in supporting Kyoto. (Although the Kyoto targets are proving hard to meet: only five countries in the EU at the moment are on course to meet the reductions in emissions they have signed up to.) Over the period 1992–2002, all EU15 states have maintained or reduced their energy intensity. The case of Ireland, where high economic growth has gone along with improvements in energy intensity, shows that countries that start from a low economic base do not necessarily have to devour energy as they catch up with more developed ones. This example is important when one considers potential high levels of growth in the new member states. However, environmental policies have to be brought in much closer conjunction to the economic and social programmes, both at the national and the EU level – as argued earlier. The concentration of EU thinking on 'social exclusion' does not touch at all upon programmes of lifestyle change now at the centre of welfare reform.

I would conclude that we need, not a Lisbon-minus, but on the contrary a *Lisbon-plus*.[6] The Lisbon Agenda was never detailed or persuasive enough in two core areas: social justice and the environment. So far as the former goes, at the European as well as at the national level (as argued earlier), we need to get over an unfortunate polarity that has haunted efforts at reform. The defenders of social justice see themselves as having to block efforts to help less well-performing states become more competitive and generate more jobs. They are not persuaded by the references to reducing social exclusion made by those pressing for reform, and fear that an 'Anglo-Saxon model', which cares much about markets but little about social justice, is taking over Europe.

The argument needs to be made and sustained (as I have tried to show in this book) that Lisbon-style reforms promote social justice and welfare rather than undermine them. And this argument cannot just be an abstract or value-driven one: it must state chapter and verse. All is not for the best in the best of all possible worlds, and compromises and adjustments that need to be made have to be pointed out. Where there are losers, the fact needs to be clearly indicated, coupled to a specific analysis of what can be done to improve their lot.

The proposed Global Adjustment Fund is at least a step in the right direction. A version of this idea was proposed in the Sapir Report. The idea was officially endorsed at the December 2005 meeting of the European Council. It gained support in the wake of the French and Dutch 'no' votes, since anxieties about potential job losses played such a significant part in this outcome. The Fund will be limited to a budget of €500 million a year. Member states will be able to draw upon the resources provided to offer retraining and job search allowances for workers who are laid off as a result of 'major structural changes in world trade patterns'. Strict criteria are involved to ensure that claimants do not use the money to prop up failing industries. The existence of the Fund shows that the EU 'cares' about the plight of those who fare poorly as a result of

[6] I owe this idea to conversations with Roger Liddle and Patrick Diamond. See their contributions to Anthony Giddens, Patrick Diamond and Roger Liddle (eds.), *Global Europe, Social Europe*. Cambridge: Polity, 2006.

economic change. But it is clearly no more than a gesture, given the limited resources involved.

The special budget review promised for 2008 should be used to secure real change in the distribution of resources – although given national intransigence, the omens are not good. The Sapir and Aho Reports have pointed out what is needed. The EU budget should be directed away from agriculture towards programmes that enhance growth, placing a particular emphasis upon innovation. Even with recent reforms, the Common Agricultural Policy (CAP) is a massive anachronism (and infamously so to most disinterested observers). Over 40 per cent of the budget is spent on 2–3 per cent of the EU's workers.

Regional Disparities

The Lisbon Agenda bears directly upon the issue of social and economic disparities between member states and between regions, one of the main concerns of the EEC/EU since its early days. 'Cohesion' and 'convergence' have long been spoken of as goals on the European level as a whole. The Treaty of Rome stated that the successful progress of the EU could be attained only by 'mitigating the backwardness of less favoured regions'. While convergence is sometimes presented as a simple process of poorer member states and regions drawing closer to the richer ones, things are more complex than that. Once the EU has been established, and as it expands, new dynamics are introduced within nations and across borders.

The very goals of convergence and cohesion themselves can be in conflict. Convergence means the process of macroeconomic integration, while cohesion means the raising of the living standards of poorer nations and regions to become closer to the richer ones. To further convergence, states might have to introduce policies that threaten cohesion. For instance, they might have to reduce subsidies within their own borders, which could in turn worsen existing disparities of income or wealth.

The EU has undergone six successive expansions. The level of economic inequality, both between nations and between regions, has initially increased with all of these, the exception being in 1995 when Austria, Finland and Sweden joined. Following each expansion, prior to the latest one in 2004, economic disparities overall tended to decline quite rapidly. The dispersion levels in the 1990s increased only among the original six member states, but for an understandable reason: the reunification of Germany, East Germany being much poorer than the West.[7]

Of the four poorest states in the EU15 prior to the 1980s, Ireland has performed by far the best. From a per capita GDP measure of 56 per cent of the EU average in 1973, the country had moved to 110 per cent of that average by 2002. Portugal was also at 56 per cent of the average on accession in 1985, but had only reached 72 per cent by 2002. Spain has made very considerable progress politically, but less in relative economic terms – it moved from 74 per cent of average EU GDP in 1985 to 77 per cent in 2002. However, the gap between the wealthiest and poorest regions within the EU has actually grown over the past thirty years. The least wealthy region in 1977 was four times poorer than the most affluent one. By 1996 it was more than five times poorer. A more telling figure is the total proportion. Between 1977 and 1996 the per capita income of the five most deprived areas in the EU barely changed in relative terms. In 1977 it was 44.5 per cent of the EU average; in 1996 it was 44.7 per cent of the average. The income of the five most wealthy areas, on the other hand, increased from 206 per cent of the EU average in 1977 to 224 per cent by 1996.

The poorest regions are not always found in the poorest countries; nor are the most affluent regions necessarily in the wealthiest states. The regional stretch in some countries is large. The most affluent region in the EU is in Germany, but its poorest areas are poorer than most other regions in the Union as a whole, including regions in Spain, Portugal and Greece. Germany is a reasonably egalitarian country when assessed in terms of the distribution of individual incomes. However, the income dispersion between the richest and poorest regions in Germany is the highest in the EU15.

---

[7] Carol M. Glenn, 'Regional convergence and regional policy in the European Union', Valdosta State University, GA, June 2000. <www.eu-center.org/research/working%20paper/papers/39.carol.m.glen.doc>.

The entry of ten new member states in 2004 has substantially increased regional variations. About 92 per cent of the population of the new member states live in regions where GDP per head is below 76 per cent of the EU25 average, and 66 per cent live in regions where it is lower than 50 per cent of the average.[8] GDP per head in Bulgaria and Romania is less than 30 per cent of the EU25 average. When those two countries join, which should be in 2007 or 2008, the number of people living in regions with income below 75 per cent of the EU average would be more than double the current figure. It would grow, in fact, from about 73 million to some 153 million. The disparity between the EU average and their average GDP per head would also double, rising from about 30 per cent below average to 60 per cent below.

The structural funds and the cohesion fund are the main community resources available to help reduce disparities between states and regions. The cohesion fund was introduced in 1993 to help improve economic development in the EU's poorest countries. Countries with a GDP of less than 90 per cent of the EU average are eligible for the funds. Transfers from the structural and cohesion funds add about 3 per cent to investment in Spain, and 8–9 per cent in Greece and Portugal. They contribute about 4 per cent in what was East Germany, and 7 per cent in southern Italy. These funds are supplemented by loans from the European Investment Bank – totalling €20 billion in 2002. These various funds have contributed to economic development both in regions and in nations. GDP in Spain in 1999 was estimated at 1.5 per cent higher than it would have been without intervention. Comparable figures for Ireland are 3 per cent and for Portugal 4.5 per cent.

The enlargement to twenty-five members did not go along with increased budget contributions from existing member states. Hence the number of regions qualifying for assistance was reduced, and the structural funds were targeted more towards the poorest regions. However, this change may mean that reduction in the disparities between regions will be even more difficult to achieve.

[8] European Union, 'Third Report on Economic and Social Cohesion (Executive Summary)', p. iv; available online at <www.northsea.org/nsc/documents/eu_policies_beyond_2006/cohesion3_summary_en.pdf>.

Why are regional variations apparently so deeply entrenched? It may be simply that, in relative terms, the funds involved are so small – the structural funds amount to less than 0.5 per cent of EU GDP. Policies followed within countries have much more potential and actual impact – and they do not always act to reduce regional disparities. A study covering the EU15, for example, found that some key national policies devoted to improving competitiveness – such as those promoting R&D – were slanted towards the richer regions within their particular countries. The more affluent a region is, the more the government spends on facilitating R&D within it; the poorer the region, the less is spent. Given that such investments should spur economic growth, the result is likely to increase the regional disparities that already exist.[9]

Poor regions are so for different reasons. Within the more affluent states, they tend to be regions of industrial decay – visible expressions of the decline of manufacture and the rise of the knowledge/service economy. Such decline is often accompanied by urban dilapidation – for example, in some northern areas in the UK, property in certain streets or micro-neighbourhoods has become to all intents and purposes valueless. In the Nordic countries, the poorer areas by contrast are rural – they consist of sparsely populated regions in harsh climatic zones. In southern Italy, poor regions span the urban and the rural – their poverty comes from their lack of economic development, coupled to traditional familialism. These differences are recognized in the allocation of structural funds, but given the breadth of the problems and the thinly spread nature of the resources, their impact is necessarily limited. Of all the regions in the EU, southern Italy seems most impervious to change. In 2002, only 43 per cent of the population aged 18–65 was in work, the lowest rate not only in the EU15 but also in the EU25.

The large differences in income level between nations and regions mean that one of the ideas sometimes offered for more levelling across the EU – a Europe-wide minimum wage – (as stressed

---

[9] Luc Soete, 'A knowledge economy paradigm and its consequences', in Anthony Giddens, Patrick Diamond and Roger Liddle (eds.), *Global Europe, Social Europe*. Cambridge: Polity, 2006.

in chapter 1) is a non-starter. Some have suggested that a European minimum income could be calculated in each member state.[10] However, such a proposal would not in any sense be a true minimum wage, since the variations would be so large. Imposing a universal minimum wage would be a tactic insensitive to the large institutional differences between countries and to variations in the nature of their economies; and the regional issue would be exacerbated, since a one-size-fits-all policy would be actively counterproductive.

What policy conclusions can we draw from the above considerations? Some suggestions follow. First, policy-makers both within nations and at the European level should give more attention to the EU itself as a source of economic divergence. Not just EU-level policies, such as the development of the Single Market, but the interaction of policy and socio-economic change too can affect the goals of social justice within nations and between regions. The EU is not a state; neither is it simply a free trade area. Its identity is contentious, because it is in the nature of an ongoing experiment. But this situation means that its dynamics as a system are not well understood, since they do not necessarily parallel those of nation-states. The regions, for example, are no longer just part of nations, but of a supranational entity.

On the pan-European level, there are interconnections between changing life-patterns and inequalities. For instance, rising levels of income have made foreign travel easier, facilitated by such arrangements as the Schengen agreements, which have eliminated border controls among the states that have signed up to them (fifteen countries, including Norway and Iceland from outside the EU). EU anti-monopoly regulations, together with privatization of state airlines by individual countries, have allowed for cheap air travel within Europe as well as across the world. One consequence within the UK has been the impoverishment of seaside towns. Towns that in the 1960s were relatively affluent, such as Hastings or Broadstairs on the English south coast, have become among the poorest in the country. The holidaymakers who used to frequent

---

[10] Dominique Strauss-Kahn, *A Sustainable Project for Tomorrow's Europe.* Project presented to Romano Prodi, 2004.

them, coming mainly from lower socio-economic groups, now holiday in Spain, Portugal or Greece. In the meantime, resorts in those countries that were once poor have become increasingly affluent. Impoverished seaside towns and their hinterland areas may be harder to regenerate than erstwhile manufacturing areas, since the stock of transferable skills is less. In a sense, they have moved in the opposite direction from most other areas. They were already in the service economy, but the services they offer have become superseded and displaced.

Second, on the European, like the national, level we should remember that poverty is diverse, not a simple and single phenomenon – as the above examples show. As in the case of poverty of individuals, it will not do to concentrate only on the poor regions themselves. Some policies might be concentrated on influences external to those regions – others could conversely be focused upon their micro-dynamics. A new orientation of policy on the EU and national levels seems urgent, given that there has been such little progress in reducing inequalities between poorer and richer regions. Part of the problem is that we simply don't have the research materials. The study of individual and local poverty was transformed once time series and international data became available; such data do not exist on a pan-European level.

A third conclusion to be drawn is that the use of structural funds should be linked to good governance. In less-developed countries, long experience has shown that large sums of money can be absorbed with no visible change happening. Without improvements in governance, no amount of external aid or investment is likely to have any effect – as has happened in southern Italy. Good governance doesn't only mean efficient and non-corrupt political leadership; it means also a lively civil society – active and effective third-sector organizations. Much the same applies to regions, and to cities and subdivisions within them. An instructive example is the success of some of the autonomous regions in Spain, some of which have also created regional identities where none existed before. Self-esteem isn't only important on the level of the individual. Regions and localities that have pride in their identities can both leverage change and promote themselves externally.

Good governance is likely to be crucial in breaking through cycles of regional advantage that can otherwise build up. Although there have been such widespread fears of social dumping, foreign direct investment tends to go to the more affluent nations and regions rather than the poorer ones – let alone the poorest. Ireland has become much richer than it was previously partly because of the foreign investment it has attracted; but investment continues to flow into the country. In 1999–2001 investment inflows made up about 21 per cent of GDP in Ireland, a country that now has the second highest level of GDP per head in the EU. The figures are 15 per cent for Denmark, and 13 per cent in the Netherlands. The countries with the smallest inflows were poor ones: Spain (1.5 per cent), Italy (1 per cent) and Greece (under 1 per cent).[11]

An almost identical pattern is found among the regions. The lowest inflows are into the regions that need direct investment most. The former East Germany – if one excludes Berlin – received only 2 per cent of the total inflows into Germany between 1998 and 2000. In Italy, less than 4 per cent (of a very small sum in any case) went to the south. This situation has partly been reversed in the case of the new member states, however.

Innovation, R&D

We must hope that some poor regions, like 'backward' nations, will be able to leapfrog directly into advanced sectors of the knowledge/service economy. For this to happen, they will need substantial investment in IT and in education. The Lisbon Agenda, of course, placed a very defined emphasis upon education, especially higher education, plus research and development, in its programme for Europe's economic regeneration. The mid-term review of the strategy continues to talk forcefully of 'knowledge and innovation – engines for sustainable growth'. As elsewhere, the formal targets set are currently not being met. R&D budgets in the EU are supposed to reach 3 per cent of GDP by 2010. Business R&D

[11] See Pervez Ghauri and Lars Oxelheim, *European Union and the Race for Foreign Direct Investment in Europe*. London: Elsevier, 2006.

spending is to rise to two-thirds of total investment, as is already the case in the US; at present both lag well short.

However, critics have pointed out that setting percentage targets is a questionable approach.[12] The 3 per cent target is made up of 1 per cent to be contributed by the state and 2 per cent by private industry. The segment that is supposed to expand is precisely that over which governments have no direct control. The targets are not focused in terms of results. Why should firms have any interest in increasing proportional expenditure on R&D for its own sake? If they do make new investments, it is because they believe that scientific advances or ideas can help them perform better. If they can, however, firms will apply the same economic reasoning to R&D that they use in other areas of their activity. They will reduce expenditure on R&D as far as possible, to pare down costs, and perhaps outsource it to small high-level companies.

The 3 per cent objective, based on comparison with the US, takes no account of economic differences between America and the EU. The profits and income tax regimes of the US differ from those of most EU countries, involving different regulations and incentives. Moreover, some of the research carried out in relation to business in the US is state-funded – especially R&D that has potential military implications.

There are other reasons too to have reservations about the Lisbon interpretation of R&D in relation to the knowledge/service economy. Luc Soete has argued convincingly that the relationship between research, innovation and socio-economic development is changing as the knowledge/service economy matures.[13] 'Old-style' R&D is no longer as relevant as it was; and it is no longer so important that R&D is produced endogenously. How innovation processes are understood has changed significantly over recent years. Although presented as radical, the Lisbon attitude to R&D embodies an approach that is coming into question. That approach is based on an industrial model, with incentives for firms to invest in upgrading of their workforce internally, and presumes a close relation between firms and universities or other higher education establishments.

[12] Soete, 'A knowledge economy paradigm'.
[13] Ibid.

Hence discussion is concentrated on technological aspects of knowledge creation, shortage of scientists and engineers, and the requirement to develop European integration in research. These may be desirable objectives, but Soete suggests that they miss some core kinds of 'knowledge' that the knowledge/service economy needs. The 'knowledge' in the new economy is certainly in part scientific and technological – as the very impact of information technology shows. But even more important are creativity, the testing of new ideas and the opening up of new markets according to changing patterns of demand. For example, there is nothing especially technological about the success of Starbucks, which either catered to a latent taste, or helped develop that taste, or a bit of both. Many successful enterprises or new services are in some sense technology dependent, but technology is rarely, if ever, the sole driving force of their market success. iPods make use of major technological advances, but they carved out a new market in some large part because of stylistic appeal, clever design and effective marketing.

There is a major point of connection here with activating labour market policy. The production of 'knowledge' increasingly occurs in networks, which might be quite far-flung, rather than in hierarchical corporations (which themselves tend to become flattened in terms of their authority systems). Perhaps, as Gunther Schmid has proposed, artistic and media labour markets might be the harbingers of the future as much as those for more traditional scientific and technological occupations.[14] Most artistic and creative workers are in loosely organized networks, not in permanently dependent employment relationships. The seniority principle plays only a small part, and payment by fixed working hours is much less important than in the standard employment contract. Whereas old-style occupations demanded constant and specific skills, newer knowledge-based ones are more fluid. There seems to be an unending appetite for novelty and originality, which, in conjunction with shifts in taste, drives innovation. That innovation in turn is not

---

[14] Schmid, 'Towards a theory of transitional labour markets', in Bernard Gazier and Günther Schmid (eds.), *The Dynamics of Full Employment: Social Integration Through Transitional Labour Markets*. Cheltenham: Edward Elgar Publishing, 2002.

linear, but driven by various 'break-outs' from pre-established ways of doing things.

The creative economy in the US has grown by 20 million net jobs since the late 1980s; rather than technological advance as such, it explains a good proportion of America's economic success. The creative economy now accounts for nearly half of total salaries. The entertainment industry produces twice as many jobs as engineering. Significantly, given labour shortages, companies are now taking steps to upgrade employees, and dissolve barriers that stop low-skilled workers from making progress. An example is Best Buy, a retail firm selling consumer electronics. Schemes allowing for the acquisition of skills allow employees to progress quickly from in-store customer service into management positions.

There is an additional consideration. How far should we depend upon R&D that is specifically confined to a European setting? It is not clear that national or EU R&D percentages have any real significance for economic performance.[15] As companies develop more complex transnational divisions of labour, R&D and other sources of new ideas will come increasingly from around the world. With a more global patenting regime, permitting widespread use of innovations – and the immediate assimilation that today's communication systems permit – relevant R&D might have little impact on the domestic economy within which it takes place. Firms will consider their investment not from a local but from a global perspective.

It certainly matters that locally the expertise to make use of innovation is there – investment in science, technology and other sources of innovation is undeniably important. But the capacity to make effective use of scientific and technological advances may often be as significant as actually originating them. Product cycles, moreover, whether in goods or services, become shorter than they were, because of the intensity of competition transferred more onto a global scale.

The old-style system was founded upon a simple division between those who produce knowledge and those who apply it in commercial contexts – R&D laboratories and universities on the one hand, and business firms on the other. The motivation of the

---

[15] Soete, 'A knowledge economy paradigm'.

knowledge producers, seen from this perspective, is not mainly to generate new ideas or findings as such, but to supply outputs capable of reasonably fast practical implementation. These patterns persist in more industrial settings, such as the chemical, pharmaceutical and electronic consumer goods industries, but not in the burgeoning service sectors. Efficiency gains, or the pioneering of new markets, depend much more on flexible networks and the fusion of technology with other forms of creativity. In research areas relevant to economic success in service provision, success is likely to come from global access to knowledge sources, the development of joint standards and even quite often the diffusion of new products to developing countries. Research on energy-saving technologies and resources to combat climate change provides a very clear example.

The Commission has recently suggested that spending on R&D within the EU countries is only likely on current trends to rise to 2.2 per cent by 2010. China is increasing its investment in R&D at double digit rates and on current trends will overtake the EU in proportional terms by that year. This circumstance is not especially worrying in itself, since China will be busy making up gaps that existed previously. It will to some extent be competing in areas that the advanced economies have largely abandoned, although, for reasons given earlier, this situation is changing fast. The EU societies have to keep ahead by building on more established research institutions, but more crucially by keeping ahead in terms of product development and market innovation. The disquieting thing is that these processes in many cases and in many countries in the EU seem even less well developed than traditional R&D.

Higher Education

R&D implies higher education. Growing awareness of the economic significance of universities and colleges was one of the factors prompting the Lisbon Agenda in the first place. Some analysts thought that campus-based universities would become increasingly obsolete, as most learning in the future would be done on the Internet. Many new Internet-based universities were set up, some within the penumbra of the state, most established through private initiative. A few – notably the campus-less University of Phoenix – have been highly successful, but most have fallen by the wayside.

The relative failure of Internet universities – so far at least – drives home some important lessons. Brand name in universities is extremely hard to achieve. The best universities in the world tend to be among the oldest. One of the reasons is that talent in universities comes in clusters. The first question a leading academic will ask another academic about his or her department is 'Who else is there?' – what other well-known academics are in that department? Prestige among universities, seen in national or global terms, depends upon research, no matter how many hours academics spend upon teaching. Finally, prestige in rankings creates market value. A degree from Harvard, the Sorbonne or the LSE, for example, is esteemed everywhere. The market value of such degrees also depends on their scarcity.

In a speech given in Glasgow in April 2005, the President of the European Commission, José Manuel Barroso, stated that 'universities have never featured so high on the Commission's agenda'.[16] The Commission followed through on that remark by publishing a communication on universities sent to member nations. It confirms the central role of higher education in the Lisbon strategy, and specifies areas for improvement (of which there are many).

Somewhat arcane Eurospeak has been introduced to signal the EU's efforts in the higher education field. There is a European 'higher education space'. The Bologna Declaration of 1999 set out the parameters of this 'space' in terms of a range of objectives. 'Easily readable' and comparable degrees were to be established across the member states, to promote educational mobility, help integrate labour markets and increase the international competitiveness of European higher education. Other objectives were

[16] José Manuel Barroso, 'Strong universities for Europe. Speech at the European Universities Convention', Glasgow, 2 April 2005; available online at <www.eua.be/eua/jsp/en/upload/Barroso_speech.1112693429657.pdf>.

added later, including aspirations to do with the extension of lifelong learning. The Bologna Declaration was a commitment undertaken by national governments, it being accepted that education in general and higher education in particular are not within the province of common European policy. The community's role is limited to encouraging cooperation between member states.

Five benchmarking goals have been set in conjunction with the Lisbon Agenda. All member states have agreed to reduce by half the gender imbalance among graduates in mathematics, science and technology by 2010, starting from a baseline of 2000. The percentage of young people aged 25–29 having at least upper-secondary education is to reach 80 per cent or more. In addition, an average of 15 per cent or more of the population aged 25–64 is to be involved in lifelong learning; in no country is the proportion to be lower than 10 per cent.

It is widely accepted that universities in the EU at all levels lag behind their American counterparts. Few European universities make it into the world top hundred when measured in terms of research criteria. In many countries in the EU, universities are over-crowded, the faculty demotivated and poorly paid. For these reasons there is a continuous seepage of some of the best scholars and researchers to the US. Most do not return. There are manifest contradictions in the policies of some EU states about universities in relation to the knowledge/service economy. The numbers of students in university have increased rapidly everywhere, but funding has remained largely static; so the quality of education offered is often poor. Moreover, surveys show that the regular links between universities, research institutes and business in R&D are on average weaker than in the US.

Universities do not exist just as adjuncts to business, or as a resource for the economy. We have to think about the wider mission of universities and also about their governance. Europeans have become so used to the admonition that American universities are superior to their own that it is worth pointing out that all is not well in higher education in the US. The last few years have seen a spate of criticisms of the state of universities there. It has been observed that American higher education 'has remade itself into a vast job-training programme',[17] which tends 'to promote the need for a productive citizenry rather than a critical, socially responsive, reflective individualism'. One author has spoken of 'the university in ruins'.[18]

Contrary to a commonly held view, US universities depend quite heavily upon state support, whether from the federal or the local state. In a recent analysis it was concluded that very few state universities could afford to privatize. Many 'private' universities and colleges depend quite heavily upon state finance in the shape of generous research resources. Where universities draw significant funding from business, there are serious worries about how far this situation compromises the independence of research. Yet only a few universities with large endowments are able to turn back large sources of funding offered externally.

Universities have to preserve their autonomy from the state at a time when governments are wanting to turn them to national economic advantage. One way of doing so is by reasserting the values for which universities stand. The expansion of higher education is not just about responding to the demands of the new economy. It is also about preparing citizens for a world of diversity and change. Non-vocational subjects should continue to fill their fair share of the curriculum; and the disinterested pursuit of knowledge should be the prime function of the research-based university. The problems faced in the US show that there is no easy route to resolving these issues.

In US universities there are other problems too. The fees in leading private colleges have risen so high that they are beyond the budgets of the majority of American families. Scholarships are widely available, but only in a handful of rich institutions are they sufficient to guarantee entrance to all those from poorer backgrounds who qualify for admission. The proportion of those from such backgrounds in the top echelons of American higher education is dropping.

---

[17] Diane Ravitch, former Assistant Secretary of Education, quoted in Richard Herch, 'The liberal arts college', *Liberal Education*, Summer 1997.
[18] Quote from Eric Gould, *The University in a Corporate Culture*. New Haven, CT: Yale University Press, 2003; Bill Readings, *The University in Ruins*. Cambridge, MA: Harvard University Press, 1997.

Various implications follow for Europe. In most EU countries, higher education can no longer be funded wholly, or almost wholly, by government. What made sense when a small percentage of young people went to university – and no older ones did at all – does not do so when that figure rises to over 40 per cent and the target proportion is even higher. Students must pay towards the cost of the education they receive. So long as the money goes directly to universities, it helps support their autonomy as well as providing resources to pay better salaries and provide more developed research environments for faculty. The problem is to ensure that those from less privileged backgrounds don't suffer. The systems introduced in the UK and Australia are geared to try to achieve this. Payment of fees is not upfront, as it is in the US, but deferred until after graduation; those earning below a certain level pay nothing back. The extra resources are used not only to improve salaries and working conditions, but also to set up scholarships and other sources of help for students from less privileged origins. In effect, there is redistribution from better-off students towards the less well-off.

The EU has no power to ensure that moves towards more diverse funding for higher education are made within the member states. But it could kick-start a debate. Pensions reform and reform of health care systems are universally agreed to be necessary. The same should be true of higher (and further) education, whose turnover in economic terms is now gigantic. It would be a mistake to concentrate only on science and technology. The proposed European Institute of Technology (a follow-up from the Sapir Report) is only worth persisting with if the resources that can be put into it are sufficient to allow it to compete with world leaders – and where will those resources come from?

In the best scenario there would be a coming together of (1) the need for creativity in the knowledge/service economy; (2) the preservation of the university as ranging across the arts, humanities and philosophy as well as science and technology; and (3) restoration of leading European universities to world-class status. Creativity cannot be taught as such, but is surely one of the products of a first rate university education; and there is no reason at all to suppose it is confined to science and little danger to imagine that it looms large in business studies.

Some overall policy conclusions, therefore:

1 It does not make much sense to set an overall target for R&D, particularly where most movement towards the target is supposed to come from business.
2 Old-style R&D – focused on science and technology, connecting businesses (and also public institutions) with research institutes and universities – remains of great importance. But attention has to be concentrated almost as much on the conditions under which the take-up and market exploitation of technology occurs. Both larger and smaller countries are increasingly able to exploit technology on a global level, given the right conditions.
3 Universities and colleges have a pivotal role in the knowledge/service economy. Some, indeed, have referred to them as the 'factories of the knowledge economy'. In the new economy, simply, adaptability and a cosmopolitan outlook – as well as, in many contexts, being numerate – take on a fresh importance. It makes perfect sense to expand higher education – and the EU goal of 80 per cent of younger people in post-secondary education is not excessive.
4 Steps to improve the position of universities in the EU countries are imperative, although most have to be taken on a national or regional level. It is especially important to upgrade institutions at the top end, not because of elitism, but because the leading universities tend to set the tone for the rest, and because of their essential importance for innovative research.
5 The EU can learn a great deal from the American higher education system, and must strive to reverse the flow of leading researchers who cross the Atlantic and are lost to Europe. One possibility might be to copy the Canadian example. In Canada, prestigious chairs were set up on the basis of government money, well funded in terms of salaries and working conditions. Universities could apply for these in order to attract top-class scholars. The scheme seems to have helped reverse the Canadian brain-drain to the US. Such a scheme could be applied by some of the member states, or by the EU,

or both. However, there are major stresses and strains in US higher education and the lessons of these should not be lost. Some, in fact, centre upon the increasing ties between universities and business, others on funding. There is no silver bullet answer to the question of how higher education on a mass level should be funded. It is surely obvious, however, that student contributions must be involved.

6 The expansion of higher education poses significant problems of social justice. It should provide greater avenues of social mobility for students from poorer backgrounds, but the evidence suggests that this is not happening. Policy measures are needed to bring higher education within the horizon of those who would not otherwise think of the possibility; and to provide support for those who are especially needy. We must also seek to reduce the gap opening up between those who experience higher education and those who do not.

7 Higher education is itself a very large business, which increasingly brings in independent revenue of its own – such as that from students from outside the EU. Such revenue-generation must be factored into any overall assessment of the costs and benefits of its expansion.

Ecological Modernization

One area where Europe could lead the world is in the further development of ecological modernization. It is possible that rather than further reducing competitiveness, the development of new ecological technologies – and just as important, styles of life – could be a spur to its renewal. Information technology has transformed our economies and our lives over the past thirty years. Perhaps there will be a key discovery, or set of discoveries, that will change our lives just as much over the next thirty in the environmental/energy field. As the sources of fossil fuel become more problematic and the manifestations of climate change more acute, the pressure for innovation will be well and truly on.

At the moment, Japan, rather than the EU or the US, must be considered the leader. Japan started to make environmental innovations in the 1970s. At that point its clear-air policies were well ahead of elsewhere – itself a reaction to something of a crisis, since Japan's cities had previously been among the most heavily polluted in the world. After the oil crisis of the 1970s, the Japanese made a serious attempt to reduce energy use. World consumption of oil has risen steadily, but Japan's has stayed constant since 1975, in spite of the fact that the economy has grown threefold.[19] The country has successfully introduced a conservationist culture and has diversified its energy sources. In Japan, 21 per cent of cars are vehicles with low emissions, a much higher proportion than elsewhere. 'Intelligent machines' in the major cities switch off ticket machines, escalators, lifts and other machinery when they are not in use at any one moment.

Air conditioners are required by law to be redesigned to use 60 per cent less electricity than the present average by 2008, as must other types of office and domestic machinery. The legislation has in fact produced a great deal of activity from firms making goods that must meet the criteria. So far, most of these cost more than the products they are superseding and therefore are not competitive on world markets. But they will become so as prices fall or as other countries begin to gear up seriously for energy saving.

Energy consumption in Japan per head is now only a half of that of the US – and two-thirds that of Germany, France or the UK. Five out of Nippon Steel's ten large factories are burning recyclable goods, such as domestic waste, in their factories. The corporation has reduced its dependency on oil by 85 per cent since 1974. Producing one tonne of steel uses 20 per cent less fuel than its American counterparts. The paper industry now gets 38 per cent of its power from sources based on waste recycling or other renewable energy sources.

Toyota, which became the world's biggest car-maker this year, envisages a future with accident-proof eco cars, powered by engines that can actively clean the air around them, running on congestion-free roads. Of the group's turnover of US$110 billion, 4–5 per cent is being invested in the development of non-fossil-fuel

[19] Anthony Faiola, 'Turn off the heat – how Japan made energy-saving an art form', *Guardian*, 17 February 2006.

cars. The main problem is not the technology, but the cost. The head of overseas operations at Toyota has argued that the environmental credentials of the company have been the main reason it has been able to outgrow the big US car-makers.[20]

There are signs that the US is at last taking its 'oil addiction' seriously. A report produced by the Natural Resources Defense Council in 2005 calls oil dependence 'the Achilles heel of America's economy' – and of its national security.[21] The US has currently less than 3 per cent of known oil reserves and imports 60 per cent of its oil. The NRDC calculates that, by a number of simple measures, and using available technology, US oil consumption could be reduced by 40 per cent by 2025. If current trends are sustained, on the other hand, the country will by that time consume 40 per cent more oil than it does today.

In February 2006 the Swedish government declared its intention to become the first advanced economy to wean itself off oil and natural gas completely by 2020.[22] Like Japan, Sweden reacted vigorously to the rising oil prices in the 1970s. Today, virtually all of its electricity comes from non-fossil-fuel sources (including, at the moment, nuclear power). Motor vehicles are the main consumers of fossil fuels. The country has reduced its oil dependency from 77 per cent of total energy consumption in 1970 to 32 per cent in 2003. In the same year 26 per cent of overall energy consumed came from renewable sources – compared to an EU15 average of only 6 per cent. The country aims to emulate Brazil in converting a substantial proportion of its motor vehicles within a relatively short time to bio-fuels. According to Mona Sahlin, the Swedish Minister for Sustainable Development, the fact that the country has a relatively small dependence on oil is a major competitive advantage for Swedish industry. Since 1994, the use of oil in housing and services sectors has been reduced by 15 per cent.[23]

[20] David Gow, 'Ten years down the road', *Guardian*, 31 March 2006.
[21] Natural Resources Defense Council, *Securing America*. Issue Paper, February 2005.
[22] John Vidal, 'Sweden plans to be world's first oil-free economy', *Guardian*, 8 February 2006.
[23] Mona Sahlin, 'Sweden first to break dependence on oil!', Government Offices of Sweden, available online at <www.sweden.gov.se>.

Portugal has recently announced the building of one of Europe's biggest projects in wind power. The project will generate the equivalent of 25 per cent of all wind power currently used in the EU countries. The country is planning the first commercial wave farm in the world, and is radically expanding the use of solar energy. A new solar energy plant near the town of Moura will be a dozen times bigger in terms of energy generated than the current largest plant in Europe.

The EU's sustainable development strategy recognizes that 'the per capita consumption of resources and energy in Europe is above any sustainable level'.[24] In global terms, the EU, with 7 per cent of the world's population, uses about 17 per cent of world resources per annum. The environmental strategy is supposed to be integrated with the Lisbon process, but in spite of the plethora of ambitions the strategy contains, little or no idea is given of how. On 8 March 2006 the Commission published a Green Paper on energy.[25] The paper states that one trillion euros will be needed over the next twenty years to replace ageing plants. Import dependency is rising rather than the reverse. Judged by current trends, in twenty years' time, 70 per cent of the Union's energy requirements will be imported, compared to the 50 per cent that is imported today. Six priorities are listed to promote greater energy efficiency:

1 Create a properly competitive electricity and gas market, to bring down prices and increase security of supply.
2 Improve security of supply such that a country that experiences damage to its infrastructure could be helped by others, or draw from a common pool.
3 Move towards a more renewable and diverse energy mix.
4 Improve energy efficiency and combat climate change.
5 Encourage the development of new energy technologies.
6 Develop a coherent external energy policy to create partnerships with producers, transit countries and other international

---

[24] European Commission, Communication from the Commission to the Council and the European Parliament on the review of the Sustainable Development Strategy. Available online at <http://europa.eu.int/eur-lex/lex/LexUriServ/site/en/com/2005/com2005_0658en01.pdf>.
[25] European Commission, *Green Paper on Energy*, 8 March 2006.

agencies. This would include especially new initiatives towards Russia, as the most important supplier of energy.

When the Lisbon Agenda was under development in the late 1990s, world energy prices were low and there was actually excess capacity in most member states. Energy prices rose at about the same time as the Lisbon strategy was published, in 2000. Oil and gas intertwine with issues of geopolitical security, as they always have done, but the nature of the security issues has altered. Russia and Central Asia have come much more into the reckoning as nations strive to reduce their dependence on fuel from the Middle East. The North Sea oil fields, which were useful sources of oil and gas, are becoming depleted.

Demand from the EU and from the ex-Soviet countries for gas from Russia is expected to grow at about 3 per cent a year. Yet more than three-quarters of production at Russia's largest company, Gazprom, comes from fields where resources are running out. Without more technological investment, prices could double by 2010. At the moment, such investment looks unlikely to be forthcoming. Most will have to be private, but foreign companies at the moment are denied the needed investment opportunities.

To these new vulnerabilities we have to add international terrorism. In February 2006 suicide bombers attacked the Abqaiq processing plant, the largest oil producer in the world. One analyst said: 'Damaging the facility . . . would be unleashing a hurricane that engulfs the world. Within days all governments would [have to] step in to curtail consumption in a coordinated effort.'[26] The attack involved several cars laden with bombs. One of the cars got through the outer perimeter of the security fences and exploded only one mile from the huge plant, where it would have done extensive damage. The exports from the plant supply over 10 per cent of the world's oil needs each day. It does not take much imagination to see what larger attacks, perhaps launched simultaneously at several plants and pipelines, could do.

---

[26] Carola Hoyas and William Wallis, 'Bombers foiled in Saudi oil plant raid', *Financial Times*, 25 February 2006.

The energy market in Europe has now been widely liberalized and privatized, in line with EU policy. There is not really a unified market, but rather a range of bilateral agreements – a hangover from the time when energy was cheap and plentiful. Trading is limited and each country carries spare capacity. The difference between rhetoric and reality about liberalization is large. Takeovers and takeover bids have been plentiful. For instance, in January 2006 Germany's biggest energy company, EON, made an (unsuccessful) bid for Endesa, Spain's electricity company. If it had gone through, EON would have been the largest power and gas company in the world. But when the Italian utility firm Enel hinted at a takeover of the French power and water group Suez, the French government sought to block it by announcing a merger between Suez and the state-controlled Gaz de France. France does not want 'foreign' takeovers, and other countries quite often feel the same.

Greater interconnection would bring more security as well as lowering costs. Electricity in the post-war period was treated as a national good. Some countries, such as France, had national monopolies. Others, like Germany, had state-regulated agreements between state-owned and private producers. Several directives were introduced by the Commission at the end of the 1980s, proposing greater price transparency and cooperation between member states for investment. Attempts to liberalize further met with several set-backs in the Council and European Parliament. The result has been a variety of energy policies across Europe.[27] (It should be noted that this position is not particularly different from that in the US, where there is little standardization across states.) Electricity provision functions as a network system, however, and it would be sensible to extend it Europe-wide. Indeed, it could be argued that a single energy market couldn't exist without it.

Electricity cannot be stored, but gas can. Storage on a European level is worth thinking about seriously. As Helm points out, unlike oil, gas is a regional energy source and hence security should also be considered on a regional level. Such a move need not mean a

---

[27] Atle Midttuh, 'Path dependent national systems or European convergence?', in Marie-Laure Djelic and Sigrid Quack (eds.), *Globalization and Institutions*. Cheltenham: Elgar, 2003, p. 161.

further ceding of powers on the part of member nations – it could be organized in an inter-governmental way.[28]

The EU sustainable development strategy quite rightly links energy issues and climate change, and in fact sets out to establish a 'road map' for both. As far as climate change is concerned, the road map sets out short-, medium- and long-term objectives. The more immediate ones concern meeting renewable energy targets. By 2010, 12 per cent of domestic energy consumption across the EU is to come from renewable sources and 21 per cent of electricity. Energy efficiency overall is to improve by 2.5 per cent per year and by 3.5 per cent in the state sector. The EU has staked out for itself a prime leadership position in negotiating international agreements for the second stage of an international climate change regime.

In the medium term, the EU aims at a minimum of 30 per cent reduction in greenhouse gas emissions by 2020, as compared to 1990 levels. At least 25 per cent of energy by the same year is to come from renewable sources, and 33 per cent of electricity supply. Energy consumption is to be reduced by 20 per cent compared to 1990. By mid-century, EU greenhouse gas emissions are to fall by at least 80 per cent, in line with the aim of having a fully decarbonized economy by then. At some point between 2030 and 2050, the recycling of production materials and waste, including domestic waste, is to reach 95 per cent – meaning that zero untreated waste would go to landfill. By 2010 a transport pricing system should be in place reflecting the real costs to society of the various modes of motorized travel. The aim of such a system is to halve energy consumption from internal travel by 2030. There is a stated methodology for achieving these ends, but the mechanisms for doing so are not well specified – reflecting again the limited purchase the EU has on member states for decisions of this sort. For example, there are to be 'binding requirements and incentives for energy efficiency' – but it is only the member states who can make them binding.

How could the EU emissions trading system be deepened? At the moment, the scheme is only in place until 2008, with negotiations

---

[28] Dieter Helm, 'European Energy Policy: Securing supplies and meeting the challenge of climate change', 25 October 2005; available online at <www. fco.gov.uk/Files/kfile/PN per cent20papers_ per cent20energy.pdf>.

under way to extend it to 2012. Even the latter date is too close to be within the planning horizon of companies in terms of both investment and R&D. The post-2012 framework needs active consideration immediately. In this way, the likely cost of carbon can be factored in by potential investors in new energy programmes.

Most of the initiatives taken by EU states within the existing EU directive on renewable energy are directed towards wind power. More impetus needs to be given to other renewables and how they might be integrated in a practical way with emissions-reduction targets. Bio-fuel looks to have a major future, and could be connected to the EU's development goals. For instance, there has been a proposal for investment in large-scale sugar plantations in Colombia, in Latin America, which would be used to produce bio-fuel, especially in areas where a cease-fire has been arranged with the guerrillas. The idea could help stabilize those areas and at the same time bring in energy sources to the EU. Clean coal is a possibility of major importance, especially as the technology here is advancing rapidly. Investment in nuclear energy is likely to come about whatever objections might be made against it. It is very important to consider what the implications would be at European level. Safety and security issues for nuclear power stations do not concern only the countries in which they are located. It would be advisable to establish pan-European licensing, taking into account agreed-upon safety standards and possible mutual help should a station suffer a terrorist attack.

To realize the aims the EU has set itself, ways will have to be found to stimulate the very large sums of investment needed, most of which must come from the private sector. Energy investments have some distinctive characteristics. They are mostly long term and vulnerable to unpredictable future changes, such as alterations in political ideology or technological developments. Interested parties will not make investments unless these risks are covered or at least reduced to an acceptable level. This means drawing up new forms of long-term contract, in which investors and insurers collaborate, but within an overall regulatory framework set both at the EU level and nationally. With the opening up of the Single Market, competition policy so far has concentrated mainly on short-term market competition. Modifying EU policy towards monopoly might be necessary for companies to be large enough to cope with the huge investment costs that major energy investments have.

Helm has suggested several ways in which investor-friendly regimes can be created while at the same time competitiveness is sustained or enhanced.[29] Regulatory demands in the energy sector are substantial. Energy companies that operate on a European basis at present face considerable add-on costs from the fact that each member state has its own regulatory system. Helm proposes that the EU should set up a review, on an ongoing basis, which would analyse the regulatory burden in each state and identify regulations that either increase costs or diminish competition in the energy sector.

Policy conclusions in the environmental area of course stretch well beyond the themes discussed here, at least in the way that 'environment' is ordinarily understood. Climate change, air pollution and energy security are plainly the most important ones, however, since their actual and potential consequences are so large. Some core policy implications of the foregoing discussion can be stated as follows – in some ways they summarize the themes of this book as a whole:

1 Ecological issues, especially those relating to climate change, must at this point be brought into the core of the theory and practice of social welfare. The rights and obligations of citizenship can no longer attach only to the classical framework of the welfare state, in which the environment is an externality. A positive welfare approach, linked to lifestyle change, is the way forward – not only risk management after the event, but more proactive strategies to improve life quality.

2 Ecological modernization provides an overall guiding orientation. It means seeking to generate profit-making opportunities from innovations that have environmental benefits, either through technological change or through increasing competitiveness. However, government policies – at national and transnational level – must play a central role. Policies include directly influencing lifestyle change, providing favourable conditions for R&D, and setting up appropriate tax regimes for these, plus long-term investment.

[29] Ibid.

3 Environmental issues have to be taken out of the hold of the green movement, since otherwise they appear to be in the grip of a special interest group or groups. Green concepts and terminology in general should be regarded as suspect, particularly insofar as they concern a return to 'nature', hostility towards science and technology or competitive markets.

4 We cannot treat climate change any longer as just a possibility for the future. We should act on the presumption that it is already happening, and that even in the short term its effects will worsen. This means taking measures now against known or probable dangers – for example, protecting areas vulnerable to floods and to more extreme weather conditions than those known in the past; and considering insurance and health implications. The EU should draw up a survey of vulnerabilities with national and pan-European plans of action, to be implemented as soon as feasible.

5 There are clear opportunities to upgrade and revise energy policy, as far as possible within a framework of ecological modernization. Much older plant in any case needs to be replaced. Creating the conditions for the investment needed will require initiatives at the EU level as well as national policies. The physical connection of the electricity grid and the establishment of a gas security and storage plan should play a major part.

6 The EU's stated plans for coping with Europe's energy needs and responding to climate change are ambitious, especially in the longer term. At the moment, they lack effective means of implementation, and a lot more detailed work will need to be done. But in the shorter term it might be asked whether they are in fact ambitious enough. Some countries in Europe are planning to move much faster, and how far they succeed should be closely monitored.

7 The EU's environmental involvements can make a major contribution to security. Climate change and energy management in this sense are part of a broader agenda encompassing a range of threats such as avian flu and international crime. Combating these demands transnational collaboration of the sort the EU is well equipped to provide, or to further develop.

Box 6.1 EU-level policies

1 Lisbon-plus: the Lisbon Agenda should be integrated with effective schemes for promoting social justice and with environmental citizenship. These concerns cannot be just added on to the already large list of Lisbon criteria, but have to be targeted upon certain core areas. The Global Adjustment Fund is a nod in the right direction.

2 'Convergence' is usually spoken of as a one-way process, that of reducing socio-economic differences between nations and regions. Not enough work has been done examining how new dynamics of the EU might affect those disparities, including horizontal as well as vertical integration.

3 Inequalities between regions remain a major problem, both in and across member states. Existing policies have not worked. Investment funds should be more closely linked to good governance criteria.

4 'Old-style' R&D investment remains very important. However, success in the knowledge/service economy depends upon more than scientific and technological innovation, and especially upon market innovation.

5 A great deal more can be done on the EU level to promote higher education, in relation both to economic prosperity and citizenship. However, higher education is far more than just another business. The classic goals of research-based universities – the disinterested search for knowledge and a wide-ranging syllabus across the humanities and social sciences – have to be sustained.

6 Ecological modernization offers a potential basis for enhancing EU competitiveness as well as responding to the combined challenge of climate change and energy shock. The 'managed liberalization' of energy markets can play a vital part in furthering these goals.

7 The EU can make a major contribution to handling new threats, especially those of a more global nature, where collective action and collaboration are at a premium.

All the areas discussed in this chapter are ones in which the EU can make a visible difference to the lives of its citizens over the next few years, a key contribution to re-establishing its legitimacy. They also reflect people's real concerns. Following the repudiation of the constitution, the Commission established an exercise in 'Democracy, Dialogue and Debate', in which 25,000 people from the member states were interviewed. Worries about the economic effects of enlargement and effective social protection topped the list of people's preoccupations, confirming the central importance of the social model. Most citizens remain favourable to the European project, where that project is defined in terms of investment in education and innovation, common health concerns, environmental protection and contributing to security.[30]

---

[30] Special Eurobarometer Report 21, *The Future of Europe*. Brussels: European Commission, 2006.

7

Eight Theses on the Future of Europe

I was recently in Santa Barbara, California, where there is an extensive range of second-hand bookstores. In an obscure corner of one of these I came across a work for which I paid the princely sum of $1. It was by an author called John Gunther and was called *Inside Europe*. Gunther wrote a large number of books on different nations and regions in the world. In this one, he describes how he travelled around a variety of countries of Europe, interviewing political leaders and ordinary members of the public.

His book was published in 1961. Reading it brought home to me the extraordinary range of changes that have transformed the subcontinent over the period of the forty years since then. At that time the Cold War was not so cold. Germany is described by the author as the 'fiery heart of Europe'.[1] Divided though Europe was, the Berlin Wall did not yet exist: 40,000 Berliners lived in the East but worked in the West every weekday; 7,000 did the same in reverse. By then, 3.5 million people had fled East Germany to live permanently in the Federal Republic. The Soviet Union is portrayed as an 'immutable power', more stable than the US – and its hold over Eastern Europe is seen in the same way. Three countries in Western Europe were in the grip of semi-fascist dictatorships: Portugal, Spain and Greece. Portugal had Salazar, Spain had Franco and Greece had the Colonels.

Gunther's book is some 600 pages long, but there are only four or five pages on the EEC, which is seen as an interesting development

---

[1] John Gunther, *Inside Europe*. New York: Harper, 1961, p. 11.

but a rather marginal one. Gunther's view was the characteristic one of the time, a few visionaries apart. It is only looking back from this distance that we see the Treaty of Rome, signed in 1957, as so pivotal. One of the communities it established, the European Atomic Energy Community, in fact turned out to be still-born, so Gunther's perspective was in a way not so far from the truth.

Many histories of the EU, and of post-war Europe too, are written as though there were a continuous evolution towards greater democracy and economic success. Mark Mazower's phrase, 'dark continent', is more appropriate. As Mazower stresses, the history of Europe in the twentieth century is one of discontinuities and regressions as well as advances. Europe may appear to be made up of old states and peoples, but in many respects it is not. Rather, it is 'new, inventing and reinventing itself over this century' – often, as Mazower points out, through 'convulsive transformation'.[2] Parliamentary democracies were installed in a range of countries after 1918, from Northern Europe to the Balkans. They had constitutions incorporating the most up-to-date liberal principles. In his work *Modern Democracies* James Joyce spoke of 'the universal acceptance of democracy as the normal and natural form of government'.[3] Yet twenty years on from 1918, most of the fledgling democratic states had disappeared, replaced by authoritarian regimes.

It is worth mentioning that the 'golden age' of the welfare state, which I have previously expressed reservations about, was not seen in that light by most observers at the time. In the early 1960s, for example, Richard Titmus wrote of a growing sense of disillusionment with the way welfare systems were developing. 'All the impulses and ideals of the 1940s to recreate, rebuild and replan have now collapsed', he wrote.[4]

All of which leads me to *Thesis one*: The year 1989 marks a rupture, not just in the history of Europe overall, but in that of the EU in particular. The fall of East European, and then Soviet, Communism has of course affected the whole world, which was for

[2] Mark Mazower, *Dark Continent*. London: Vintage, 2000.
[3] Cited in ibid, p. 4.
[4] Cited in ibid, p. 301.

so long in the thrall of the bipolar era. Europe, Germany and Berlin, however, were the front line, the 'fiery heart' of the Cold War, which at several points could have produced a conflagration. The EEC/EU was essentially a Cold War creation, getting its identity from a contrast with American market liberalism on the one side, and state socialism on the other. The events of 1989 more or less completely transformed the nature of the EU, not just those countries that freed themselves from Communist rule.

Yet one wouldn't know this from official EU pronouncements. The EU to its credit immediately turned its attention to the East European countries, but it accommodated their potential accession within its traditional language, that of 'enlargement'. The Union has been through successive enlargements, all of them important – especially the accession of the Mediterranean countries that had laboured under dictatorships. But opening up to the East was not just another enlargement. The EU simply could not be the same after 1989 – not just because of the problem of absorbing states much poorer than the European average and with a different socio-economic make-up or the increase in the number of member states. It was because, with an open boundary towards the East, and to the Balkans too, the identity and very nature of the EU became problematic.

Talk of enlargement hid much of this from view, as in its way did the proposed constitution. The constitution was perceived by the EU officialdom and most political leaders as a means of consolidating the already existing European project. But this approach was a disingenuous one. For it was widely apparent – not least to the public – that there were much more radical changes going on to which everyone must accommodate. Communist Europe may have been threatening, but at the same time it stabilized problems to the east of the EU, which were the responsibility of the Soviet Union. Now, the EU borders, or is close to, Belarus, Moldova, the Ukraine, Georgia and Armenia, as well as the Middle East. The accession of Turkey was, for a long time, an 'in principle' issue, but after 1989 it became a matter of practical concern.

Some of the states that have joined the EU are new ones, reinforcing Mazower's point about constant transformation. They include the Czech Republic, Slovakia, Slovenia, Latvia and

---

Box 7.1 Why the EU faces a new world

1 Open border to the East – new regional environment.
2 Expansion becomes open ended.
3 New security problems – rise of new-style terrorism, pandemics and other major risk factors.
4 Ambiguous situation of NATO – transatlantic alliance more problematic.
5 Worsening of world environmental dangers.
6 Franco-German axis loses its relevance as dominant driving force.
7 Some of main trade competitors located in developing world.

Lithuania (although the latter two did exist between 1919 and 1939) inside the EU. Outside the Union, virtually all the Balkan states are new, as are those in the group bordering Russia. Even Russia is 'new'. Compared to the situation in Europe, it is the US that is an 'old' country! It has been calculated that 8,000 miles of new borders have been created in Central and Eastern Europe alone since 1989. The results are far from being to everyone's liking. Only a small proportion of people living in Western Europe consider their borders 'unsettled'. In Central and Eastern Europe, more than half think so, in the sense that 'there is territory that is ours'.[5]

The proposed constitution did not define how the EU should restructure itself in the context of such problems. Questions raised by the latest 'enlargement' (in 2004) go beyond giving the EU a systematic legal identity, improving decision-making procedures or giving more focus to foreign policy – vital though these are, as I shall argue later. Looked at in this way, perhaps it isn't surprising that the 'no' voters in France and the Netherlands didn't stick to constitutional issues, but gave vent to more sweeping worries.

The forces that produced 1989 and the fall of the Soviet Union were the same as those that the EU has to face up to today. They

---

[5] Jan Zielonka, *Europe Unbound*. London: Routledge, 2002.

Box 7.2 Each of the elements in box 7.1 can actually add strength to the EU

1 Open border to the East embraces not only a local role, but a wider geopolitical one too.
2 The EU is a powerful force influencing democratization, the role of law and the spread of market economies.
3 EU-level collaboration offers citizens protection from new global risks.
4 The Union shoulders more of its defence responsibilities, as well as developing rapid-reaction capabilities elsewhere.
5 The EU assumes a leading role in reducing climate change risk.
6 More equal power-sharing occurs among member states.
7 The European social model successfully 'goes global'.

---

include the two sets of structural changes I have focused on in this book – changes affecting everyday life, and the changes introduced by accelerating globalization. Everyday democratization is not just confined to the Western countries; it is an influence making itself felt everywhere. Because of the ease of modern communications, it is virtually impossible for closed societies to persist. The one or two that continue, such as North Korea or Burma, are tottering on the edge of collapse.

I was in Berlin on 11 November 1989, the evening the wall was opened. People coming in from East to West showed us their maps of the city. The whole of West Berlin was blanked out on them – there was just an empty space. But they knew all about the other side of Berlin anyway, because of watching Western television programmes. Everyday democratization is not the same as consumerism. Of course many people in Eastern Europe and the Soviet Union wanted the consumer goods and the overall affluence enjoyed by the West. But they also wanted, as surveys showed, greater mobility and autonomy – in short, freedom – in their everyday lives.

With the advance of globalization, the command systems that worked well in Soviet Communism in an earlier age become dysfunctional. The same was true of the West, although those systems existed there in looser and less authoritarian forms. Taylorist influences, for example, were visible in Western management until well into the 1980s. Coupled with the advance of information technology, globalization has created powerful pressures towards the development of flexible systems of management and flattened hierarchies. Corporations that have failed to adapt have perished.

The fall of Soviet Communism and the demise of Keynesianism in the West – with its acutely important implications for the welfare state – were directly bound up with these sets of changes. Both were oriented to national demand management, a perspective that became unsustainable with the advance of economic globalization. The consequences were not as disruptive in the West as in the East, since the degree of central planning and overall economic control by the state was much lower in the former than in the latter. Chinese Communism survived only because the state relinquished control over most market mechanisms – but how stable that system will prove remains to be seen.

Thesis two: In the light of these transformations we (pro-Europeans) have to work out all over again what the European Union is for, and persuade a now anxious public. The 'why' at the moment is just as important as the 'how'.

It is not enough any longer to say that the Union, in its current or earlier versions, has created peace in Europe. Moreover, the thesis is in any case a suspect one. The economic integration of Germany and France was one of the motivations for the early formation of the EU. Germany renounced any lingering imperial ambitions in agreeing to become part of a larger collaborative entity. Yet the real threat to Europe (as Western Europe) post-1945 was no longer Germany, but the Soviet Union. Divided Germany was the focal point of this threat, not the origin of it. Peace in Europe arguably was sustained far more by the presence of NATO than by the EEC/EU. Moreover, in the war that did occur in Europe after 1989, the civil war in ex-Yugoslavia, the EU did little to distinguish itself. The conflicts in Bosnia and Kosovo were only resolved with, in the first case, the intervention of the Americans, and in the second of NATO. Only in the case of containing the struggle in Macedonia could the EU lay claim to successful involvement in the prevention of military violence.

One of the effects of the changing character of sovereignty in the global age is that territorial wars between nations are less likely than they were. There are still armed conflicts of a territorial kind in sub-Saharan Africa. There are armed non-state groups that have pursued territorial objectives in Europe, notably the IRA and ETA. And there are dangerous flash points in other parts of the world. Two nuclear powers confront one another in the shape of Pakistan and India, with the issue of Kashmir unresolved. If Iran gets nuclear weapons, an arms race could develop in the Middle East; and in East Asia the question of Taiwan is still hanging in the air.

But for the majority of countries there are no nations likely to conquer their territory, or indeed that have any interest in doing so. Virtually all states in North, Central and South America are in this category. So are those of the EU, North Africa, Russia, Central and East Asia and Australasia. Weak states rather than strong states today provide most of the problems with which the world has to deal. Most nations today face dangers and risks, rather than the threat of invasion from other states. Global terrorism is one of these new risks. It is quite different from the sort of terrorism associated with Northern Ireland and the Basque country. The IRA and ETA had the aim of establishing new nation-states – in the one case unifying a divided country, and in the other creating a nation-state in a nation without a state.

The new terrorism is geopolitical, a creature of globalization and mass communications. Al Qaeda, like other jihadist organizations, has cells in many countries. Its aims are very general, and extremely ambitious – nothing less than a return to Islamic rule in states ranging from Pakistan through to North Africa and even southern Spain (former Al Andalus, now known as Andalusia). Moreover, it will not hesitate to use large-scale violence if it can. Under a worst-case scenario, 60,000 people could have died on 9/11 in New York and Washington, not 3,000 as actually happened. Al Qaeda's aims are territorial, but it is not a state. It is more like a malign NGO, driven by a sense of mission. It is hardly an invading force, but, together with other radical groups, a major source of risk for many countries – especially were nuclear terrorism ever to become a real possibility.

National identity in the past has been formed and sustained in opposition to others – to enemy states, in other words, or coalitions of such states. The Cold War divisions were the last version of this dynamic. Many nations, including those in the EU, now have to define their identities in a different manner. It does not follow that nation-states are about to disappear, because they are not. It could be that we are seeing something of a return to the nation-state in the world at large. After all, under the current American administration the US has explicitly decided to put its own interests first and has actively denied multilateralist principles. As Condoleezza Rice put it, America should proceed from 'the firm ground of the national interests, not from the interest of an illusory international community'.[6] Geopolitical relations are very much as major states' leaders define them. By interpreting the international system as based upon force and violence, the Bush administration has helped to some degree to make it come true. Moreover, the two big rising countries, China and India, are nation-states (as well as nuclear powers).

Yet as everyday democratization proceeds, and globalization intensifies, new cross-cutting networks develop; cities and regions push for more autonomy, while nations develop common interests. Both China and India might have a different political form some years from now. There are clear signs of emerging transnational regionalism everywhere, from Latin America to Africa to Asia. Mercosur in Latin America may have suffered set-backs, but there is continuing involvement of Latin American countries in other networks (including with the EU). The Association of South-East Asian Nations (ASEAN), together with Korea, Japan and China, has issued a joint report suggesting enhanced political, economic,

---

[6] Condoleezza Rice, 'How to promote the national interest', *Foreign Affairs*, January 2000; available online at <www.foreignaffairs.org/20000101faessay5 -p0/condoleezza-rice/campaign-2000-promoting-the-national-interest.html>, p. 4.

environmental and cultural cooperation.[7] The African nations are seeking to get together too.

Thesis three: The 'why' of the European Union can readily be specified once we grasp the nature of the world to which it must now relate.

The classic role of the Union from its early days is still highly important, although it is being redefined. That is to say, the EU exists to bring *economic benefits* to its members that they otherwise would not have. Small and medium-sized countries can prosper in the global economy – look at the cases of Taiwan, South Korea, Singapore, Chile and Australia. However, the Single Market brings advantages that more isolated countries miss out on. These are not primarily to do with immediate economic gains, which are in any case difficult to calculate. The most important advantage lies in having a very large, stable market close to hand – which counts for a lot even in an IT-dominated age. This is why the developed countries in Europe that have not become members of the Union – Norway, Iceland and Switzerland – nevertheless have such close and complex economic ties with it. They are not simply free-riders, because they have the intrinsic disadvantage of not having any direct influence over decisions that affect them.

The *social model* (in its diversity) is a basic part of the reason for the existence of the EU. Habermas and Derrida were right about that (see chapter 1). Initially this position sounds odd, because Europe's welfare systems largely developed independently of the EU institutions and the EU still lacks power over them. Yet Europeans as a whole, as surveys show, see the care and protection offered by welfare provisions as central to their lives. Research in the US shows quite different attitudes there. The social model is hence a key part of 'Europeanness', but in an evolving way. In Cold War Europe – and prior to the intensifying of globalization – the welfare state had a different role from that needed today, for reasons explored in this book. It was organized under the aegis of

---

[7] Association of South-East Asian Nations, *Towards an East Asian Community, Report of the East Asia Vision Group*, 2001; available online at <www.mofa. go.jp/region/asia-paci/report2001.pdf>.

Keynesianism, was based on traditional work/family patterns, and its overall economic effects were not part of its rationale. The case has to be forcefully made, as I have tried to do, that Europe's welfare systems can make a positive contribution to competitiveness in a post-industrial context. It is no longer a question, as Habermas and Derrida argued, of protecting citizens from the buffetings of the market. The state – and the EU – must sometimes intervene in order to facilitate market exchange, or to make it more efficient. Far from being inconsistent with social justice and social welfare, such innovations are crucial for furthering them.

The claim that *sovereignty pooled is sovereignty gained* has real meaning – strengthened rather than weakened by emerging trends in world society. We know that power is not a zero-sum game. As Talcott Parsons pointed out long ago, new institutional arrangements can generate more power than existed before, rather like money; like money there is then more to redistribute.[8] The main legitimating principle of the EU should be that by cooperation and the pooling of resources, member states get more (real, as opposed to formal) sovereignty than they would otherwise have.

One example among many, so far as external sovereignty is concerned, is the leverage the EU has in trade policy. This was already true at the time of GATT, where the EEC was a leading partner because of the collective trading weight of its founding members. It has been said that during the 1960s the negotiating power of the six, represented by the Commission for the first time, matched that of the US, 'thus marking the end of a period of unchallenged American leadership in the post-war international trading system'.[9] However, in the expanded marketplace of today, the EU has a much more extended role to play, especially in the context of the WTO.

The EU can help provide *security* for its citizens well beyond anything individual nations can offer. In current times, the Union has no choice but to be a geopolitical actor, in ways that were not the case in earlier periods. This is exactly because the current round of 'enlargement' is so different from earlier ones. In earlier

---

[8] Talcott Parsons, *Talcott Parsons on Institutions and Social Evolution: Selected Writings*. Chicago: University of Chicago Press, 1985.
[9] Loukas Tsoukalis, *What Kind of Europe?* Oxford: Oxford University Press, 2005, p. 70.

phases of the EU's development, the conditions of joining were relatively straightforward, since the nations signing up were more or less on a par in terms of economic and political development. The reasons why so many wished, and wish, to join now are not the same as those of the original members, with the partial exception of Spain, Portugal and Greece. They are now much more transformational in nature. What happens in the lead-up to accession is as important as accession itself. Countries want to join to gain access to the now massive European market, benefit from the funding that becomes available to them, be part of an organization of world influence, and to secure political and legal stability for themselves.

Sustaining a *zone of peace* within and around the EU, still to be fully secured within the area of the Balkan states, is a prime task. However, the EU can and should have a fundamental role in protecting citizens from new-style risks, including those stemming from climate change, global terrorism, pandemics and international crime. The EU can be far more effective in minimizing such risks than its member states could ever be acting alone.

The EU stands for *general values* that it embodies and defends. I take these to be: cultivating and protecting democracy within the Union and externally; creating unity out of diversity, a phrase that is much more than just a slogan, referring as it does to the cosmopolitan nature of the EU; promoting solidarity within and across the Union, in the various senses of that term distinguished earlier; a commitment to collaboration in the face of external threats; and providing for a constructive engagement with wider world problems and conflicts. These values in essence tie together the foregoing points.

The spread of democracy from the 1970s onwards, led by the EU, is by any token a great success story. In spite of some pre-war parallels, there has never been a situation before where so many European states are liberal democracies. Moreover, they are part of the same overall community, with equal rights and responsibilities. As Timothy Garton-Ash says, 'If that's not a story to be proud of, what is?'.[10] However, with an open border towards the East, it is

[10] Timothy Garton-Ash, *Free World*. London: Allen Lane, 2004.

no longer at all clear where the expansion of the EU should stop – and here citizens are right to demand more clarity.

Thesis four: For the reasons just listed, the EU has to be a political project. To decide what kind of political project, we have to go beyond the antithesis between the federalists and the inter-governmentalists. We could start, as it were, at the two edges of opinion. The idea that the EU should become a federal state goes back well before the founding of the EEC itself – to before the Second World War in fact.[11] It continues to have its exponents today.[12] The most famous version of this view in recent years was that given by the former German foreign minister, Joschka Fischer, in a lecture in Berlin in May 2000.[13]

Federalism (I shall argue below) is an archaic mode of thinking in the contemporary world, not the best way of working out how the EU should develop in the future. Yet Europe cannot be, as Margaret Thatcher wanted, from an opposing position, driven only by 'willing and active cooperation between independent sovereign states'.[14] The EU has moved well beyond such a scenario already. The Union cannot be seen as just a council of nations, a sort of regional UN with economic pretensions. The Single Market and the Single Currency presume integration, as does the body of law that the EU has built. The EU is not a super-state, and will not become a super-state. It is not, and will not be, a superpower either, at least in the sense that term had in the Cold War period. A super-power is an agency capable of deploying its forces and protecting its interests around the world. The US is the only actor capable of so doing for the indefinite future. Europeans have to come to terms with the fact that Europe is no longer the main pivot of global

---

[11] See Arthur Salter, *The United States of Europe*. London: Allen and Unwin, 1931.

[12] Guy Verhofstadt, *A United States of Europe*. London: The Federal Trust for Education and Research, 2006.

[13] Joschka Fischer, 'From confederacy to federation – thoughts on the finality of European integration'. Lecture given at Humboldt University, Berlin, 12 May 2000; available online at <http://europa.eu.int/constitution/futurum/documents/speech/sp120500_en.pdf>.

[14] Margaret Thatcher, 'The Bruges Speech'; available online at <www.margaret-thatcher.org/speeches/displaydocument.asp?docid=107332>.

Box 7.3 What the EU is (and should be)

1 A regional power, not a super-state or superpower.
2 A democratic association of semi-sovereign nations, drawing upon collective capabilities.
3 The democratic nature of the EU is not primarily representational but deliberative.
4 Seeks to deploy the power of network government, both in its own functioning and on the world scene.
5 Member states accept constitutional discipline as an 'autonomous act', not as an act of becoming subordinate to a higher authority.
6 The de facto constitutional settlement the EU already has is a firm basis for its transnational character. Its basic institutional form, depending upon the triad of Commission, European Council and Parliament, will not alter, except around the margins.
7 The EU 'goes global' in terms of its adaptability to the changes associated with the global age.
8 Adopts the perspective of assertive multilateralism.
9 The EU is, after all, European! – because of (i) its location, (ii) its cultural inheritance and (iii) its symbols.

---

concerns. In this sense, several centuries of world history have come to an end. However, Europe can, and should, aim to be a developed regional power, with some considerable clout in world affairs.

Some of the differences of opinion and viewpoint that exist about what the EU is and what it should be are linked to the 'big three' states. The UK official line has long been an inter-governmentalist one, even if not in recent years as extreme as that held by Mrs Thatcher. Leading German politicians and thinkers have tended to think of Europe in terms of a federal model akin to their own national one. French leaders tend towards a more centralized view of the EU, which, however, they see as still sustaining national interests. Traditionally, they have seen European and French interests as identical (less so now). Some small member nations have favoured a federal view, but most are wary of it, seeing their influence as threatened and diminished by such an idea. The new member states are quite strongly inter-governmentalist: having just escaped the control of the Soviet Union, they have no wish to sign up to another super-state. The divergences between these views appear so large that it would seem impossible to reconcile them. It *is* impossible to reconcile them in their conventional form but we should learn to think about each in a new way.

Federalism (I believe) is a dead project, but the federalists have something to teach us, which is the importance of decision-making and leadership. If these qualities cannot be further enhanced, the EU is likely to be condemned to stagnation and relative impotence in world affairs. Improved leadership and decision-making are not the same as federalism and can be achieved without anything like a fully-fledged federal system.

A Europe that is too inter-governmental (which is the situation at the moment) has serious limitations. It allows national interests too often to override common ones; the larger nations routinely dominate the smaller states. The familiar pattern whereby national leaders take the credit at home for the positive accomplishments of the EU, while blaming the EU for what goes wrong nationally, is reinforced. Significant power must be held by the Commission and the Commission leadership. If there is not effective leadership, in the Council as well as the Commission, drift and inertia result. It is up to the European Parliament, and not only the nations, to monitor the activities and proposals of the Commission.

The EU is an experiment in government without a state. Finding a formula for a political Europe is now as urgent a task as renewing the social model, and indeed interconnected with it. Andrew Moravcsik has convincingly argued that there already exists a 'European constitutional settlement', based on an institutional equilibrium.[15] The proposed constitution, he argues, would have

---

[15] Andrew Moravcsik, 'In defence of the democratic deficit: reassessing legitimacy in the European Union', *Journal of Common Market Studies*, 40/4 (2002).

added little to this. The EU is primarily a form of deliberative democracy, and will remain so. Its democratic nature comes primarily from the fact that proposed policies have to be discussed in an open manner and decisions as far as possible reached through consensus. As one author puts it: 'EU institutions should be read as a supranational version of deliberative ideals and interpreted with a view to compensating some of the shortcomings of the constitutional nation-state.'[16]

The constitutional nature of the EU is best understood in the terms proposed by the theorist of jurisprudence Joseph Weiler. Weiler makes it clear why the EU is neither a super-state nor an association of sovereign nations. It is worth quoting him in some detail:

> Constitutional actors in the member states accept the European constitutional discipline not because as a matter of legal doctrine, as is the case in the federal state, they are subordinate to a higher sovereignty and authority attaching to the norms by the federal principle, the constitutional *demos*. They accept it as an autonomous voluntary act, endlessly renewed on each occasion of subordination, in the discrete areas governed by Europe, which is the aggregate expression of other wills, other political identities, other political communities.[17]

The fact that compliance is 'an autonomous voluntary act' does not mean every decision taken in the EU has to get the agreement of all parties concerned, which would be impossible. It means that acts of compliance, and the legal apparatus that has been built up, involve equals. Europe is inevitably cosmopolitan, says Weiler, because of the different nations and cultures it comprises. However, citizens in the EU become accustomed to laws and norms created by the collective will of member states. Such norms are

---

[16] Christopher Lord, *Democracy in the European Union*. Sheffield: Sheffield Academic Press, 1998.

[17] Joseph Weiler, 'Europe's *Sonderweg*', in K. Nicolaidis and Robert Howse (eds.), *The Federal Vision*. Oxford: Oxford University Press, p. 68. For an interesting discussion of the same quotation, where, however, the author reaches different conclusions from mine, see Glyn Morgan, *The Idea of a European Superstate*. Princeton: Princeton University Press, 2005, pp. 114–20.

learned through the operation of the Union itself, not through abstract ideals. We are prepared to submit to the decisions of a polity composed of 'others' because of the conviction that they share similar values. Hence, the EU 'is a construct which is designed to encourage certain virtues of tolerance and humanity'.[18]

Thesis five: There should be no return to the constitution as such. I write as someone who felt ambivalent about the constitution, for reasons already given. In large part it ignored the need to provide a new rationale for the Union post-1989 or to address the worries many felt about 'enlargement'. Moreover, no one seemed able to decide whether the constitution was a major new endeavour or a relatively unimportant one. It was a political breakthrough for Europe, or a mere tidying-up exercise, according to taste.

Its failure, nevertheless, is a serious business. There is no consensus among member states about what to do next. Some want to proceed with ratifying – five countries have done so since the French and Dutch referendums. It is hard to see the point, though. French and Dutch political leaders insist that asking their citizens to vote again, or ratifying the constitution in parliament, are not options – it is 'inconceivable', as some have said. Some of those who are carrying on ratifying are opposed to anything that carries the flavour of renegotiation. 'Cherry-picking' is out. Others, faced with these difficulties, speak of reviving the idea of a two-speed Europe, with an inner group moving ahead of the rest. How this strategy could work with two of the founder members left on the sidelines is not clear.

Yet a further approach has recently surfaced. The French and Dutch voted down the constitution in large part because they were anxious about what would happen to jobs and social protection. In fact, the constitution had little or nothing to say about such matters. Why not add some sections on these issues and re-present the whole thing to the voters?[19] A 'social protocol' could be added

---

[18] Joseph Weiler, *The Constitution of Europe*. Cambridge: Cambridge University Press, 1999, p. 301.
[19] Angelica Schwall-Düren, *The Way out of Europe's Constitutional Crisis*. Berlin: Friedrich Ebert Stiftung, April 2006.

to the existing text. It would guarantee certain basic aspects of different countries' social protection systems. For instance, it would guarantee the persistence of the traditions of *service publique* in France. The notion, however, is not exactly a compelling one. The idea of preserving in aspic some of the very social provisions that are holding nations, and Europe, back is not exactly a sensible way forward.

What to do? The situation is not quite as difficult as it appears. Some 90 per cent of what was in the constitutional document already existed in the shape of the various treaties already in place. So it is the extra 10 per cent that we have to concentrate upon. 'Cherry-picking' is the wrong term to describe such a process, since what can be lifted out is simple and internally consistent.

It would help if there could be a short, agreed-upon mission statement (as proposed by the Commission to mark the fiftieth anniversary of the Treaty of Rome), answering the question 'What is the EU for?' in a post-1989 situation, within which suggested constitutional changes could be integrated. The surveys carried out following the refusal of the constitution showed that a high proportion of Europe's citizens back the EU, but when asked what the EU is for, not many have any answers.

The most important change for the future has to be in decision-making. The procedures instituted at Nice are too time-consuming and ineffective. Minorities can block decisions indefinitely should they want to. The procedure of passing on the presidency of the EU every six months, to put things politely, does little to ensure consistent and forceful leadership. A step towards greater continuity of leadership will be taken in January 2007, when Germany, Portugal and Slovenia will team up to provide a 'combined' presidency of the Council. The constitution proposed a new President of the Council, to be elected by members every two and a half years, which is surely a much better arrangement.

Further down the line, I would have no aversion to merging the presidencies of the Council and Commission into a single office. This idea was rejected in the run-up to the constitution as being too 'federalist', even though, to my mind, it has nothing intrinsically to do with federalism at all. The proposal in the constitution to unify

---

Box 7.4 Structural problems of the EU, 2006

1 The constitution was the wrong tactic, at the wrong time, but rejection is a serious set-back. Leaves major defects in decision-making processes.
2 Renewed economic dynamism is the key both to restoring legitimacy and the EU's power in the world. But the EU governing institutions have only limited purchase over the reforms needed.
3 National governments tend to play to home audiences.
4 Introduction of the euro has not given a kick-start to growth.
5 Debates about the social model are polarized, producing a false antithesis between markets and social justice.
6 Tensions exist between large and small member states, and between rich and poor.
7 Citizens are unwilling to contemplate spending more on defence.
8 The pattern of expenditure in the budget is quite out of line with the investment needs of the EU.

---

the posts of High Representative for Foreign and Security Policy and the Commissioner for External Relations is also sensible, and must at some point be implemented. I don't believe the EU has a future of any substance if it stays too inter-governmental. I don't think holding this view makes me a 'federalist'. The EU will not become a nation-state writ large. However, it does need clear mechanisms for decision-making and leadership. Accountability would be greater in such a system than the current one. In the Council at the moment, for example, there is no place where the buck (euro) stops. The system of six-month presidencies means that accountability is inherently elusive.

What therefore *is* the European Union? I don't think it is good enough to leave its nature undefined – to think of it as an 'unidentified flying object', as Jacques Delors once said in a celebrated quip. It is not sufficient to define it only in terms of what it is not –

not an organization on the way to federalism, and not a form of inter-governmentalism. Nor do I think it will do to compare the EU to a bicycle that can only keep upright when it is going along.

I would define the EU as a *democratic association* (or community) of *semi-sovereign nations*. I don't regard 'semi-sovereign' as a contentious term. Far from sovereignty being indivisible, it is always partial, internally and externally. The Union is an association, because any member state can leave (although this right was only formalized in the constitution). The EU is not a post-national entity, because the component nations do not disappear, and they retain large capacities for independent action. The EU differs from the UN, however, because formal sovereignty has been pooled, such that each member takes on board decisions handed down in EU courts. It is democratic, but primarily in the sense of deliberative democracy.

In his lecture of 2000,[20] Joschka Fischer spoke of the 'finality' of the European Union, but in a version I do not think practical or desirable. So what might the finality of the EU be – the point at which it will no longer be going through changes and revisions to its basic form? Here is how I would see it. Finality is likely to involve more developed forms of deliberative democracy than currently exist, almost certainly geared at some point to electronic communication. It will be a system that hopefully balances dynamic and effective leadership with the preservation – and indeed the enhancement – of national and local democracy. Protecting democracy could be of key importance. The 'dark continent' has had too disturbing a history to suppose that the future will be smooth going.

In writing this book, I have been conscious of how loosely one uses the term 'Europe'. 'Europe' has several different meanings. It can refer to the subcontinent as a whole and therefore includes countries like Norway, Switzerland or Serbia. It can mean the governing institutions of the EU – the Commission, the Council and so forth. Or it can refer to the collectivity of EU member states. The third of these is perhaps the sense in which the term is used least often, but in some ways it is the most important. 'Europe' could

---

[20] Fischer, 'From confederacy to federation'.

become a 'learning machine' for the exchange of ideas and practices, in politics and in economics.

The open method of coordination is, in a sense, an attempt to do this, but it still operates only on the intersection between the Commission and the member states. Why not have more horizontal forms of dialogue and policy-making, involving a range of groups and organizations? These could be issues-networks, such as suggested on a global level by J. F. Rischard in his book *High Noon*.[21] They would involve some representatives from member governments, civil society groups and businesses, and be organized by the Commission. Concerning problems such as reducing dependency on fossil-fuels, they could ask questions such as: 'What is the time-scale of needed changes?' 'Where do we want to be 20 years from now?' 'What are the options?'

Instead of empty talk about subsidiarity, there could be real attempts made at devolution or the everyday involvement of citizens. These wouldn't so much involve returning specific.powers to the nations as experimenting with possibilities of bottom-up involvement. 'New governance theory' suggests that there are ways of involving concerned citizens directly in the work of government – involving deliberative democracy at the local level, e-democracy, public conversations, participatory budgeting, and alternative dispute resolutions.[22] In several states in the US, for instance, there has been a dramatic growth in the use of new governance processes.

Finality means having a developed European public sphere, no matter how slow the progress at the moment. For this to happen, there must be agreement about a common language, which all citizens are encouraged to acquire. This language has to be English. English is no longer the language of particular nations. It is the global language. Finality means the setting of boundaries to the Union and recognizing that these are unlikely to change, an issue on which I shall elaborate in what follows. It means having command of sufficient power for the Union to play a significant

---

[21] Jean-François Rischard, *High Noon: 20 Global Problems, 20 Years to Solve Them*. New York: Basic Books, 2003.
[22] L. M. Salomon, *The Tools of Government: A Guide to the New Governance*. Oxford: Oxford University Press, 2002.

role in world politics, not just as one great power among others, but as a pioneer of transnational governance.

Thesis six: The same factors that are causing nations, large and small, to agonize about their identities apply also to the EU. Consider, for example, the United States. Over recent years, a whole spate of books has appeared puzzling about what the US 'is' and what it should stand for.[23]

Samuel Huntington identifies a range of possible identities that could be attributed to the US. Are we, he asks, a 'universal nation', which incorporates and expresses values common to all humanity?

> Or are we a Western nation with our identity defined by our European heritage and institutions? Or are we unique with a distinctive civilization of our own, as the proponents of 'American exceptionalism' have argued throughout our history? Are we basically a political community whose identity exists only in a social contract embodied in the Declaration of Independence and other founding documents? Are we multicultural, bicultural or unicultural, a mosaic or a melting-pot?[24]

Or is the US, as others have proposed, none of these, but a new empire?[25]

Michael Walzer has suggested that every American also has another identity.[26] No one is just an American. People are Irish-American, Hispanic-American, African-American, and so on. There isn't anyone outside this dualism, because 'Anglo-American' is also an identity – although for writers like Huntington, not just one among many others. Hyphenated identities have begun to appear within European nations – such as 'Asian-British' or 'Caribbean-British' – and one can only presume that they will become more common.

---

[23] See, for example, Peter Brimlow, *Alien Nation: Common Sense About America's Immigration Disaster*. New York: Harper Perennial, 1996.

[24] Samuel Huntington, *Who Are We?* New York: Free Press, 2004, p. 9.

[25] Niall Ferguson, *Colossus: The Rise and Fall of the American Empire*. New York: Penguin, 2004.

[26] Michael Walzer, 'What does it mean to be an American?', *Social Research*, 71/3 (1990).

But we do not have hyphenated identities at the European level. When people say they are happy to be both German and European, or maybe Bavarian, German and European, they are saying something important. They are making a declaration about cosmopolitanism. But nobody defines him- or herself as 'German-European', and it seems unlikely that such self-descriptions will become more widespread in the future. Whatever 'Europeanness' is, it will not mimic being 'American', nor will multiple identities be dealt with in the same way.

Jürgen Habermas has sought to define European identity in terms of a set of abstract principles, which he labels 'constitutional patriotism'. The EU is founded upon principles of liberty, democracy, respect for human rights and the rule of law.[27] He recognizes that the justifications for what is now the EU in its early days no longer suffice – controlling German power and ending interstate war. The principles he identifies, however, can be detached from the nation-states in which they originally developed, and transferred to a transnational level.

The thesis of constitutional patriotism has been widely criticized, and in my view rightly so. It seeks to avoid all notions of commonality and belonging. Whatever one thinks of Huntington's version of what makes up America's identity, he cogently dismisses the idea that it can depend only on moral/legal norms. Perhaps it isn't surprising that Habermas seems recently to have shifted his position somewhat. Europe, he now says, must involve 'an affective attachment to a particular ethos', something which is 'a specific way of life'.[28] Here we come full circle. For what is this way of life? Well, it is none other than that defined by the European social model. However, he takes the familiar line that the social model is a 'defence' against globalization, a view which I think is wrong.

In my view, for the EU to flourish there must be something for citizens to belong to, and that something must be a community. It is not accidental that through its various incarnations the EU has consistently called itself a community. A community can be

[27] Jürgen Habermas, *The Postnational Constellation*. Cambridge: Polity, 2000.
[28] Habermas, 'Why does Europe need a constitution?', *European Union Institute*, 2001, p. 8.

Box 7.5 What the EU should do

- avoid attempted revival of the constitutional treaty;
- new mission statement, oriented to the post-1989 world;
- decision-making processes sharpened, with extensions of majority decision-making;
- greater leadership capabilities for Council/Commission;
- single foreign minister;
- real consolidation of military capability, geared towards rapid reaction capabilities;
- take difficult decisions about finality, including boundaries, and develop coherent regional policy;
- introduce 'new governance' procedures, coupled to greater transparency;
- fundamental restructuring of the EU budget.

---

cosmopolitan, and the EU certainly is so. It can and does involve generally shared values – readily identified in trans-European surveys. A community should have an overall sense of purpose, a rationale. What this might be, post-1989, I have suggested earlier.

One of the keys to creating a more integrated European identity in the future is likely to be education, especially further and higher education. Since the setting up of the Single Market, the number of Europeans gaining qualifications outside their own countries has accelerated. Both companies and governments want well-travelled, cosmopolitan staff. European identity is distinctive in this sense, that it must be cultivated in parallel with national cultures – themselves internally diverse and contested. As in the economic and political spheres, this is not a zero-sum game. The one identity does not ipso facto subvert the other.

A community has to have some principles of inclusion, and therefore of exclusion. Boundaries are in some sense inevitable. There must be 'others' but it does not follow that relations with others have to be hostile or defined through antagonism. Good neighbours are just as much neighbours as bad neighbours are. But what exclusionary principles should the EU apply?

The 'European project' could be defined in terms of almost indefinite extension, as would in fact follow from the idea of constitutional patriotism, which appears to set no boundaries. The Council of Europe includes Russia and the Ukraine. If Europe stands only for principles, why should membership be denied in the future to any nation at Europe's outer border, and why should not those borders extend indefinitely? Should a successful constitutional democracy at some point emerge in Georgia or Armenia, why not include them? Morocco applied for membership of the EU in 1986, only to be turned down on the grounds that it is not European. But it is not at all obvious that it is not. After all, 'Europe' was for centuries largely centred around the Mediterranean, including most of what is now North Africa.

It is significant that no one speaks of expansion to the West (or only very few do[29]), even though in terms of communications the Atlantic barely exists any more. If principles were all that defined the EU, the US and Canada would be more plausible members than the Ukraine or Russia – much of their history, as nations, is 'European'. The fact that this possibility is not entertained shows that the EU already has one generally accepted boundary.

De facto borders are emerging around the EU to the East and South at this point. There is a range of countries which, if they made applications, could not be refused as accession candidates. These include Iceland, Norway, Switzerland and all the Balkan countries should they make sufficient progress. The EU has commitments to Bulgaria, Romania and Turkey. For the moment there are no other plausible candidates for the near future, which should give the Union time to get its house in order.

The eventual outer limit should probably be the above group of countries plus, perhaps one day, the Ukraine, Moldova and Belarus – but no extension to the Caucasus, or beyond Turkey (therefore not Israel), or to North Africa. Why? Not because 'here Europe ends' in some historical or cultural sense, but for a series of other reasons. The EU cannot indefinitely base its foreign policy on the

[29] Jeremy Rifkin mentions the possibility that Canada might eventually join the EU – giving as a parallel the fact that Hawaii is an American state even though it is many miles away from the US mainland. Jeremy Rifkin, *The European Dream.* Cambridge: Polity, 2004.

attractions of potential membership. It cannot do so, otherwise its relations with its near-neighbours become too confused. Moreover, the EU has to retain – and further develop – its capabilities as a political actor, which it can only do if it has effective decision-making. If it is indefinitely expanding, that capacity will dwindle rather than increase.

The EU faces major problems ahead in settling its boundaries, however. The Union cannot expand indefinitely if it is to be a community rather than only a set of constitutional principles and agreements. Yet it cannot readily 'announce' where its future outer boundaries should be drawn. The EU could say we stick where we are – no further countries for the foreseeable future can aspire to accession status. The Ukraine, Moldova and Belarus can never become full members.

Such a stance might be welcomed by Russia, but it would seriously inhibit the chances of the three ex-Soviet republics of modernizing, politically and economically. If the EU, on the other hand, says openly that the path is there for the three to join at some point, Russia and perhaps other adjoining states might see such a statement as an imperialist one. The dilemma is difficult, because the status quo is wholly unsatisfactory – it sends mixed messages, as noted earlier. We have already had a glimpse of its implications, with the action Russia took to cut off gas supplies to Ukraine and demand that the country switch rapidly to paying full market prices. These actions resulted from the Orange Revolution and the declared ambition of the country to join the EU.

Boundaries are currently being discussed by EU leaders under the heading of 'absorption capacity' – how many further countries the EU can absorb without serious dislocation. This debate is not really centred upon the ex-Soviet provinces, however, but covertly or more openly upon Turkey. Turkey's accession is divisive within the existing EU countries for a diversity of reasons – its size, geographical location, its low level of economic development and the fact that it is a predominantly Islamic society. The great danger at the moment is that the schizophrenic attitudes of EU leaders towards Turkey will produce a situation that is the worst of all worlds.

The EU should much more whole-heartedly back the decision it has already taken: to accept Turkey as an accession country. Many pro-Europeans in Turkey, from different sides of the political spectrum, feel let down by the half-hearted nature of the embrace that has been offered by the EU. Turkey is a member of every European organization short of the EU itself, and is a long-standing member of NATO. To be sure, there are major hurdles to be overcome before Turkey's accession could become a reality, including the stand-off over the future of Cyprus. Yet should the EU turn its back on Turkey at this point, the result could be a slowing of economic growth in the country, political polarization and an embittered society, one turning East rather than West. Those who currently talk of putting obstacles in Turkey's way should reflect on whether they really want a struggling, divided, possibly antagonistic state on their doorstep. A democratic, liberal, prosperous Turkey as a member state of the Union is a far more attractive prospect than a failing Turkey looking in from the outside.

Thesis seven: In pursuing its geopolitical goals, the EU should have recourse to a variety of forms of power. The American author Robert Kagan touched upon quite a few sensibilities in Europe with his contrast between *power* (the US) and *weakness* (the EU).[30] An agency with power (the US) will use it, while one with little or no power (the EU) will elevate its weakness into lofty principles of collaboration. As Kagan put it, drawing on the best-seller about male and female attitudes by John Gray,[31] the Europeans are from Venus, the Americans are from Mars. The US is 'masculine', because it possesses the use of force and is not afraid to use it to achieve its ends. The EU tries to get its way (because it has no other options) by the 'feminine' arts of persuasion and seduction.

It is a mistake, however, to use 'power' in this narrow way and certainly to contrast it to 'weakness'. The embrace of international law, collaboration to limit the effects of climate change – these are themselves forms of power. Violence without negotiation does not

[30] Robert Kagan, 'Power and weakness', *Policy Review*, 113 (2002).
[31] John Gray, *Men are from Mars, Women are from Venus*. London: Harper Collins, 1993.

work, or is at best very limited, because it can produce no stability (as we see in the case of Iraq). Yet persuasion without the possibility of effective sanctions is inherently limited too, as is shown in the case of the EU's failed attempts, at the time of writing anyway, to dissuade Iran from developing its nuclear programme.

Kagan's distinction parallels that made by Joseph Nye between hard and soft power. Hard power is the use of sanctions to obtain compliance, including the threat or actual use of force. Nye defines soft power as where a country or other organization achieves the outcomes it wants 'because other countries want to follow it, admiring its values, inculcating its example'.[32] But the distinction is again a misleading one. It is misleading in part because of the very terminology. 'Soft' implies weakness and vulnerability. Yet the forms of activity that fall under the category of soft power are not necessarily like this at all. What is soft about assertive bargaining in the context of the WTO, for example? There is nothing especially 'hard' where military intervention produces a crumbling society wracked by internal divisions, as has happened in Iraq.

However, the main objection that should be made to the distinction between soft and hard power is that it subsumes too much under a single dichotomy. Compliance, and therefore the use of power – because *all* the categories listed below are forms of power or potential power – can be achieved by:

- providing a model to be emulated by the other;
- diplomatic engagement, the use of persuasion;
- voluntary collaboration to reach shared objectives;
- the use of incentives;
- getting the other to participate in a legal or rule-bound system (like the WTO);
- the use of coercive sanctions (such as economic sanctions);
- the threat or the use of violence.

In practice these are not always separate from one another. Some presume others. For instance, the rule of law is not ordinarily

[32] Joseph Nye, *The Paradox of American Power*. Oxford: Oxford University Press, 2002, p. 8.

effective if it is not in some sense backed up by coercive sanctions. Multilateralism – governance by consultation and persuasion – is an intrinsic feature of the EU, and is a principle of wide applicability in an interdependent world. However, the idea that the capability to use force should be left to others makes no sense. The EU should adopt a stance of what one could call *assertive multilateralism* – an approach which stresses the importance of international law, negotiation and reconciliation, but recognizes that the threat of use of force may be necessary to back them up. Multilateralism is rarely an all-or-nothing thing. There will only be infrequent occasions where the majority of nations in the world see eye to eye. The EU will also have to make room for 'principled bilateralism' – situations in which one or more member states make interventions that have overall Union support (for instance, the British in Sierra Leone in 2000).

Such a view does not imply that the EU should be one element of a new balance of power between equally influential agents. The EU is not a nation-state writ large and the point is not to act as a counterweight to the US or other powers or groups of powers. The EU is pioneering a transnational system of government which in principle other areas of the world could draw from – or, where mistakes are made or dead ends encountered, learn from.

The EU must have military capability, one of the issues that, in spite of repeated attempts, has remained somewhat bogged down. The EU has more soldiers under arms than the US, but lags seriously behind in terms of technological capacity. Since NATO's Defence Capabilities Initiative was launched in the late 1990s, a series of attempts has been made to upgrade Europe's defence capacities. In the conflict in Kosovo the US military saw the EU states as especially deficient in precision strike, mobility, intelligence, and control and communications.[33] The American Senator Jesse Helms remarked at the time that the EU 'could not fight its way out of a wet paper bag'.

Some adjustments have been successfully made. The EU15 governments in 1999 committed themselves to provide a collective

---

[33] Hans-Christian Hagman, *European Crisis Management and Defence*. Oxford: Oxford University Press, 2002.

force, deployable in non-EU territories within sixty days and capable of being sustained for twelve months. In 2004 this initiative (not yet fully realized) was joined by a proposal to set up a series of 'battle groups', capable of rapid and sustained deployment, each consisting of some 1,200–1,500 troops.[34] In 2003–4, some 60–70,000 European troops, excluding those involved with NATO, were deployed outside the EU.

The European Security Strategy, drawn up in 2003 by the High Representative for Foreign Policy Javier Solana, was a significant document. It was the first systematic attempt to identify the risks the EU faces in a post-1989 world. It recognized the new levels of interdependence of world society and listed the major threats to EU security: new-style terrorism, nuclear proliferation, regional conflicts, state failure and transnational crime.[35] There was an explicit acknowledgement that armed force will sometimes be needed to cope with these problems, alongside other strategies.

Yet it fell short of developing a completely effective approach to new problems and the role of force in countering them. An emphasis upon peacekeeping and nation-building is all very well, but necessarily inadequate if there are not the forces to keep the peace while reconstruction is going on. Kagan's caustic observation that the Americans do the dishes and Europeans the drying up still captures the core of the truth. (Another version is the US 'kicks in the door' and the EU 'cleans the house'.)[36]

This situation is as unstable as that of the unreformed European social model, with which it is in fact closely tied. Before 1989, Europe was a protected zone, able to devote itself to its own socio-economic development; and old habits die hard. Europe's foreign policy consists largely in enlargement and the attractions of potential membership for neighbouring states. I have argued that this approach has run its course, at least as an ever-extensible principle.

---

[34] William Wallace, *Is There a European Approach to War?* London: European Foreign Policy Unit Working Paper, March 2005.

[35] For an analysis, see François Heisbourg, 'The "European security strategy": Is it for real?', ESF Working Paper No. 14, 2003.

[36] François Heisbourg, 'The "European security strategy is not a security strategy"', in Steven Everts et al., *A European Way of War*. London: Centre for European Reform, 2004.

We need the counterpart of a Lisbon Agenda for foreign policy; and this must be translated into terms accessible to the general public.

Can the EU in fact develop a coherent and integrated foreign policy? After all, member states tend to guard their autonomy of action here just as much as they do in respect of taxation and welfare. Yet if changes are made in EU governance, we can envisage more effective foreign policy than the Union has been able to muster so far. The divisions that opened up over the Iraq war are not likely to be repeated in most of the foreign policy areas the EU must confront. The Union has no federal authority that can override the collective or individual decisions of its member states; but this situation can be a source of strength as well as a problem. It can inhibit rapid decision-making in crisis situations, but the need to find consensus can also protect against irresponsible ventures.

To expand the EU's role in the wider world must, however, minimize what might be described as *euro-hypocrisy*, a phenomenon that at the moment is uncomfortably widespread. There are at least three areas where it is visible, at least to outside observers if not always to Europeans themselves. One concerns the willingness with which Europeans have become accustomed (as Kagan points out) to sheltering behind US military power – while at the same time being prepared to castigate the Americans for their failings. Europe's welfare systems are flouted in some part by a reluctance of national electorates to invest in the modernization of their armed forces and weapons systems.

The second is the failure of the European states to re-examine their colonial past, especially in the light of their new-found cultural diversity. The Europeans were the aggressors in world society for a long time. Talk of European values can ring hollow to those in less developed parts of the world still struggling with the long-term residue of colonialism. When democracy was developing in Europe, and lasting right up to the 1960s, it was specifically denied to colonial subjects.

Africa, the Middle East and parts of Asia were divided up more or less arbitrarily by the European colonial powers. Many of their current difficulties come from this inheritance, supplanted in a seamless way by the Cold War. Battles between the two super-powers were fought out by proxy in these parts of the world.

Europe's future will depend in some large degree upon its abilities to build pluralistic societies and counter racism. I am not suggesting that the ex-colonial nations all make public apologies for their past. But the propagation of today's European values will be unsuccessful if not accompanied by a realistic acceptance of the seamy side of European adventurism. As Chris Patten says, we must avoid sounding like 'those leaders who suggest we dwell on a higher moral plane in Europe . . . conveniently managing to file and forget gas chambers, gulags, and our Christian heritage of flagrant or more discreet anti-Semitism and Islamophobia'.[37]

Finally, hypocrisy towards the developing world is obvious in Europe's agricultural protectionism and its foot-dragging attitudes towards change. The EU wants to be a major force in helping poorer parts of the world develop. Yet the persistence of the CAP, even with the concessions that have been made to Third World producers, sends a different message.

My final thesis: Contrary to appearances, this is a time of *opportunity* for Europe – the opportunity to recharge economically and to be in the vanguard of change. The European project appears to many to be lapsing. Even some of its most dedicated supporters are experiencing doubts or second thoughts. Thus, one remarks that for years he was sanguine about the future of the EU, and noted how it attracted interest around the world. But 'for some time now', he says, 'I have been less confident. . . . Clouds are gathering and maybe even a storm is brewing.' The European endeavour today 'lacks excitement'.[38]

Others have gone further. The historian Niall Ferguson, for example, suggests that the European Union 'is an entity on the brink of decline and perhaps ultimately even of destruction'. It won't disappear, certainly not in the short term, but might fade into relative obscurity. This is what has happened, he points out, with organizations like OECD, now an agency for economic analysis and reporting, but once upon a time a prototype for the reconstruction of

---

[37] Chris Patten, *Not Quite the Diplomat*. London: Allen Lane, 2005.
[38] Pascal Lamy, *Towards World Democracy*. London: Policy Network, 2005, pp. 27 and 31.

Europe following the Marshall Aid programme. One day, the EU may too 'be no more than a humble data-gathering agency with expensive but impotent offices in the city of Brussels or elsewhere'.[39] The cluster of problems it faces, economic, political and organizational, Ferguson argues, is simply too great.

Those problems are real. As Marx once said of capitalism, the EU could collapse under the weight of its own contradictions. Capitalism didn't collapse, but went on to new strengths. The EU can do so as well, given that it becomes, and stays, reform-minded. The single most important factor that would restore legitimacy for the EU would be the successful recasting of the social model, as described in this book. It is by no means an impossible task, as I have also sought to show. In principle, the more developed EU states have many competitive advantages in the new global arena. Much is often made of the idea that the European Union is a product of elites, rather than having been sanctioned by the will of the people. I take issue with this assertion, since the EU has been built, or acceded to, by democratically elected governments, and in a cumulative fashion. I have suggested that rather than a turn against elites, there is something else going on. That something is a course of development that implied continuity – after 1989 – when in fact there was rupture.

---

[39] Niall Ferguson, 'The end of Europe?', American Enterprise Institute Bradley Lecture, Washington, 1 March 2004, p. 2.

Appendix: Open Letter on the Future of Europe

This letter – written with Ulrich Beck – was published in more than 30 newspapers in the EU countries and elsewhere over a space of about three weeks in June 2005. In a way, it was our counterpart to the letter of Jürgen Habermas and Jacques Derrida with which I opened this book. Like their letter, it gave rise to lively discussion.

The proposed European Constitution is dead. The people of France and the Netherlands have spoken. But what sentiments underlay their 'non' and their 'nee'? A confusion of ideas and feelings, probably: 'Help, we don't understand Europe any more'; 'Where are Europe's boundaries?'; 'Europe is not doing enough for us'; 'Our way of life is being swamped.'

The Constitution is dead. Long live . . . ! What? It's up to pro-Europeans to say. We shouldn't allow the Euro-sceptics to seize the agenda. We have to react to and cope with the 'no' in a positive and constructive way.

The EU is the most original and successful experiment in political institution-building since the Second World War. It has reunited Europe after the fall of the Berlin Wall. It has influenced political change as far away as Ukraine and Turkey – not, as in the past, by military, but by peaceful means. Through its economic innovations, it has played a part in bringing prosperity to millions, even if its recent level of growth has been disappointing. It has helped one of the very poorest countries in Europe, Ireland, to become among the richest. It has been instrumental in bringing democracy to Spain, Portugal and Greece, countries that had previously been dictatorships.

It is often said by its supporters that the EU has sustained peace in Europe for more than 50 years. This claim is dubious. NATO and the presence of the Americans have been most important. But what the Union has achieved is in fact more profound. It has turned malign influences in European history – nationalism, colonialism, military adventurism – inside out. It has set up or supported institutions – such as the European Court of Human Rights – that not only reject, but legislate against, the very barbarisms that have marked Europe's own past.

It is not the EU's failure, but its very successes that trouble people. Reuniting Western and Eastern Europe would have seemed an impossible dream less than 20 years ago. But even in the new member states, people ask: 'Where does all this stop?' These feelings tend to stimulate an emotional return to the apparent safe haven of the nation. Yet if the EU were abolished overnight, people would feel less rather than more secure in their national and cultural identities. Let's say, for example, that the Euro-sceptics in Britain got their way and the UK quit the EU altogether. Would the British then have a clearer sense of identity? Would they have more sovereignty to run their own affairs?

No they would not, is the answer to both questions. The Scots and Welsh would almost certainly continue to look to the EU anyway, perhaps leading to the break-up of the United Kingdom. And Britain – or England – would lose rather than gain sovereignty, if sovereignty means real power to influence the wider world. For so many issues and problems today originate above the level of the nation-state and cannot be solved within the boundaries of the nation-state.

The paradox is that, in the contemporary world, nationalist or isolationist thinking can be the worst enemy of the nation and its interests. The EU is an arena where formal sovereignty can be exchanged for real power, national cultures nurtured and economic success improved. The EU is better placed to advance national interests than nations could possibly do acting alone: in commerce, immigration, law and order, the environment, defence and many other areas.

Let us start to think of the EU not as an 'unfinished nation' or an 'incomplete federal state', but instead as a new type of cosmopolitan project. People feel afraid of a possible federal superstate and they are right to do so. A resurgent Europe can't rise up from the ruins of nations. The persistence of the nation is the condition of a cosmopolitan Europe; and today, for reasons just given, the reverse is true too. For a long time the process of European integration took place mainly by means of eliminating difference. But unity is not the same as uniformity. From a cosmopolitan point of view, diversity is not the problem, it is the solution.

Following the blocking of the Constitution, the future of the EU suddenly seems amorphous and uncertain. But it shouldn't do! Pro-Europeans should ask themselves three questions: Do we want a Europe that stands up for its values in the world? Do we want a Europe that is economically strong? Do we want a Europe that is fair and socially just? The questions are close to rhetorical, because everyone who wishes the EU to succeed must answer positively to all three.

Various quite concrete consequences follow. If Europe is to be heard and valued on the world scene, we cannot suddenly declare an end to expansion, nor can we leave the EU's system of governance as it is. The Union is a means of promoting the spread of peace, democracy and open markets. There is virtually no hope of stabilizing the Balkans, for example, if the prospect of EU accession is cut off. The eruption of further conflict there would be a disaster. The EU will lose massive potential influence geopolitically if it decides to keep Turkey out.

Similar considerations apply to governance. The EU cannot play an effective global role without more political innovation. The proposals to reform the leadership of the Council, and to have a single EU foreign minister, should be kept in play. More effective means of taking mutual decisions are needed than the cumbersome method left over from the Nice agreements. And the proposals in the Constitution to have more consultation with national parliaments before EU policies are instituted are surely both democratic and sensible.

Political and diplomatic influence, however, always reflect economic weight. It is here above all that pro-Europeans must urge the

Commission and the leaders of member states to action. We know that the 'no' votes in France and the Netherlands were motivated substantially by social and economic anxieties – anxieties that fed into the larger fears noted above. Despite its other successes, the European Union is simply not performing well enough economically. It has much lower growth levels than the US, not to mention less developed countries like India and China.

Europe simply must gear up for change. But along with reform we must preserve, and indeed deepen, our concern with social justice. The British Prime Minister, Tony Blair, has called for a Europe-wide debate on this issue. We believe he is right to do so. Some countries have been remarkably successful in combining economic growth with high levels of social protection and equality – especially the Nordic countries. Let's see what the rest of Europe can learn from them, as well as from other successful countries around the world.

The rejection of the Constitution does allow – let's hope it forces – Europeans to face up to some basic realities and respond to them. The European Union can be a major influence on the global scene in the current century. It is what pro-Europeans should want to happen. Let's make it happen.

Index

Notes: The abbreviation ESM = European Social Model; glossary definitions are shown by '(g)' after the page number.

absence from work 24–5
activating labour market policy xi(g),
   90–1, 179–80
active labour market policy 90
active trust xi(g), 116–17
activism 100–2
addictive behaviour 79–80, 137, 149,
   151–2
ageing society 6–7, 138–44, 149
   see also older people
ageism 86, 140, 141
Agenda 2010 33–4
agriculture 171, 229
Aho Report 166–7, 171
Aiginger, Karl 11–12, 13
air travel 175–6
Al Qaeda 205–6
alcoholism 136, 151–2
Anglo-Saxon welfare capitalism 9, 10
assertive multilateralism xi(g), 226
'at risk' groups 67–70
Australia 128, 185
Austria 19, 89
autonomy see freedom

banking rules 20
Barroso, José Manuel 166, 182
Belarus 222, 223
Belgium 89, 118, 126, 161–2
benefit dependency 100–1, 118, 119
Beveridge, William 96

'Big Mac' jobs 62, 63, 64, 68–9, 86–7, 88
bio-fuel 194
birth rates 6–7, 13–14, 36, 38, 69, 94–5
blocked societies xi(g), 32–40
Bluitgen, Kåre 130
Bologna Declaration (1999) 182–3
boundaries, EU 221–4
Brillat-Savarin, Jean 152
Britain see UK
Bulgaria 173, 222
business start-ups 38, 80, 142

Canada 123–4, 125, 128, 186
capital markets 57–8
carbon markets 155–6
care, attitudes of 112–13
career mobility 68–70
carers 143
cars 135, 144–5, 150, 156, 162, 188–9
Castells, Manuel 22–3
Central and East European states 40–3,
   201–2
   1989 events 3, 200–1, 202–3
   EU boundaries 222–3
   EU fund investment 173
   EU as political project 212
   picture of in 1961 199
   poverty 42, 74
   regional disparities 173, 177
   Services Directive 56
   social dumping 43–7

Central and East European states (*cont.*)
    social model typology 9
    see also specific countries
change, attitudes to 66, 67
charitable organizations 102
child care 73, 93, 94, 95
children 13–14
    French welfare policies 13–14,
        36
    obesity 146
    poverty 31, 71, 75, 78, 92–4
    social justice policy 91–5
China
    globalization 8–9
    outsourcing 4, 47, 48–9, 51–2
    research and development 181
    survival of Communism 204
choice 109–12
    lifestyle 137
    public-service reform 82
    state school systems 14
citizen-consumers xi(g), 104–6
citizenship 119–22, 123–4
    environmental 160–3, 195, 197
    new governance theory 218
civil liberties 102, 104
civil society organizations 102, 105, 160,
        176
civility 113
class 61–70, 98
    health and 136–7, 151
client empowerment 82, 103, 106–7,
        109–10
climate change 154, 155, 156–7, 158, 193,
        195, 196
cognitive development 94
cohesion
    EU 171
    social *see* social solidarity
cohesion fund 173
Cold War 201, 228–9
colonialism 228–9
Common Agricultural Policy (CAP) 171,
        229
communications technology *see*
        information and communications
        technology (ICT)
Communist states
    1989 events 3, 200–1, 202–3
    picture of in 1961 199

post-1989 *see* Central and East
        European states
    see also China
community, EU as 220–1
community integration 113–14
company ownership, France 35
competitiveness *see* economic
        competitiveness
compulsive behaviour 137
consensus politics 40
conservative welfare capitalism 9, 10
constitution, EU 5, 25, 30–1, 198, 201–2,
        212–13, 214–19
constitutional patriotism 220
consumer-citizens xi(g), 104–6
consumption of services 106–9
convergence 171, 197
corporatist welfare capitalism 9, 10
cosmopolitans 67
Coulborn, Theo 153
country of origin principle 53, 54, 55–6
creativity 66–7, 179–81, 185
cultural diversity 27, 35, 103, 117–19,
        134
    see also immigration and immigrants
cultural integration 102, 104
culture, child poverty 94
currency union *see* monetary union
Czech Republic 42, 201–2

defence capability 226–7
Delors, Jacques 216
democracy 200, 209–10, 213, 217, 218,
        230
    see also everyday democratization
'Democracy, Dialogue and Debate' 198
Denmark
    anti-immigrant sentiments 25, 133
    business start-ups 38
    economic performance 11–12, 19, 177
    education 12, 14
    environmental policies 161
    family policies 13
    freedom of speech 130, 131, 132–3
    gender equality 13, 63, 73
    health care 13
    individual action plans 101–2
    information technology 12
    labour market 12, 21, 101–2
    pension reform 14, 24

Index

poverty 75
social justice 73
Derrida, Jacques 1, 207
developing economies
euro-hypocrisy 228–9
globalization 47–8
see also China; India
diabetes 145, 148
diet 137, 145, 146, 147–8, 150, 151, 152
disabled people 24–5, 101
diversity *see* cultural diversity
domestic services 143–4, 160–1
domestic work 72–3, 92–3, 95
drug use 151–2

East European states *see* Central and East
European states
eating habits 136, 137, 145, 147–8, 150,
151, 152
ecological issues *see* environment
economic competitiveness
energy sector 194–5
environmental policies 158–9, 197
future of EU 230
global markets 8–9
Lisbon Agenda 167
social justice and 55–7
see also economic performance
economic inequalities *see* socio-economic
inequalities
economic integration
migrants 126–8
reason for EU 204, 207
economic performance 4–6, 11–12,
171–7
blocked societies 34–5, 37–8
ex-Communist EU states 42, 46, 173
impetus for change 30–1
Lisbon Agenda 15–16, 18–20, 167–8
new egalitarianism 91
reason for EU 207, 208
regional disparities 172
Single Market 52
see also economic competitiveness;
labour markets
economic rights 98, 104
education and training
ageing society 142
blocked societies 36, 39
class 69

creativity 180, 185
EU identity 221
flexicurity schemes 51
Global Adjustment Fund 170–1
higher 181–7, 197
blocked societies 36, 39
class 69
developing economies 48
Lisbon Agenda 177, 178, 181–3
impetus for ESM reform 31
inequalities 24, 78, 79, 80–1, 184, 185,
187
learning credits 81
Lisbon Agenda 177, 178–9, 181–3
Nordic policies 12, 13, 14, 22–3
positive welfare 97, 103
pre-emptive re-employment schemes 80
social justice policy 71
child poverty 94
inequalities 78, 79, 80–1, 187
transitional labour markets 88, 89
in traditional welfare state 98
USA 28, 112, 183–4, 186–7
user choice 111–12
egalitarianism, new xii(g), 91
electricity 159, 189, 190, 192, 193, 196
emigration *see* immigration and
immigrants
employment *see* labour markets
employment insurance 88–90
empowerment 82, 103, 106–7, 109–10
energy 9, 155–9, 161, 162, 169, 187–95,
196, 197
ensuring state xi(g), 97
environment 153–63
cars 135, 150, 156, 162, 188–9
China 51–2
ecological modernization 187–96, 197
Lisbon Agenda 165, 169, 190, 191,
197
Esping-Andersen, Gøsta 9–10, 11, 72
Estonia, economic performance 42
ethnic minorities *see* minority groups
euro-hypocrisy xi(g), 228–9
'Europe', use of term 217–18
European Central Bank 19, 20, 165, 168–9
European Court of Justice 165
European Monetary Union (EMU) *see*
monetary union
European Security Strategy 227

237

European social model (ESM) 1–29
  ageing society 140–1
  definition 2
  EU-level policy-making 164–98
  future of EU and 230
  identity and 220
  impetus for change 30–1
  reason for EU 207–8
  scope for reform 31–58
  social justice 27, 55–7, 59–61, 70–84
European Union (EU) 164–98
  ageism 141
  birth rates 6–7, 69, 94–5
  blocked societies 32, 39
  boundaries 221–4
  budget reviews 18–19, 171
  Common Agricultural Policy 171, 229
  constitution 5, 25, 30–1, 198, 201–2,
    212–13, 214–19
  cultural diversity 27, 117–19
  decision-making 212–14, 215–17
  'Democracy, Dialogue and Debate' 198
  economic performance 4–6, 11–12,
    171–7, 207
  enlargement 6, 26, 201–2
    accession state reforms 40–3
    boundaries 222–4
    geopolitics 208–10
    people's preoccupations 198
    regional disparities 171–3
    social dumping 43–7, 55, 177
  environment 155–6, 158, 169
  federalism 210, 212, 215–17
  finality 217–19
  foreign policy 227–9
  future of 199–230
  Global Adjustment Fund 170–1, 197
  globalization 6–9, 26, 44–5, 47–52
  identities 219–21
  impact of 1989 events 200–4, 230
  inter-governmentalism 211, 212–13,
    216–17
  language 218
  leadership 212, 215–16
  Maastricht Treaty, 'Protocol 14' 60
  military capability 204–5, 226–7, 228
  opportunities for 229–30
  obesity 135, 146–7
  picture of in 1961 199–200
  as a political project 210–14

positive welfare 27
  power 224–9
  reason for 204–10, 215
  seat-belt wearing 144–5
  Services Directive 52–7
  Social Chapter 60
  Social Charter 60
  social justice 27, 55–7, 59–61, 169, 170
    inequalities 74–7, 82, 83, 92–3
    regional disparities 175
    transitional labour markets 86
  sovereignty 208, 213, 217
  strains on the ESM 3, 4–9, 11–24, 26–9,
    200–1
  values 209
  see also Lisbon Agenda; monetary
    union; *specific member states*
Eurorealism xii(g)
everyday democratization xii(g), 66
  events of 1989 203
  lifestyle 137, 138
  social solidarity 115–16
  welfare delivery 106–7, 109
ex-Communist states *see* Central and East
    European states

families 7, 13–14
  blocked societies 34, 38
  reunification of migrant 128
  risk/opportunity distribution 68
  social inheritance 93–4
  social justice 72, 73, 93–4
federalism 210, 212, 215–17
Ferguson, Niall 229–30
Finland
  ageing society 140
  anti-immigrant sentiments 25
  economic performance 11–12, 22–3
  education 12
  family policies 13
  global markets 57–8
  labour market 12, 90
  lifestyle change 146–8
  pension reform 14, 24, 140
  poverty 75
  technology 12, 22–3, 57–8
Fischer, Joschka 210, 217
flexicurity 12, 25, 51, 56–7, 78, 80
Florida, Richard 66–7
food corporations 149–50

foreign policy, EU 227–9
Fortuyn, Pym 25
France
  ageing society 140
  business start-ups 38
  economic performance 11–12, 19, 31
  energy market 192
  EU constitution 5, 30–1, 44, 214–15
  EU as political project 211–12
  family policies 13–14
  formation of EU 204
  freedom of speech 131
  gender equality 85
  impetus for change 30–1
  minority groups 35, 36, 121, 126
  social dumping 46
  social model reform 31–2, 34–7, 40
  social model typology 9, 10, 11
free-market philosophies 105–6
freedom (personal autonomy) 97, 99, 104,
    137, 149, 151, 203–4
freedom of speech 102, 104, 129–33, 134
Freud, Sigmund 137
Friedman, Thomas 49
fuel *see* energy
fundamentalism 131–2

Garton-Ash, Timothy 209
gas supplies 157, 190–1, 192–3, 196
gender issues
  ageing society 143, 144
  higher education 183
  new egalitarianism 91
  pay 13, 63
  seat-belt wearing 145
  social justice 72–3, 85, 92–3, 95
  transitional labour markets 85, 92
geopolitics 9, 157, 191, 205–6, 208–10
Germany
  business start-ups 38
  economic performance 11–12, 19, 31,
    177
  energy market 192
  EU fund investment 173
  EU as political project 211
  events of 1989 203
  family policies 14
  federalism 40
  formation of EU 204
  gender equality 85

immigrants 123, 126, 138
impetus for change 31
outsourcing 50
picture of in 1961 199
regional disparities 172
social dumping 46
social justice 73, 85
social model reform 31–4, 40
social model typology 9, 10, 11
welfare delivery 106–7
Global Adjustment Fund 170–1, 197
global terrorism 191, 194, 205–6
global warming *see* climate change
globalization xii(g), 4, 6–9, 26
  demand management and 204
  France 34–5
  Nokia 57–8
  research and development 180–1, 186
  social dumping 44–5
  social model reform 47–52
  transitional labour markets 85
'golden age' 3, 200
governance 176–7, 218
Greece
  EU fund investment 173
  impact of accession to EU 44, 45
  investment inflows 177
  overweight population 146
  poverty 75
  seat-belt wearing 145
  social model typology 9
  street veto power 40
green movement 153–5, 196
greenhouse gas emissions 193–4
Günther, John 199–200

Habermas, Jürgen 1, 207, 220
Hakim, Catherine 72–3
health
  ageing society 139, 140, 141–2, 143–4
  environmental factors 153
  lifestyle 136–8, 141–2, 144–52
  positive welfare 97
  under-employment 24–5
health campaigns 136
health care 13, 36
health services 108, 109–10, 111
heart disease 147–8, 149, 150
Helm, Dieter 192–3, 195
Helms, Jesse 226

Index

Hemerijck, Anton 10–11
higher education 181–7, 197
  blocked societies 36, 39
  class 69
  developing economies 48
  Lisbon Agenda 177, 178, 181–3
Himanen, Pekka 22–3
household inequalities 63, 72, 73, 92, 93–4
household service provision 143–4
Hungary 41–2, 74, 75
Huntington, Samuel 219, 220
Hvam, Frank 130

Iceland 207, 222
identities 206, 219–21
illegal immigrants 125, 126, 127–8, 129
immigration and immigrants 117–34
  assimilation 25, 120–2
  citizenship 119–22, 123–4
  class divisions 67
  freedom of speech 129–33, 134
  illegal 125, 126, 127–8, 129
  managing 126–9, 134
  multiculturalism 27, 35, 120, 122–6, 133
  poverty 76–7
  unemployment rates 6, 118, 126–7
income
  child poverty reduction 93
  inequalities *see* socio-economic inequalities
  redistribution 70, 82–3, 91, 94, 118
  transitional labour markets 87–8
India 4, 47, 48, 49, 50, 51
individual action plans (IAPs) 101–2
inequalities *see* socio-economic inequalities
information and communications technology (ICT)
  ageing society 142
  developing economies 4, 48
  environmental issues 161–2
  globalization 8, 48, 49–50, 57–8
  investment levels 12, 22–3
  Lisbon Agenda 177
  see also Internet
inheritance tax 83–4
initiative, positive welfare 97
innovation 177–81, 197
  creativity 66–7, 179–81

environment and 153, 155–6, 187–9, 195
in ESM *see* European social model (ESM), scope for reform
EU-level policy 166–7, 171, 177–81
see also research and development; technological change
inter-governmentalism 211, 212–13, 216–17
Internet, education 80, 81, 182
interventionism 100
Iran 9, 157, 205, 225
Iraq 1, 157, 225
Ireland
  East European workers 43, 46
  economic performance 14, 172, 173, 177
  energy use 169
  social model typology 9
Islam, the West and 130–3
Islamic population, France 35
Islamic rule, Al Qaeda's aims 205–6
Islamic society, Turkey 223
Islamophobia 125, 229
Italy
  economic performance 11–12, 19, 31, 37–8, 177
  energy market 192
  EU fund investment 173, 174, 176
  gender equality 14, 63, 85
  immigrants and immigration 125, 128
  impetus for change 31
  social justice 73, 85
  social model reform 31–2, 37–9, 40
  social model typology 9

Japan 140, 146, 187–9
Jensen, Jane 93
Joyce, James 200

Kagan, Robert 224, 227
Keynesianism 3–4, 19–20, 204
knowledge/service economy xii(g), 22–3
  class 61–5, 69
  creativity 179–80
  higher education 183
  inequalities 74
  Lisbon Agenda 15–20, 26–7, 59–60, 177–9
  occupational divisions 61–3

Index

research and development 177–81, 197
self-esteem 99
size 59
social justice 72, 74, 88–9
social mobility 69–70
transitional labour markets 88–9, 99
see also Services Directive; services
   sector
Kok Report 17, 18, 165–6
Kornai, Janos 42
Kosovo 204–5, 226
Kymlicka, Will 123, 125–6

labour markets 20–2
   '50/40/10' society 65
   activating policy xi(g), 90–1, 179–80
   ageing society 139–41, 142–3
   at-risk groups 68–9
   'Big Mac' jobs 62, 63, 64, 68–9, 86–7,
      88
   birth rates 69, 95
   blocked societies 33–4, 36–7, 38
   class structure 64
   EU enlargement 26, 43–4, 46
   ex-Communist EU states 41, 42–3
   flexibility 21–2
   flexicurity 12, 25, 51, 56–7, 78, 80
   freedom of movement 43–4, 46
   Global Adjustment Fund 170–1
   immigrants 6, 118–19, 126–8, 129, 133
   impetus for welfare reform 31
   individual action plans 101–2
   inequalities 74, 78–82
   knowledge/service economy 22–3, 74
   lifestyle issues 138
   Lisbon Agenda 15, 16, 18, 19–20, 59,
      168–9
   monetary union 168–9
   Nordic reforms 12–13
   occupational divisions 61–3
   outsourcing 50–1
   regional disparities 174–5
   self-esteem 99, 101
   Services Directive 52–4, 55, 56–7
   social dumping 43–4, 46, 81, 177
   social justice policy 71, 78–82, 84–91
   social mobility 26
   transitional xiii(g), 84–91, 92, 99, 138,
      143
   under-employment 24–5

language, EU 218
Latvia 41, 42, 201–2
Layard, Richard 137–8
Le Grand, Julian 110
legal rights 98, 104
Leibfried, Stephan 75, 76
Leisering, Lutz 75, 76
Lenoir, René 64
liberal welfare capitalism 9, 10
life-course
   poverty 76, 77
   transitional labour markets 84–7,
      92
   transitions 68, 103
life-goals 97
lifestyle
   change xii(g), 135–63
   class divisions 65–6, 67
   environment 153–63, 195
   negative–positive welfare shift 97, 98,
      99, 103
Lisbon Agenda 15–20, 26–7, 59–60, 105,
      164–71
   education 177, 178–9, 181–3
   environment 165, 169, 190, 191, 197
   research and development 166–7,
      177–9
Lithuania 41, 42, 202
lone-parent families 13–14, 93
low-paid jobs 79

Maastricht Treaty, 'Protocol 14' 60
Malta 146
manufacturing sector 4
   class structure 61
   globalization 7, 47–8, 49, 57–8
   size 59
   social mobility 26
market–welfare state relation 104–7
Marshall, T. H. 98, 104
Marshall, Tom 150
Maxmin, James 107
Mazower, Mark 200
mental illness 25, 136, 137–8
Merkel, Wolfgang 71, 77
middle class 61
Middle East 157, 192
migration *see* immigration and immigrants
military capability 204–5, 226–7, 228
minimum wage 19–20, 22, 174–5

Index

minority groups 103, 117–34
  French social model 35, 36
  multiculturalism 27, 35, 120, 122–6,
    133
  poverty 76–7
  qualifications 69
Moldova 222, 223
monetary union 34, 39, 165, 168–9, 210
Moravcsik, Andrew 212–13
multiculturalism 27, 35, 120, 122–6,
  133
multilateralism xi(g), 226
multiple deprivation 65, 77
Muslims 35, 121, 125, 129–33

national identities 206, 219–21
national solidarities 117
nation-states 205, 206, 220
NATO 204–5, 226
negative–positive welfare shift xii(g),
  97–134
Netherlands
  anti-immigrant sentiments 25
  consensus politics 40
  economic performance 14, 177
  EU constitution 5, 25, 214–15
  gender equality 85, 93
  temporary employment scheme 89
network society 114
networks, creative 179–80
new egalitarianism xii(g), 91
Nokia 57–8
non-governmental organizations (NGOs)
  102, 160
Nordic states 11–15
  consensus politics 40
  economic performance 11–12
  education and training 12, 14, 22–3
  environmental policies 159
  gender equality 13, 63, 73, 85
  pension systems 14, 24, 140
  poverty 12, 63, 75, 76, 93–4
  regional disparities 174
  social model typology 9, 10–11
  see also Denmark; Finland; Norway;
    Sweden
Nordic welfare capitalism 9, 10
Norway 207, 222
nuclear power 155, 159, 194
Nye, Joseph 225

obesity 135, 136, 137, 145–7,
  148–9
obligations 98–9
obsession-compulsion 137
occupational divisions 61–3
off-shoring 47
oil 9, 157, 158–9, 188, 189, 191
older people
  ageing society 6–7, 138–44, 149
  'Big Mac' jobs 86
  life crises 77
  risks and opportunities 68, 70
  see also ageing society
Ollila, Jorma 57–8
'open method of coordination' (OMC)
  15–16, 165, 167–8
opportunity distribution 68
Östros, Thomas 54
outsourcing 4, 47, 48, 49
overweight population 145, 146

paper use 161–2
Parsons, Talcott 208
passive trust xii(g), 115–17
patriotism, constitutional 220
Patten, Chris 229
pension funds 159–60
pension systems 24
  ageing society 140–1
  Germany 33–4
  Italy 38–9
  Nordic states 14, 24, 140
personal autonomy see freedom
personalization of services 107
Pisani-Ferry, Jean 168
Poland 41, 42, 146
political parties 63–4
political project, EU as 210–14
political rights 98, 104
political systems 39–40
politics of second chances xii(g), 86
pollution 51–2, 135, 153, 156, 158, 162,
  188
Portugal
  energy sources 190
  EU fund investment 173
  impact of accession to EU 44, 45, 172,
    173
  obesity 146
  poverty 76

Index

seat-belt wearing 145
social model typology 9
positive welfare xii(g), 27
 shift to 97–134
post-industrial society xii(g), 62
 see also lifestyle
poverty 7, 74–7
 active trust 116
 at-risk groups 68
 children 31, 71, 75, 78, 92–4
 class structure 63, 64
 defining social justice 71
 definition 74
 ex-Communist EU states 42, 74
 France 36
 healthy eating 151
 new egalitarianism 91
 Nordic states 12, 63, 75, 76
 regional disparities 176
 social activism 102
 social exclusion 64–5, 77
 social justice policy 77–84, 92
 UK 31, 75, 76–7
power, EU 224–9
preventative welfare xii(g)
product leasing/renting 160–1
prosperity, positive welfare 97
protectionism 47, 49, 55–7, 81–2, 229
public health campaigns 136
public services
 client empowerment 103, 106–7,
  109–10
 delivery 82, 106–9
 ethos 108–9
 notion of 96, 104–5, 112
 targets 110
Putnam, Robert 116–17

racism 120, 123, 124–5, 133–4, 229
recycling 158, 193
redistribution, wealth/income 70, 82–4,
 91, 94, 118
redundancy, social justice policy 80–2, 89
 see also transitional labour markets
regional disparities 171–7, 197
regional power, EU as 211
regional solidarities 117
regionalism 206–7
religious groups 125, 129–33
renewable energy 190, 194

research and development (R&D) 177–81,
 197
 Aho Report 166–7
 Nordic states 12
 regional disparities 174
 universities 183, 184, 186, 197
retirement 24
 ageing society 139–41, 143
 at-risk groups 68, 70
 EU-level policy-making 165
 Germany 33–4
 Italy 38–9
Rice, Condoleezza 206
rights 98, 102, 103, 104
Rischard, J. F. 218
risk
 environmental 55
 individual–state transfer 97
risk distribution 68
Romania 173, 222
Russia 157, 191, 223
 see also Soviet Union

Sahlin, Mona 189
Sapir Report 17–18, 166, 171
Scandinavia *see* Nordic states
Schmid, Günther 87–8, 179
schools
 child poverty 94
 choice over 111–12
 Nordic policies 14, 94, 112
seaside towns 175–6
seat-belt wearing 144–5
second chances, politics of xii(g), 86
security
 of class groups 66, 67–8
 in employment *see* flexicurity
 EU role 208–9, 226–7
 welfare state role 97
self-esteem 99, 101, 152, 176
self-help groups 152
service economy trilemma 10–11
services, welfare *see* welfare
Services Directive 52–7
services sector
 'Big Mac' jobs 62, 63, 64, 68–9, 86–7,
  88
 outsourcing 4, 47, 48, 49–50
 product leasing/renting 160–1
 regional disparities 175–6

services sector (*cont.*)
  size 59
  strains on ESM and 4
  see also knowledge/service economy;
    Services Directive
sickness 24–5
  see also health
single currency *see* monetary union
Single Market
  advantages 207
  energy investments 194–5
  EU as political project 210
  Lisbon Agenda 17, 165
  Services Directive 52
single parent families 13–14, 93
Slovakia 41, 42, 146, 201–2
Slovenia 41, 42, 74, 201–2
Smith, Timothy 36
smoking 136, 147
social activism 102
Social Chapter 60
Social Charter 60
social class *see* class
social cohesion *see* social solidarity
social dumping 43–7, 55, 81, 177
social exclusion 64–5, 72, 77, 79–80,
  136–7
social investment state xiii(g)
social justice 55–7, 59–61, 70–3
  children 91–5
  education and training 71, 78, 79, 80–1,
    88, 89, 94, 187
  inequalities 73, 74–84
  Lisbon Agenda 27, 59–60, 169, 170
  regional disparities 175
  transitional labour markets 84–91, 92
  user choice 111
social mobility 26, 69–70
social model *see* European social model
social protection 72, 214–15
social solidarity 112–17, 118–19, 134
socio-economic inequalities 23–4, 74–84
  active trust 116
  'at risk' groups 67–70
    see also children, poverty
  China 51
  convergence 171, 197
  cultural diversity 118
  education 24, 78, 79, 80–1, 184, 185,
    187

ex-Communist states 42, 43
France 36
free-market philosophy 105–6
healthy eating 151
household 63, 72, 73, 92, 93–4
income redistribution 70, 82–3, 91, 94,
  118
India 51
regional 171–7, 197
service user choice 111–12
social exclusion 77
social justice 59–61, 73, 77–84, 92–4,
  111, 175
wealth redistribution 70, 82–4, 91, 118
women 13, 63
see also poverty
Soete, Luc 178, 179
Solana, Javier 227
solar energy 190
solidarity *see* social solidarity
sovereignty 208, 213, 217
Soviet Union
  collapse of Communism 3–4, 200–1,
    202–4
  picture of in 1961 199
  reason for EU and 204
Spain
  economic performance 14, 31, 172, 173,
    177
  education and training 31
  energy market 192
  EU fund investment 173
  governance 176
  immigration 128
  impact of accession to EU 44, 45, 172
  obesity 146
  social justice 73
  social model reform 31
  social model typology 9
  women's pay 63
Sperling, Gene 55, 80
start-up businesses 38, 80, 142
state, role of 96, 97, 98–9, 104–5, 112,
  207–8
structural funds 173–4, 176
sustainable development 189, 190–8
Sweden
  anti-immigrant sentiments 25
  child poverty 75, 93–4
  East European workers 43, 46

economic performance 11–12, 19, 21
education 12, 14, 23
energy sources 189
family policies 13
gender equality 13, 73
health care 13
immigrant employment rates 127
labour market 12
pension reform 14, 24
schools 14, 112
Services Directive 54
sickness and disability 24–5
Switzerland 207, 222

targets, public service 110
tax credits 93
taxation
child poverty 94
economic performance 21
environmental aims 155–6, 162
ex-Communist EU states 41
foodstuffs 150
globalization 44–5
income equality 23–4
income redistribution 82–3, 91, 94
wealth redistribution 82–4, 91
technological change
at-risk groups 68
creativity 179
environmental effects 153
globalization 7, 180–1
labour market flexibility 21
see also information and
communications technology;
innovation; research and
development
terrorism 130, 191, 194, 205–6
Thatcher, Margaret 210
Titmus, Richard 200
Toyota 188–9
trade
East European countries 45–6
EU leverage 208
Global Adjustment Fund 170–1
growth of 4, 50
protectionism 47, 49, 55–7, 81–2, 229
trade unions 33, 40, 53–4
training *see* education and training
transitional labour markets xiii(g), 84–91,
92, 99, 138, 143

transitions, life-course 68, 103
trust
active xi(g), 116–17
passive xii(g), 115–17
Turkey 222, 223–4

UK
citizenship for immigrants 120–2, 124
East European workers 43, 46
economic performance 14, 19, 31
education and training 31
environment 157, 158
free-market philosophy 105–6
gender equality 85
immigrant employment rates 127
lifestyle change 148–9, 150
mental illness 137–8
multiculturalism 124–5, 126
obesity 146, 148–9
poverty 31, 75, 76–7
reactions to Services Directive 53–4
regional disparities 174, 175–6
seat-belts 144
service user choice 110, 111
social model typology 9, 10, 11
tax credits 93
wealth redistribution 83–4
Ukraine 222, 223
under-employment 24–5
underclass 65
unemployment
'50/40/10' society 65
active labour market policy 90
ageing society 141
at-risk groups 68
birth rates 69, 95
blocked societies 33, 36–7, 38
class structure 64
EU and USA compared 6
ex-Communist EU states 41, 42–3
Global Adjustment Fund 170–1
immigrants 6, 118–19, 126–7
Nordic policies 12
outsourcing 50
regional disparities 174
Services Directive 56–7
social dumping 46, 81
social justice policy 78–82, 84–91
transitional labour markets xiii(g),
84–91

unemployment (*cont.*)
  under-employment and 25
  welfare delivery 106–7
  see also flexicurity
unemployment benefits 88, 89
  immigrants 118, 119, 127
unions 33, 40, 53–4
universities *see* higher education
upper class 61
USA
  ageing society 139–40
  birth rates 6–7
  creativity 67, 180
  diabetes 145
  ecological issues 135
  economic performance 5–6, 16, 22–3
  education 28, 112, 183–4, 186–7
  energy consumption 188, 189
  and EU military capability 205, 226,
    228
  globalization 48–50
  healthy eating 151
  immigrants and immigration 118, 119,
    120, 127, 128, 133–4
  inequalities 28, 184
  national identity 206, 219
  obesity 135, 145
  positive life-goals 97
  power 224
  re-employment schemes 80, 81
  religious groups 131
  research and development 178, 183
  seat-belt wearing 144, 145

values, EU 209
van Gogh, Theo 25
Van Parijs, Philippe 118

wage insurance 88–90
Walzer, Michael 219
war
  Iraq 1, 157, 225
  Yugoslavia 130, 204–5, 226
waste 158, 161–2, 193
water 157, 158, 160

wealth inequalities *see* socio-economic
    inequalities
wealth redistribution 70, 82–4, 91, 118
Weiler, Joseph 213
welfare
  client empowerment 103, 106–7,
    109–10
  delivery 82, 106–9
  dependency on 100–1, 118, 119
  use of term 96–7
welfare state
  negative–positive shift 27, 97–134
  notion of 96–7, 98–9
  reason for EU 207–8
  see also European social model
Wilkinson, Richard 136
wind power 190, 194
Wolff, Martin 7–8
women
  ageing society 141, 142, 143
  caring roles 143, 144
  employment rates 16
  EU policies compared 13–14, 73
  in knowledge/service economy 63, 72
  life-course preferences 72–3
  new egalitarianism 91
  risks and opportunities 68, 69
  transitional labour markets 85, 87,
    92
work foundations 89
working class 61, 63–4, 65
work–life balance 25

young people
  'Big Mac' jobs 86–7
  education policy 183, 186
  employment rate in Poland 41
  French employment contracts 36–7
  obesity 146
  poverty 94
  seat-belt wearing 144–5
'youthing society' xiii(g), 139–44
Yugoslavia, civil war 130, 204–5, 226

Zuboff, Soshana 107